TEACH YOURSELF

# CARD GAMES

an authoritative collection of
card game classics, favourites and recent discoveries
for beginners, regulars and explorers

# David Parlett
## Hodder & Stoughton

A MEMBER OF THE HODDER HEADLINE GROUP

*To Albie Fiore*

*British Library Cataloguing in Publication Data*

Parlett, David
  Card Games. – (Teach Yourself Series)
  I. Title  II. Series
  795.4

ISBN 0-340-59204-4

First published 1994
Impression number  10 9 8 7 6 5 4 3 2 1
Year              1998  1997  1996  1995  1994

Copyright © 1994 David Parlett

Typeset by Rowland Phototypesetting Limited, Bury St Edmunds, Suffolk.
Printed in Great Britain for Hodder & Stoughton Educational, a division of Hodder Headline PLC, 338 Euston Road, London NW1 3BH by Cox and Wyman Limited, Reading, Berks.

# CONTENTS

# — INTRODUCTION —

The delightful thing about card games is that there are so many of them, which means there is something to suit every taste. Not only that, but the stock is being constantly replenished. New games and novel variations of old ones are being constantly developed; games from other countries – especially from Eastern Europe, recently – are finding their way into the British repertoire. Even such apparently unchanging fixtures as Contract Bridge are not entirely immune from revision.

So there is always room for a new and up-to-date book of card games, and here it is. (Some passages of text presenting basic rules of standard games and describing sample deals are, however, where unaffected by the passage of time, taken unchanged from my earlier *Card Games for Everyone*.)

This one is designed for beginners, regulars, and explorers. Speaking as an explorer, I am glad to be able to include a description of a genuine Russian version of the game Preference, of the French Barbu, and of a game adapted from one of Chinese origin which my circle insists on referring to as 'the Bum Game', from a free translation of its French equivalent *Trouduc*. Anyone who enjoys experimenting with new games will find plenty to occupy them here, and will endorse my warm thanks to field researchers and correspondents who have been kind enough to share their discoveries with me.

For regular players, I hope my approach to the description and discussion of well-known card games will be found helpful, especially in settling divergent views on how to deal with unusual situations. In this connection I must remind regular players of a point well known to explorers but often ignored or disbelieved by beginners – to wit, that very few games have universally accepted 'official rules'. By far the majority of popular games are played with minor variations, elaborations and 'house rules' that vary from town to town and even from school to school, a 'school' being any informal group of players who play together regularly. Collecting card games is rather like collecting folk songs, which one percipient writer has characterised as being 'everywhere different yet everywhere the same'.

But I have written this book especially with beginners in mind. To help them particularly, I include sample hands and illustrated notes on strategy and tactics wherever a game is of sufficient depth to warrant such an approach. Although I have excluded witless games of chance, some will yet be found whose skill factor will be readily apparent to any intelligent ten-year-old, and so require no superfluous and patronising comments of my own.

I have also catered for beginners by the structure of the book and in the way I cross-refer between simpler and more advanced games of the same type. Let me explain.

All Western card games can be usefully divided into two groups, namely, those that do and those that don't involve the play of 'tricks'. The most advanced and prestigious games, headed by Bridge but also including Whist, Solo and Euchre, are all of the trick-taking variety, and anyone who wishes to make the most of the pleasures of card-play by playing intelligent games (as opposed to money-changing inanities like Baccarat) should start by getting grounded in the basic principles of trick-play. An ideal way of doing this is to start with simple trick-taking games for two. Whether your companion is a relatively experienced player or also a learner is equally advantageous: if the former, you can solicit their tolerance and benefit from their advice; if the latter, both of you can start at a low level and learn from your own and each other's mistakes. And, either way, you can get your necessary learning experience without feeling intimidated by anyone else looking on.

This book therefore opens with a collection of two-player trick-taking games proceeding from the simplest to those of greater elaboration and potential depth. From these you can pass on to the sections on three- and four-handed trick-taking games, each of which, again, starts with the simplest and proceeds to the more complex examples. Incidentally, it is important to note that by 'simplest' I mean those with simple rules and structures easily explained and grasped. This is not the same as trivial or childish. Games with simple rules, like Whist and Solo, may be

Each card is thus uniquely identified by rank and suit, as for example 'Two of clubs', 'Queen of hearts', 'Ace of spades', though they are generally printed with the suit first: ♣2, ♡Q, ♠A. Its identity by rank and suit is inscribed in the top left-hand corner, so that you can readily identify all the cards in your hand without having to fan them out too widely. (Please note that I often use the initial T for Ten although this does not appear upon the card itself. Example: In some games the top cards rank A T K Q J instead of A K Q J T).

Card games derive their motivation and interest from the psychological tension induced by the fact that individual cards are identifiable only from the front and not from the back. Invariably, the cards are first randomised by shuffling, then dealt face down to players, who hold them in such a way that each player knows only the cards held by himself, not those of anybody else. For this reason, card games are technically described as games of 'imperfect information'. Intelligent card games, however, as opposed to simple betting games, hinge on the process of acquiring information by a variety of methods, including observation, inference and deduction. (Yes, by cheating too; but this complicates the issue.) They are therefore better characterised as games of 'developing information', for this is precisely what they are all about.

## The card-playing set-up

*Players.* Most games are designed for, or have variations for, a specific number of players. If played by the wrong number, the balance of a game will be upset, and its enjoyment spoilt. Patience is played by one, and many good games by two or three. Four may play alone or in two partnerships of two, in which case partners sit opposite each other across the table. Games for five or more tend to be more chancy and less skill-rewarding.

*Seating and partners.* In case of disagreement as to who sits where, players may each draw a card at random from a pack spread face down in a row, the highest rank drawn conferring first choice of seat, and so on downwards. Two or more tied players will draw again to break the tie. The same draw may be used to establish partnerships. In Bridge, for instance, those drawing the two highest cards play as partners against those drawing the lowest. In games for four or fewer, it is usual to refer to the players by their compass positions at the table, i.e. North, East, South, West.

*Rotation.* In Britain, the turn to deal and play usually passes to the left, or clockwise around the table as viewed from above. However, this varies from country to country, and serious card-players generally prefer to play whichever way round is appropriate to the country of origin of the game being practised. As the exact rotation makes no real difference to the play, I will only mention in passing which way round is customary for any particular game, and leave you to do as you please.

*Game structure.* Most card games involve several deals or hands of play. Depending on the game, a hand of play may last anything from less than one minute to ten or more. To make the play worth while, and to balance out the receipt of 'good' and 'bad' hands, a game therefore consists of several deals. It may be played:

- for an agreed length of time,
- up to a target score, set either by the rules of the game or by prior agreement,
- for as many deals as specified by the rules of the game.

*Shuffle and deal.* Whoever drew the highest card usually deals first, and the turn to deal passes to the left. Before dealing, the dealer shuffles the cards in order to randomise the pack. You can't learn shuffling by words, only by observation and practice. In most card games (other than Bridge), anyone has the right to shuffle on demand, but the dealer has the right to shuffle last. He then offers the pack to his right-hand neighbour, who initiates a 'cut' by lifting the top half and placing it on the table. The dealer then completes the cut by placing the bottom half on the the top. The purpose of this rigmarole is to ensure that no-one can see the bottom card of the pack and so identify a card held by another player. It will, of course, be frustrated if the dealer is careless enough to hold the pack at an upright, outward angle when dealing.

The deal is made by distributing cards face down one at a time around the table, the first card of each round going to the player at Dealer's left (variously called 'eldest', 'forehand', etc) and the last to himself. Some games specify that cards be dealt not one at a time but in batches of two or three. Such a rule makes a significant difference and should not be ignored. In some games, the whole pack is dealt out. In some, for various purposes, a few neutral cards may be dealt face down to the table as a spare hand or 'widow' or 'talon'. In some, a batch or stock of cards will be left face down, from which players draw additional cards in the course of play so that all are eventually used. In others, the undealt cards are left untouched and play no part at all, except to increase the chance factor by making the acquisition of 'perfect information' impossible until it is too late to do anything with it.

## Tricks

Most Western card games are based on playing cards to tricks.

A trick is formed when each player in turn has played a card face up to the table. It therefore consists of as many cards as there are players. The leader – the first to play – is normally allowed to play any card he likes. The others are then normally required to furnish a card of the same suit as the one led, if possible, until the trick is complete. Whoever played the highest card of the suit led wins the trick, turns it face down in a squared-up pile before him, and then leads the first card to the next trick.

Normally, a card of a different suit from that led cannot take the trick. However, many games permit one suit to be designated 'trump' (from 'triumph'). In such games, a player unable to follow suit to a plain-suit (non-trump) lead can beat the suit led by playing a trump. The rule of trick-winning therefore becomes: The trick is taken by the

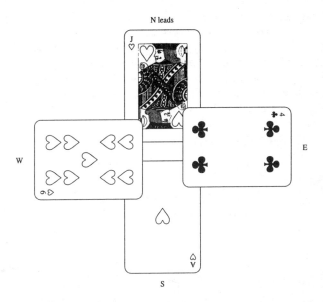

**Figure 1: Playing tricks** (1) Playing at no trump, North leads the Jack of hearts. The others, playing in clockwise rotation, must follow suit (play hearts) if they can. East cannot follow, and discards a club. South wins the trick with his Ace, it being the highest card of the suit led. (2) With clubs trump, the trick is now won by East, who is permitted to trump (or 'ruff') by virtue of having none left of the suit led. Had West been unable to follow, he might have won the trick by 'overtrumping' with a club higher than the Four.

highest card of the suit led, or by the highest trump if any are played. Most trick games follow this rule, though exceptions will be encountered.

Here is an example. Of four players, assume that North leads clubs, and that two players have no clubs to play:

North ♣9, East ♣Q, South ◇K, West ♡2.

If the game is played at no trump, East's Queen wins because it is the highest card of the suit led. South's King, though ranking higher, is of the wrong suit.

If hearts are trumps, West's Two takes the trick, as it is the highest (only) trump played. If diamonds are trumps, South's King is the winning card. And if clubs are trumps, East wins again, because a trump suit cannot itself be trumped.

Of many ways of selecting a suit for trump, the commonest are these. In older and simpler games the last card of the pack is turned face up and its suit becomes trump automatically. In more highly developed games a trump suit (or 'no trump') is nominated by the player who contracts to win the greatest number of tricks in return for so doing. Such games are usually preceded by an 'auction' in which players 'bid' to nominate trumps by increasing the number of tricks they offer to win. For greater interest the suits may be graded in a specified order of superiority, so that a bid can be overcalled not necessarily by raising the number of tricks but by bidding the same number of tricks in a higher-ranking suit, or at no trump, which beats every suit. This is the distinguishing feature of Contract Bridge.

## Scores and pay-offs

The amount you win or lose is particularly interesting in card games, most of which produce more varied results than the simple '1 for a win, 0 for a loss, ½ for a draw' of chess. Card games fall into two types as to the way in which scores are made or recorded.

1  'Hard-score' games are played directly for cash, or for objects representing cash, such as chips or counters. Settlements are made at the end of each deal, so that each deal is a complete game in itself. A session of play has no overall game structure, and can end at any point.

2  'Soft-score' games are played for notional points recorded in writing on suitable scoresheets. In this case a game consists either of a specified number of deals, or of as many deals as it takes for a

player or partnership to reach a specified target score. This gives the game an overall structure, to which additional scoring interest may be attached – for example, bonuses for reaching the target score soonest, or penalties for failing to reach a minimum level. Additionally, scoring considerations may influence one's strategy of play ('playing to the score').

All gambling games are played for hard score, and games of chance invariably for cash, but it does not follow that all games played for hard score are 'gambling games' in the popular sense of depending more on chance than skill. Solo Whist, for example, is almost invariably played for hard score, and for cash at that, but it can be a game of great skill, and only an accident of social history has deprived Solo of the sort of highly developed scoring system that has contributed so greatly to the success of Contract Bridge.

Most games of skill are played for the 'soft score' of points recorded in writing. At end of play, these may or may not be converted into the 'hard score' of cash settlements between the players. The more skill-demanding the game, the greater the tendency for interest to attach to the play itself rather than to its capacity for determining cash settlements. Many play such games 'for small stakes' as a matter of temperament or tradition. Others will not play for money at all. Whatever one's attitude to playing for money, it must be admitted that it is the gambling origin of card games that has led to their fascinating scoring systems, and (consequently) to the unique feature of card games whereby one's strategy is often governed by the various scoring possibilities of a given hand.

# —— SURVEY OF —— CARD GAMES

There are hundreds of different card games, but many are minor variations on one another, and all can be fitted into a few large families by their basic mechanisms of play as follows.

## Trick-taking games

Most Western card games involve the play of tricks, as described in the preceding section. Given this underlying mechanism of play, trick-games fall into three large groups according to the object of the game.

In *plain-trick* games, players aim to win an agreed minimum number of tricks. They may or may not get credit for winning more ('overtricks'), but are invariably penalised for falling short ('undertricks'). Rarely, the aim of the game may be to win a specific number of tricks, neither more nor fewer.

In *point-trick* games, individual cards have point-values, and players aim to gain a minimum number of points from cards captured in tricks. In such games it is possible to win by taking a few tricks containing many card-points, or to lose by taking many tricks of relatively little value.

*Negative or trick-avoidance* games are self-explanatory. The main object may be to lose every trick (*misère*), or to win as few tricks as possible (plain-trick avoidance), or to avoid capturing penalty cards in tricks (point-trick avoidance).

Some trick games also incorporate features associated with non-trick games, such as trying to collect particular combinations of cards.

## Going-out games

There is a large family of games in which the aim is to get rid of all your cards before anyone else, or at least to avoid being the last to run out of cards. Typically, each in turn must play a card to the table which matches the last card played in some specified way. If unable, they not only fail to get rid of a card, but in some games must also draw extra cards by way of a penalty.

## Collecting games

There is a large family of games in which the object is to collect matching combinations of cards, typically a *suit-sequence* of three or more cards, such as ♣8–9–T–J, or a *set* of three or more identical ranks, such as ♣8–♡8–♣8. Most of these belong to the Rummy family, characterised by the 'draw and discard' principle borrowed from Mah-Jong. Each in turn draws the top card of a face-down stockpile or a face-up wastepile, lays out a set or sequence on the table if possible, and adds a discard to the wastepile. Card combinations are known as 'melds', and to lay one out is called 'melding'. In primitive Rummy games the main aim is to get rid of all one's cards in melds and so be the first to run out of cards, thus relating them to 'going-out' games described above. In later and more advanced games the main aim is to score points for making and enlarging as many melds as possible, and only to go out when well ahead on points.

## Arithmetical games

A few games are based on adding the face value of cards either collected or played out. They do not constitute one big family but several un-related small families, each with one or two principal members (Pontoon, Cribbage, Cassino, One Hundred). They often overlap with other families.

## Gambling games

All games are gambling games if played for money, but, as a technical classification, this heading refers to games involving little or no actual card play. At the lower end of the intellectual spectrum are games like Baccarat, where players do little more than bet on the outcome of cards turned at random. The intelligent end is dominated by Poker. Contrary to popular opinion, Poker is as deep and skill-demanding a game as Bridge. The difference is essentially not of degree but of kind. In Bridge, players make their moves with cards; in Poker, they leave their cards untouched and make their moves with cash, or objects representing cash. Just as it is impractical to play Bridge for 'hard score', so it is impossible to play Poker for 'soft'.

# 1

# TWO-HANDED
# WHIST GAMES

## *Trick games for learners*

The point of trick-play lies in trying to deduce from the play which players hold which key cards, so that you can then play your own to best advantage. The sooner and more accurately you manage to do this, the more cards still remain in your hand from which to develop subsequent winners. It's true we are talking about assumptions and probabilities rather than plain certainties, but this doesn't detract from the principle involved. An intelligent assumption is always better than a blind guess.

In a two-handed game this element will, of course, be lacking if you start by dealing out all the cards out between you, as it is a matter of simple visualisation to work out what the other player holds. Several ways of overcoming this problem are illustrated in the following simple Whist games, which will make a good introduction to the basic principles of card-play.

A Whist game is one involving the following distinctive features:

- It is played with 52 cards ranking A K Q J T 9 8 7 6 5 4 3 2.
- All tricks are of equal value and the aim is to win more of them than anyone else.
- The first card played to a trick fixes a suit that must (if possible) be followed by everyone else who plays to the trick.

- The trick is taken by the highest card of the suit led or by the highest trump if any are played, and the winner of each trick leads to the next.
- Points accrue not only for tricks won but also for 'honours', i.e. for being dealt Ace, King, Queen and Jack of trumps, or any three of them. Some players dislike the idea of scoring for luck rather than skill and prefer to ignore honours. Where applicable, agree beforehand whether or not to count them.

# German Whist

*Deal.* Deal six cards each, in ones, and stack the rest face down. Turn the top card of the stock face up. The suit of the turn-up is trump for the whole play of the hand.

*Play.* Non-dealer leads to the first trick. The winner of each trick, before leading to the next, draws the top card of the stock and adds it to his hand, and waits for the loser to draw the next (which need not be shown). He then turns the next stock card face up so that both can see which card the next trick-winner will get.

*Score.* When the stock is empty, six last tricks are played to finish off both hands. The winner scores 1 point for each trick taken above thirteen. If tied, the winner of the next deal scores double.

*Notes.* A technical problem with this game is that there is no way of checking whether a player has *revoked*, i.e. failed to follow suit though able to do so. It may be unreasonable to assume players will cheat, but it is not unreasonable to expect a game to be so designed as to make genuine mistakes readily detectable. On these grounds, the following game is preferable.

# Chinese Whist

Also known as **Scarecrow**.

*Deal.* Deal 12 cards face down in a row on the table before each player, then 12 more cards face up across them, one to one. Deal a final card to the hand of each player. Dealer then announces a trump suit.

*Play*. Non-dealer leads. The leader to a trick may play his hand card if he still has it, or any one of his face-up cards. The follower has the same options, but must follow suit if able. Before each new trick is led, any down-card whose covering up-card has been played is itself turned face up.

*Score*. Score 1 point per trick taken above thirteen.

*Game*. Keep dealing and playing until one player has scored 13 or more points.

# Humbug Whist

*Deal*. Deal four hands of 13 cards each. Turn the last card (of Dealer's hand) face up to determine trumps.

*Exchange*. The aim is to win seven or more of the 12 tricks played. Each player examines his hand and announces whether he will play with the cards as dealt or throw them in and take the spare hand on his right instead. He may not examine the spare hand first, and, having once picked it up, is not allowed to change his mind. If Dealer exchanges, he may not keep the card turned for trump, but the trump suit remains the same anyway.

*Play*. Non-dealer leads to the first trick and normal Whist rules apply.

*Score*. The winner scores 1 point per trick above six.

*Honours* are then scored provided that:

• It was previously agreed to count them,
• The score for honours is not sufficient to win the game.

If your playing hand contained all four honours, add 4 for honours; if three, score 3 if your opponent held none or score 2 if he held one. If one player held no honours or only one, the other scores 2 for honours regardless of his hand. If both held two, neither scores for honours.

*Game*. Keep dealing and playing until one player reaches an agreed target score, e.g. 5, 7 or 10.

*Notes*. Exchanging cards gives you the advantage of knowing 13 cards out of play. It is therefore worth exchanging if your hand is worth less than four probable tricks and contains only one honour, or none.

*Variant*. The last card is not turned for trump. Instead, Dealer may name a trump suit or pass. If he passes, Non-dealer must name trumps. Whoever names trumps may not exchange hands, but his opponent may.

# Double Dummy

*Deal.* The two players sit south and west of the table (not opposite each other) and South deals. Deal four hands of 13 cards face down and one at a time. Expose Dealer's last card to establish trumps. Each player turns face up the cards of the hand dealt opposite him and arranges them in suits for ease of examination. Thus each player can see the 13 cards of his own hand and two 13-hand dummies, enabling him to deduce the hand of his opponent.

*Play.* West leads; South plays from his dummy; West plays from his dummy; and South plays from his own hand. The normal rules of following and trumping apply. Whoever wins a trick leads from his own hand or his own dummy depending on which of them furnished the winning card.

*Score.* Score 1 point for each trick taken above six.

*Honours.* The score for honours (if admitted) is 4 for all four or 2 for any three, regardless of whether contained in one hand or split between a live hand and its corresponding dummy. Honours are not counted if the player concerned stood at 1 point short of game at the start of the deal, or if their holder's opponent has reached the target score.

*Game.* By previous agreement, game is 5, 7 or 10 points.

*Notes.* Double Dummy is a good game for beginners at cards whose ultimate object is to learn Bridge.

# Honeymoon Bridge

Though neither a brilliant way of adapting Contract bridge for two, nor the best way of passing time on a honeymoon (Bezique is better), this Bridge-style adaptation of German Whist at least introduces you to the basic principles of scoring at Contract Bridge, so that you will have that much less to learn when you approach the proper four-hand game.

*Preliminaries.* The first half is played just like German Whist, except that the 13 tricks so played have no scoring value. As soon as the last card has been drawn from stock there is an auction to determine which player will choose trumps in return for contracting to win a majority of the 13 tricks to be played with the final hand.

*The auction.* Each in turn, starting with the last trick-winner, must bid or pass. A bid states the number of tricks above six which the player proposes to win and the trump suit (or none) desired for that purpose. The lowest bid is 'one club', an undertaking to win at least seven tricks (6+1) with clubs as trump. Each subsequent bid must be either numerically higher, or numerically equal but higher in suit. For this purpose the suits rank from low to high in this order: clubs, diamonds, hearts, spades, no trump. Thus 'one club' can be overcalled by 'one' or more of anything else, but 'one spade' can only be overcalled by 'one no trump', and 'one no trump' only by raising the level to two or more. The highest possible bid, 'seven no trump', is an undertaking to win all 13 tricks without a trump suit.

If one player bids a contract which the other believes can be beaten, the latter may announce 'double'. The doubled player then has three options:

- To pass. The contract stands, and whoever wins will score double.
- To make a higher bid. This cancels the double and keeps the auction going.
- To redouble. This means the bidder thinks he can certainly win his contract, and throws the onus back on the player who doubled. If the latter passes, the contract stands, and whoever wins scores quadruple. Alternatively, the doubler may cancel the quadruplication by making a higher bid to keep the auction going.

The auction ends when either player passes. The last bid made is the contract; the player who bid it is the declarer; and the opening lead is made by the declarer's opponent, who is referred to – traditionally but illogically – as the defender.

*Score.* A 'rubber' is the the best of three games, i.e. the first to win two games wins the rubber. A game is won by the first player to reach 100 or more points 'below the line', over as many deals as it takes. A player who has won one game is said to be vulnerable, and is subject to certain additional penalties or bonuses.

Each player's scoring column is divided into an upper and a lower half by a line drawn horizontally across the middle. Only scores made 'below the line' count towards winning the game, and scores are only made below the line for the number of contracted tricks won by the declarer. If he wins more tricks than contracted, he scores for the contracted number below the line and for excess tricks, known as 'over-tricks', above. If he fails to win as many as contracted, neither player scores below the line, but the defender scores above the line for the number of tricks by which Declarer fell short of his contract ('undertricks').

- For a successful contract, Declarer scores below the line for each contracted trick depending on the trump as follows:

| minor suit | (♣ ◇) | 20 per trick |
| major suit | (♡ ♠) | 30 per trick |
| no trump | | 40 for the first trick |
| | | 30 for each subsequent trick |

These scores are doubled or quadrupled if the game was doubled or redoubled respectively.

Overtricks are normally scored above the line at the same rate. For example, a Declarer who bids 'two spades' and makes three (by winning nine tricks) scores 60 below the line and 30 above. If, however, the contract is doubled or redoubled, overtricks score respectively 100 or 200 each regardless of suit, and this doubles again to 200 or 400 if the doubled player is vulnerable. For winning a doubled or redoubled contract, Declarer scores 50 or 100 above the line 'for the insult'.

For winning a 'small' or 'a grand slam', i.e. successfully contracting to win six or seven respectively, Declarer scores an additional 500 or 1000 above the line, increased to 750 or 1500 if vulnerable.

- For a failed contract, Defender scores above the line for each undertrick as follows, regardless of the trump suit or no trump:

| Undoubled | 50 | (100 if Declarer vulnerable) |
| Doubled, first undertrick | 100 | (200 vulnerable) |
| each subsequent | 200 | (300 vulnerable) |
| Redoubled, first undertrick | 200 | (400 vulnerable) |
| each subsequent | 400 | (600 vulnerable) |

- For honours, a player who in the final playing hand held AKQJT of trumps scores 150, or 100 for holding any four of them. At no trump, a player who held all four Aces scores 150 for honours. These scores apply regardless of who held them and of whether the contract was made or defeated.

*Game and rubber.* When either player reaches or exceeds 100 below the line, another horizontal line is drawn across beneath it and a new game started from a score of zero. This does not affect scores made above the line.

When either player has won two games the rubber is at an end. That player adds a bonus of 500 for the rubber, or 700 if the loser did not win a game. Finally, all the scores in both columns, both above and below the line and for the rubber, are added together, and the difference between the two totals is the margin of victory.

# 2

## ECARTÉ

### Where a sense of timing counts

This game is easy enough to be learnt by beginners but deep enough to give enjoyment to experts. It was a popular casino game in 19th-century Paris, having evolved from the ancient French card game of Triomphe, from which the word 'trump' ultimately derives.

The basic idea is simple. Each player receives five cards, and the aim is to win at least three of the five tricks played, or, better still, all five. What makes it interesting, not to say subtle, is that the hands are not necessarily played as dealt. Instead, both players keep throwing out poor cards and drawing (hopefully) better replacements, until one of them is satisfied with his hand and undertakes to win at least three tricks without any further exchanges.

As in many card games, the dealer is referred to as 'younger' and non-dealer as 'elder' hand.

### The game

*Cards*. Use a 32-card pack, with nothing lower than Seven. It is convenient to use two packs, one being shuffled while the other is dealt, and to have five counters each as a scoring aid (though this is not essential).

*Deal*. Decide first dealer by any agreed means, after which the deal alternates. Shuffle, offer for cutting, then deal five cards each in batches of two and three. This may be $2 + 3$ or $3 + 2$ on your first deal, but whichever it is you must stick to for the rest of your deals in the same game. Place the undealt cards face down to one side to form a stock. Turn up the top card and lay it on the table beside the stock. The suit of the turn-up is the trump suit for the deal. If the turn-up is a King, the dealer marks 1 point for it.

*Object*. In each deal the object is to win three or four tricks (the *point*), for 1 point, or all five (the *vole*), for 2. The game is won by the first to reach 5 points after several deals. If counters are used, each places five on the table at his own left and transfers one to his right for each point marked.

*Rank*. Cards rank from high to low in each suit as follows: K Q J A T 9 8 7. Note the intermediate position of the Ace.

*Discarding*. If elder hand is satisfied with his cards, he may begin play by leading to the first trick. If not, he may *propose* a change of cards by calling 'Cards'. In this event, younger may either accept the proposal, in which case both can exchange cards as explained below, or else refuse, in which case elder must lead. (It should be noted that if elder plays without proposing, and loses, he loses double; similarly, younger loses double if he refuses the first proposal and fails to win.)

If the proposal is accepted, elder rejects face down from his hand as many cards as he does not want, announcing this number clearly. Younger does likewise, and then deals from the top of the stock first as many cards as elder needs to complete his hand, then as many as he needs himself. Now the same situation obtains. Elder may play or propose; if he proposes, younger may accept or refuse; if he accepts, more cards are exchanged in the same manner. It should be noted that younger, having accepted a proposal, thereby obliges elder to discard at least one, but need not himself exchange any if he then decides not to.

This continues until either play begins or cards run out, in which case play must begin anyway. Note that the turn-up is not part of the stock and may not be dealt as a replacement. If not enough cards remain to fill both players' hands, such cards as do remain go to elder. If either player is forced to retrieve one or more of his last discards because not enough replacements remain in stock, he must do so before seeing the cards he is dealt.

*Marking the King*. If either player holds the King of trumps he may mark one point for it provided that he announces 'King' before playing a card to the first trick, or as he does so if he plays it to that trick. If he fails to announce it in time he is too late, as the King may not be marked in retrospect. If marking the King brings a player's score to 5, the hand is not played out.

*Play.* Elder leads to the first trick, and the winner of each trick leads to the next. The second player must not only follow suit if able, but also win the trick if he can. If unable to follow suit, he must play a trump if he has any. The trick is won with the higher card of the suit led, or the higher trump if any are played. (In leading to the first trick, it is traditional for elder to announce the suit of the card he leads.)

*Score.* The winner marks 1 point for taking three or four tricks, 2 points for taking all five. But if elder played without proposing and lost, younger scores 2 whether he took three, four or five tricks. Similarly, elder scores 2 if younger lost after refusing elder's first proposal. Note that this increased value applies only if the hand was played with the cards originally dealt, no discards having been made, and only if the player who accepted his hand as good fails to take three tricks.

*Revoke.* If a player revokes, by failing to follow suit or to win the trick or to play a trump when able and required to do so, his opponent may upon discovery of the offence call for the hand to be replayed with the same cards. If the offender wins, he scores in the usual way but first subtracts one point from his total as a penalty. If he loses, there is no penalty.

*Game.* The game may be lengthened by agreeing that a rubber is won by the first player to win two games, for which there is a bonus of 2 points. Alternatively, play up to a previously agreed total of game points such as 5 or 10. For this purpose it may be preferred to count 1 game point if the opponent has scored 3 or 4, 2 if he scored 1 or 2, and 3 if he scored nothing at all.

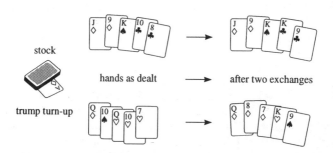

**Figure 2: Ecarté** With diamonds turned for trump, North proposes and South accepts. After two such proposals and exchanges, North rashly leads the club King, and loses (see text).

## Notes on play

The whole point of the game lies in deciding, when you have the choice, whether to play with the cards held or to propose (or accept a proposal) to change cards. Roughly speaking, a hand is playable when it contains at least three cards which are trumps or Kings. Looked at another way, it is advisable to discard all cards which are neither trumps nor Kings, and not to discard fewer than three. But there are exceptions to this principle, governed by such factors as whether you are younger or elder, hold or lack the King of trumps, and the state of the score.

From a score of love-all, there are certain types of hand upon which elder's best move is to play rather than propose. Such hands are called *jeux de règle*, 'obligatory plays', for the reason that, in casino play, the house player is obliged to play if dealt one of them – otherwise he is likely to find himself rapidly redundant and without a reference. It should go without saying that anything better than the following minimum *jeux de règle* is equally 'obligatory'. On the other hand, completely mechanical play is boring in its predictability, and more excitement may be squeezed out of playing the occasional shaky hand or sometimes proposing on a good one.

*Three or more trumps.* No matter how low they are, or what the non-trumps may be, a hand with three trumps is worth playing. Remember that there are only eight cards in each suit, and that one trump – the turn-up – is out of play, thus making it unlikely that younger will have more than one of the other four trumps. Best procedure is to lead the highest trump. If it is not taken you will almost certainly win three trump tricks, and if it is you will expect to win the other two trumps and make an eventual third trick by leading a suit your opponent cannot follow.

*Two-trump hands.* A hand with two trumps is playable if the other three cards are all of the same suit, or include a King or a guarded Queen. From the first of these, lead the highest card of the plain suit, and keep doing so at every opportunity. Two trumps and a singleton King is playable provided that the other two cards, if of different suits, are not both lower than Ten. Lead the King, unless the other two are of the same suit, in which case lead the higher of them. From two trumps and a guarded Queen (*i.e.* a Queen accompanied by at least one other of her suit), lead the Queen. Other two-trump hands are playable if the three non-trumps are generally high and not all of different suits, even down to Jack of one suit and Ten, Nine of another. Generally, lead the higher of the two-card plain suit.

*One-trump hands.* Playable if they contain K–Q–J of another suit, or if the other four cards are of the same suit and include the King, which should be led. Also playable is a hand consisting of a trump, a Queen, and another Queen twice guarded, from which the guarded Queen should be led. Risky is one trump plus two guarded Queens. At least one of the guards should be not lower than Ten.

*No-trump hands.* A hand devoid of trumps is playable if it contains three Queens or at least four court cards, provided that they are not all Jacks. (But four Jacks and another trump is playable – see below.)

By and large, younger may refuse a proposal if he holds a hand that would be a *jeu de règle* with the positions reversed, though some patterns need to be somewhat stronger. Although the fact that elder proposes suggests that his hand is too weak to play, this does not make younger's that much stronger by comparison, since he is likely to be forced into trumping earlier and lacks the initiative to start with his strongest plain suit. In particular, a one-trump hand containing K–Q–J of another suit only merits a refusal if the fifth card is also a court, while a two-trumper with three in a plain suit similarly requires the best plain card to be a court.

Possession of the King of trumps is a key factor in play, as it scores as much as winning the point in its own right, which may prove enough for game, and also increases one's chance of winning the vole while ensuring defence against it. The latter considerations also apply to the Queen of trumps when the King has been turned up. It follows that a hand qualifying as a *jeu de règle*, or a refusal, may nevertheless justify one or two discards for the sake of the vole. For example, suppose spades are trumps and you hold:

♠K Q ♡K Q ♣7

Although you have a certain four tricks and possible vole as it stands, you may propose in the hope of discarding the Seven and drawing a spade, heart or high card in its place. If refused, you will score 2 for the point in any case.

The *jeux de règle* should be known by heart, as an astute player may learn much from your indecisiveness or air of calculation if you do not play, propose, accept or refuse immediately and evenly. For much the same reason, the astute player, having dealt, will not look at his own cards until elder has made his first decision, in order to avoid giving anything away by inadvertent grimaces (or whoops of delight). And it is the height of folly to give way to force of habit by arranging one's cards in rank and suit.

Normal procedure in play is to lead the top card from one's longest plain suit. This is the suit most likely to force younger into trumping, and it is a general principle that where both players hold the same number of trumps the one first forced is most weakened. If the lead holds, continue the suit until it is trumped; but if you also hold the top trump it may profitably be led second before the forcing suit is continued. Trumps should be led only if four or more are held, or with three in hand if the top two are consecutive. From two trumps, a singleton King and two low cards, lead one of the low cards if both are of the same suit, and the King if both are different. With weak trumps and high plain cards, it is well to lead the high cards and keep changing the suit to avoid being trumped. If you manage to win the first three tricks in this way, lead the trump fourth with a view to the vole.

So far we have considered hands strong enough to have been led from without proposing. What happens when you have to lead from a poor hand on which you have proposed, but have been refused, depends on whether the hand is only poor, or so desperate that the vole may be won against you. In the latter case the important thing is to take a trick as soon as possible. Lead any King, or, if you have none, your highest single card – 'single' in the sense of being the only one in its suit. It is not advisable to lead from a guarded plain suit, such as Q–A, as you have more chance of making a trick from it if your opponent leads into that suit. If the situation is not desperate, prefer to lead one of two consecutive cards in the same suit.

If you win the first two tricks and find your opponent out of trumps, always continue with a non-trump King if you have one, and then lead a trump fourth. He will then prefer to discard from your King-suit if possible in order to preserve a possible defence in some other suit against the fifth lead. If then your fifth card is of the same suit as your King, you will win the vole. If not, you may gain nothing extra in the short run, but will have played consistently and so stand a better chance of succeeding with the ruse when the opportunity next presents itself. Otherwise, an astute opponent will notice that you only play King-then-trump when the King is guarded, and will not fall for discarding the wrong suit to the trump lead.

If left with a trump and a plain card when three tricks have been divided, lead the plain card if you have won two tricks, the trump if only one. This gives you the best opportunity of winning the point.

The best time for younger to mark the King is when about to play to the first trick. This has the advantage of withholding useful information that might otherwise have influenced elder's lead. There is rarely much point in sinking the King (deliberately refraining from marking it). Younger may do so when he stands at three towards game against elder's four and elder plays without proposing, as younger will score two and the game anyway if elder loses, and will lose anyway if elder wins the point.

Similarly, elder may sink when he has three to younger's four and younger refuses the first proposal. If when your opponent stands at four points you lack the King and it is not turned up, you should be prepared to play on a riskier hand than normally, as the more exchanging you allow to take place, the greater his chance of winning outright by drawing the King. In these circumstances it doesn't matter if you play immediately or refuse the first proposal, as a score of two is not better than of one to the player with four.

Finally, if your opponent proposes when he stands at four points to your three, refuse if you have even an outside chance of winning the point. It is true that he will win the game if you fail, but to have proposed at all at such a score indicates a very weak hand.

Unless, of course, he was bluffing. And this is the point at which all clever stratagems come to nought, for Ecarté, more than any other trick-taking game except Le Truc, is wide open to the sort of intuitive play which tends to unnerve 'calculating' players by confusing them.

## Sample game

*First deal.* Bertrand deals, the first card going to Armand. He turns up ◇A, and the hands are:

> A:  ◇J 9 ♠K ♣T 8 *proposes*
> B:  ◇Q ♠T ♡Q T 7 *accepts*

The new hands are:

> A:  ◇J 9 ♠K ♡J ♣7 *proposes*
> B:  ◇Q ♠J A 8 ♣J *accepts*

And again:

> A:  ◇J 9 ♠K ♣K 9 *plays*
> B:  ◇Q 8 7 ♡K ♠9

The play proceeds: ♣K ◇7, ♡K ◇9, ♣9 ◇8, ♠9 ♠K, at which point they have two tricks each. Bertrand's Queen wins the last trick and gives him the point. Had Armand played his original hand he would have won, but by constant exchanging he permitted Bertrand to gain three trumps to his own two. Score: A = 0, B = 1.

*Second deal.* Armand deals, turning up ♡K for which he marks a point.

> B:  ♡T ♣Q T ◇9 ♠9 *proposes*

A:   ♡J ♣J ♢K Q ♠8 *refuses*

Armand considers Bertrand's proposal to be made from weakness and a desire not to lose the initiative, and refuses on the strength of his four court cards. But Bertrand, despite his feeble hand, correctly refrains from leading his guarded suit and succeeds in winning the first, third and fourth tricks as follows: ♠*9* ♠8, ♢9 ♢**K**, ♢Q ♡**T**, ♣**Q** ♣J, ♣**T** ♡*J*. Bertrand marks two for having won after a refusal, and the scores are now A = 1, B = 3.

*Third deal.* Bertrand, before turning up ♢9, deals:

A:   ♢J T ♠J ♡Q ♣A *proposes*
B:   ♢Q ♠K 9 ♡8 7 *accepts*

Then after exchanging:

A:   ♢J T 7 ♣7 ♡9 *proposes*
B:   ♢K Q ♠K A T *refuses*

Bertrand, if he had the lead, would hope Armand had not more than two trumps and would play for the vole. As it is, he thinks he has good prospects after a second request for cards. But not so. Armand leads ♢J and Bertrand announces the King as he plays it. There follows ♠K ♢*7*, ♡*9* ♢**Q**, ♠A ♢*7*, ♣*7* ♣**T**, and Armand gains the point. Score now: Armand = 2, Bertrand = 4.

*Fourth deal.* Armand deals, turning up ♠T:

B:   ♢K Q ♡Q T ♣7 *proposes*
A:   ♠K ♣K Q ♡J 8 *refuses*

If Bertrand proposes needing only one point to game, Armand's hand gives him more than a fighting chance. Upon trumping the first trick, Armand marks his King: ♢K ♠**K**, ♣**K** ♣7, ♣**Q** and Armand wins the point. In leading the Queen rather than switching to hearts, Armand hopes that Bertrand either had been dealt no trumps, or, if he had, could still follow suit to clubs, in view of the fact that it was the lowest of all he had thrown to the King. Score: Armand = 4, Bertrand = 4.

*Fifth deal.* Bertrand deals, turning up ♣8:

A:   ♣7 ♡K Q ♠Q 9 *plays*
B:   ♣T ♡J 9 ♢ K Q

Armand now plays to the score, preventing Bertrand from drawing the King (if he had it, he would already have announced it and won), and hoping his opponent has not more than one trump. The play proceeds: ♡*K* ♡9, ♠**Q** ♣*T*, ♢K ♣7, ♡*Q* ♡*J* – giving Armand point and game.

# 3

## —————— PUT ——————

## *A game of fun but ill repute*

Although no-one (to my knowledge) regularly plays this old English tavern game, castigated by 17th-century moralists as one of ill repute, it is so easy to learn and fun to play that it would be a pity to omit it from the core curriculum of card game learners. It is essentially a game of bluff rather than calculation.

*Cards.* 52, ranking 3–2–A–K–Q–J–T–9–8–7–6–5–4 in each suit, with Three the highest card and Four the lowest.

*Object.* The game is won by the first player to score 5 points over as many deals as necessary, or to win a majority of the three tricks played in any deal.

*Deal.* The player drawing the highest Put card (Three high, Four low) deals first and the deal alternates. Shuffle thoroughly and deal three cards to each player, one at time.

*Play.* Tricks are played to unusual rules. Any card may be led, and the other player may also play any card: there is no need to follow suit and there are no trumps. The trick is taken by the higher card, and the winner of one trick leads to the next. If cards of equal rank are played e.g. two Threes, two Aces, or whatever, the trick is tied and belongs to neither player. In this case it is put to one side, and whoever led to it leads to the next.

*Putting and throwing.* Either player, when about to lead to a trick, may do one of three things:

- Throw his hand in, thus conceding the deal and 1 point to the opponent.
- Lead a card without saying anything. His opponent must then play.
- Say 'Put', which is short for 'I put it to you that you should throw your cards in while you have the chance'. If the opponent follows this advice, the deal ends and the putter scores 1 point. If not, the putter leads and the other must play.

*Score.* The game is won outright, regardless of points scored, by the player who wins two tricks in a deal, or one trick if the other two are tied. If each player wins one trick and one trick is tied, the result is a draw by 'trick and tie' and there is no score for that deal. If neither wins outright, the winner is the first player to score 5 points for concessions.

*Notes.* It is obvious that neither player will reach 5 points, because as soon as he reaches 4 the other will have no incentive to concede. Having nothing to lose, he may as well play the hand out on the off-chance of winning outright. This is not necessarily a defect in the game, though there may be a defect (of omission) in the only original source from which all later accounts of the game derive. What it means, in effect, is that in the course of one game you have four chances of throwing your cards in without penalty. The points are not a score so much as a way of keeping count of your used opportunities. Of course, you could agree that an outright win earns a double game or stake, and a win on points only a single, in which case they become a score rather than a count.

*Variant.* The game becomes more interesting if you shorten the pack to (say) 32 cards by stripping out all the lower ranks from Four to Nine. There is, indeed, an equivalent French game called le Truc – 'the Knack' – which is played with a 32-card pack ranking 6–7–A–K–Q–J–T (yes, really!). The winning of two tricks, or one and two ties, scores 1 point. However, each player may offer, or threaten, to double the value of the game when about to play to a trick, allowing the other to throw his hand in to prevent the double from taking effect. The first to reach 12 points wins the game, and the first to win two games wins the rubber.

# 4

## —— ALL FOURS ——

### A family of Jack games

All Fours is another old English tavern game, specifically a Kentish one, though it was probably came over from the Low Countries with the return of Charles II and his court. Here a special role attaches to the Knave of trumps, which was originally given the name 'Jack' to distinguish it from the other Knaves. This stuck, and became pretty well established as the name of the lowest court card in the 19th century, when cards were first produced with corner indices, as 'J' for Jack has obvious advantages over 'K' for Knave – or is it King?

All Fours has given rise to a whole family of games on both sides of the Atlantic, including (in America) California Jack, Seven Up, Auction Pitch, and Dom Pedro, and (in Britain) Don and Phat.

Here follows the original version, for two players. It is followed by All Fives and California Jack, also for two.

### —— All Fours ——

*Cards*. A standard 52-card pack.

*Game*. The winner is the first player to reach a previously agreed total, formerly 11 points in the English game but now 7 in the American – whence the alternative title 'Seven Up'. This will take several deals to achieve. Scores may be recorded on paper, though a traditional method is to start with seven counters each and pay them into a pool one at a time for each point won, so that the winner is the first to get rid of his seven counters.

*Deal.* Whoever cuts the higher-ranking card deals first; thereafter the turn to deal alternates. Deal a batch of three cards face down to each player, then a second batch of three so that each receives a hand of six cards. Lay the remainder face down to one side, and turn the top card face up.

*The turn-up.* The suit of the turn-up proposes a trump suit for the deal, which may or may not be accepted by either player. If the turn-up is a Jack, the dealer scores 1 point for it.

*Object.* The object in each hand is to score as many points as possible, single points being available for one or more of the following factors:

*Turning a Jack*, as explained above.

*Gift*, as explained below in the bidding.

*High*, for having been dealt the highest trump in play.

*Low*, for having been dealt the lowest trump in play (or, if agreed beforehand, for winning it in a trick).

*Jack*, for winning a trick containing the Jack of trumps, if it is in play.

*Game*, for capturing, in tricks, the highest aggregate value of scoring-cards, valued thus: each Ace 4, King 3, Queen 2, Jack 1, Ten 10. In the event of a tie this point goes to elder hand (non-dealer) – this is to offset younger's advantage of scoring a point for turning a Jack.

It is to be noted that the first two points (turning a Jack and Gift) will not always occur, and that there can be no point for winning the Jack if it is not in play, *ie* lies in the undealt part of the pack. Two or more of the points for High, Low and Jack may be combined in one card. For instance, if a given card is the *only* trump in play, it counts one for High plus one for Low. Similarly, the Jack of trumps will count an extra point if it is the highest or the lowest in play. In the extreme case, it would count four if it were the only trump in play (High, Low, Jack) and also the only scoring card in play (giving its winner Game).

*Bidding.* The bidder is the player who eventually chooses trumps. He is not obliged to reach any particular target and is not penalised for losing, but will naturally select a suit which he thinks will yield him more points than his opponent. Elder hand has first choice: he may accept the turned suit as trump by saying 'I stand', or reject it by saying 'I beg'. If he begs, younger may also accept or reject the proposed trump, but it costs him a point to accept. He accepts by saying 'Take it', in which case elder scores 1 point for Gift and play begins. He rejects the suit by putting the turn-up to one side and 'running the cards', as follows.

*Running the cards.* To find another suit for trumps, younger first deals another batch of three to each player, so that both have nine cards, and turns up the top card of the pack again. If it is a different suit, the same procedure applies: he scores a point if it is a Jack, then elder may stand or beg, and, if he begs, younger may accept the suit by giving elder a point or reject it by running the cards yet again, dealing three more to each. This continues until either the pack runs out, in which case the hands are thrown in and the cards reshuffled and redealt by the same dealer, or a suit is accepted as trump. Whenever the turn-up proves to be of the same suit as one that has already been rejected, the cards are run again automatically. Younger may not score a point for turning the Jack of a suit that has already been rejected.

*Play.* If the cards have been run, each player makes as many discards as are necessary to reduce his playing hand to six cards again. Non-dealer leads to the first trick, and the winner of each trick leads to the next. Normal rules of trick-taking apply, but with an important exception – namely, that the second to a trick is always entitled to play a trump, even if he can follow suit. It is not permissible, however, to play from a different non-trump suit if able to follow suit to the card led. A trick is won by the higher card of the suit led or by a higher trump if any are played.

*Score.* At the end of play each reckons his score for high, low, Jack and game. It is to be noted that points are scored strictly in the order stated, and that as soon as one player has the point which brings his total to seven he has won the game. When played for money, each game is settled separately for a fixed amount.

## Notes on play

In all games of this family, custom varies as to whether the point for Low is scored by the player who happens to be dealt the lowest trump in play, or by the player who captures it in a trick – which may, of course, be the same player if he uses it to trump with, but need not always be so. In the original game it went always to the player dealt it. In modern games such as Auction Pitch it goes to the player who captures it, though there is a tendency in two-hand play to revert to the original system. There are those who argue that if the point goes to the player who wins it then credit is given for skill rather than luck.

On the other hand, it requires hardly less judgement to decide whether or not your lowest trump – the Four, for example – is in fact likely to be the lowest in play. In short, the only matter of any import is that you should agree beforehand which rule to follow.

The strategy of All Fours depends entirely on the score. At love-all you will be looking for a hand that offers at least two and preferably three of the four potential points, and without losing one for gift for the sake of getting it. At the other extreme, with only one point short of game you can safely entrump any suit of which you hold the Ace, as you will win with the inevitable 'one for High' no matter how many of the others your opponent gains.

You are bound to win the point for High if you hold the Ace of trumps. If the cards have not been run, you can reckon the King as high (and, conversely, the Three as low) about nine times out of ten, and the Queen high (Four low) about four times out of five.

Never bank on the point for Jack unless you have it yourself, and well guarded at that, normally with at least two other trumps.

The point for game is the only one that depends upon the skill with which you play your cards. In this connection, it is essential to save any Ten you hold, as its capture is usually enough to swing the point for Game. For the same reason, it is better, if at all possible, to use Aces and Kings to capture adverse leads than to lead them in their own right. As capturing cards they stand to ensure the point for Game by taking others that may also be of value, whereas, as leaders, they risk being trumped.

A hand containing three or more trumps is usually worth playing – the more so if it includes high ranks or the Jacks, the less so if it lacks these or includes an unguarded Ten. A two-trump hand may be playable if it includes the Ace or King. If you are scoring Low for being dealt it, and have the lead, you may also chance your arm on (say) Q–2 by leading the Two and hoping to force out a singleton Ace or King. If it works, you may gain Game and Low against your opponent's High only.

---

# All Fives

This increases the number of points to be played for. Game is usually set at 61 and progress recorded on a Cribbage board. In addition to the single points for High, Low, Jack and Game, the following trumps score as below to the player capturing them in tricks:

| | |
|---|---|
| Ace | 4 |
| King | 3 |
| Queen | 2 |
| Jack | 1 |
| Ten | 10 |
| Five | 5 |

This gives a maximum of 29 points obtainable on one deal if all the value cards are in play. (In counting for 'Game', the Five of trumps is also worth five, but plain suit Fives have no value.) This scoring system may be applied to Pitch and California Jack (below).

*Variant* **Pitch** is a bidding form of All Fours, and for this reason it is generally known as **Auction Pitch**, more usually played by four than by two. Starting with the non-dealer, each in turn bids to gain a minimum number of game points (High, Low, Jack and Game, as before) in exchange for the right of nominating trumps. Whoever bids the higher number establishes trumps by leading or 'pitching' a card of that suit, which starts the play. Both players score what they actually win, but the pitcher, if he fails to win as many as he bid, is set back by the amount of his bid – *i.e.*, that amount is deducted from his score. From this feature, the game is also known as **Setback**.

# California Jack

This American variation is a cross between All Fours and German Whist.

*Cards.* Shuffle the cards and get the non-dealer to cut for trumps. This is done by lifting the top half of the pack and showing its bottom card before replacing it. The suit of the shown card is trump for the deal. Deal six cards each and stack the rest face down. Cards rank in their normal order from Ace down to Two.

*Object.* To win any of the four game points for High, Low, Jack, and Game, as at All Fours, except that 'Game' requires 41+ of the 80 card-points taken in tricks as follows:

| each | Ace | counts | 4 | card-points |
|---|---|---|---|---|
| | King | counts | 3 | |
| | Queen | counts | 2 | |
| | Jack | counts | 1 | |
| | Ten | counts | 10 | |

*Play.* Non-dealer leads to the first trick. If a trump is led, suit must be followed; if not, the second is free to follow suit or trump as preferred. It is only permissible to play a different non-trump suit if unable to follow or trump. The trick is taken by the higher card of the suit led, or by the higher trump if any are played, and the winner of each trick leads to the next. Before doing so, the trick winner draws the top card of stock and his opponent draws the next. When the stock is empty the last six tricks are played out in the usual way.

*Score.* The point for High is claimed as soon as the trump Ace is dealt or drawn; those for Low and Jack as soon as the relevant card is captured; that for Game when all the tricks have been played and the card-points counted. The deal alternates, and play continues until one player reaches an agreed target, normally 7 game points. If 7 is reached in mid-game, play ceases and the point for Game is ignored.

# 5

## —————— PIQUET ——————

### *Card game for aristocrats*

Piquet, pronounced 'P.K.' the French way or 'Picket' if you prefer English, has long been regarded as one of the great card games and certainly the best for two; if by 'best' is meant that requiring and rewarding the greatest skill in play. Of French or possibly Spanish origin, it can be traced back to at least 1500. For a game that has been played in so many countries for so many centuries it is remarkable in having undergone little variation in its basic material, thereby indicating how brilliant that material is. It is a game of tremendous depth and variety, and I never tire of playing it.

The little variation it has undergone relates chiefly to overall structure. The version described here is English Rubicon Piquet, as standardized by London's Portland Club in the late 19th century. 'Rubicon' denotes the target score of 100 points. In the older form of the game, called *Piquet au cent*, anglicized to 'Saunt', the game was won by the first player to reach 100 points over as many deals as it took. In the Rubicon game, a *partie* is six deals and the loser is more heavily penalized if he fails to reach the 'Rubicon' of 100 points.

Piquet is very easy to follow once you have got the basic idea, but the rules are subject to so many niceties of detail as to make it look at first reading far more complicated than it really is – a classic case of not being able to see the wood for the trees. You may therefore find it helpful to go through the following introductory exercise, either alone or with a prospective partner, before plunging into the verbal thicket of detailed procedure.

## An illustrative hand

Take a 32-card pack, or make one by discarding all ranks below Seven from a 52-card pack. Deal out two hands of 12 cards each as follows:

| Elder (non-dealer) | Younger (dealer) |
| --- | --- |

|   |   |   |   |   |   |   |   |   |   |   |   |   |   |   |   |   |   |   |   |   |
| - | - | - | - | - | - | - | - | - | - | - | - | - | - | - | - | - | - | - | - | - |
| ♠ | . | . | Q | . | . | . | 8 | 7 | | A | K | . | . | . | . | . | . |
| ♡ | A | . | . | J | . | . | . | . | | . | K | . | . | T | 9 | . | . |
| ♣ | A | . | . | . | . | . | 8 | 7 | | . | K | Q | J | T | . | . | . |
| ♢ | A | . | Q | J | . | 9 | . | . | | . | . | . | . | T | . | 8 | 7 |

Arrange the remaining cards in the following order:

♡Q–8–7 ♠9 ♢K ♣9 ♠J–10

Spread them face down in a row, overlapping one another, with the back of the ♡Q on top. This row is called the 'talon'. In real play, of course, no-one knows what these cards are.

What will happen is this. Elder will first discard up to five cards and draw the same number of replacements from the top of the talon, then younger will discard as many as remain (typically three) and also draw replacements. They will then seek to score points for declaring certain card combinations in their new hands, and finally seek to win a majority of 12 tricks played at no trump. The purpose of the draw is therefore partly to compose winning combinations and partly to ensure a good playing hand. Before you can do this, you have to know what the scoring combinations are. They fall into three classes.

- *Point.* This is scored by the player holding the longest suit, or, if equal, the suit of greater point-value after counting numerals at face value, 10 per court, and 11 for the Ace.
- *Sequence.* This is scored by the player holding the longest suit-sequence, or, if equal, the one with the highest top card. That player may then score for any other sequences he may hold.
- *Sets.* A set is three or four Aces, Kings, Queens, Jacks, or Tens. Lower numerals do not count. A *quatorze* (set of four) beats a *trio* (three). Whoever holds the highest quatorze, or, if none, the highest trio, is entitled to score for it and any other sets he may also hold.

Let us now look at the hands with these combinations in mind.

Elder's best chance of making point and sequence lies in keeping all his diamonds. He therefore discards his Sevens and Eights and ♡J, drawing in their place ♡Q–8–7, ♠9 and ◇K.

Younger will obviously keep his high cards and his club sequence, and will hope to draw the fourth King or Ten, either of which would give him a winning quatorze since he has one of each Ace, Queen, Jack. Making the obvious discard of three low numerals, he draws in their place ♠J T, ♣9.

The playing hands are now:

| Elder | | | | | | | | Younger | | | | | | | |
|---|---|---|---|---|---|---|---|---|---|---|---|---|---|---|---|
| ♠ | . | . | Q | . | . | 9 | . | . | A | K | J | T | . | . | . |
| ♡ | A | . | Q | . | . | 8 | 7 | . | . | K | . | T | . | . | . |
| ♣ | A | . | . | . | . | . | . | . | . | K | Q | J | T | 9 | . | . |
| ◇ | A | K | Q | J | . | 9 | . | . | . | . | . | . | T | . | . | . |

Both players have a 'point of five', elder in diamonds and younger in clubs. But elder's five total 50 card-points to younger's 49, so elder scores 5 – one per card – for holding the better point.

For sequences, elder's four to the Ace is beaten by younger's five to the King. Younger therefore scores for the sequence, and would be entitled to score for any other sequences if he had any. Sequences also score 1 per card, but those of five or more carry a bonus of 10, so in this case younger scores 15.

For sets, elder's trio of Aces is beaten by younger's quatorze of Tens, which also entitles him to reckon his trio of Kings. Quatorzes count 14 and trios 3, so younger scores 17 for sets.

Elder now leads to the first trick with the scores so far at 5 to 32. He cashes his seven winners immediately – there is no point in messing about – and scores a bonus of 10 for winning a clear majority of tricks.

There is far more to it than that, of course; but if you take this sample deal as illustrating the wood you will find it much easier to pick your pathway through the trees as I now describe them to you.


## The game

*Game.* A game or *partie* is six deals, each dealing alternately. The winner is then the player with the higher total. If the loser fails to reach 100 he is 'rubiconed', and the winner gets a hefty bonus.

*Cards.* Use a 32-card pack ranking A K Q J T 9 8 7 in each suit. Whoever cuts the higher card may elect to deal first, there being a theoretical slight advantage in so doing.

*Deal.* Shuffle the cards lightly, have them cut, and deal twelve each. You may deal in batches of two or three, but whichever you choose you must stick to it throughout the partie. Spread the remaining eight face down as a talon.

*Carte blanche.* A dealt hand devoid of court cards is called a 'blank', or *carte blanche*, and may be declared for 10 points. Whoever gets it must, if he wishes to score for it, declare it immediately, and prove it by rapidly dealing his hand of cards one by one face up to the table. (*I have here simplified a complicated rule of procedure, as the feature occurs too rarely make such a fuss over.*)

*The draw.* Elder must discard at least one card, and may discard up to five, drawing the same number of replacements from the top of the talon downwards. If he takes fewer than five, he may peep at those he did not take, other than the last three, without showing them to younger.

Younger, for his part, is not obliged to draw, but may discard up to as many as remain – usually three – and similarly draw replacements from the top of the remaining talon. If he leaves any card or cards untaken, he may either reveal them to both players or leave them face down, but may not look at them himself without showing them to elder.

*Declaring point.* Elder, if he wishes to score for point, states the number of cards in his longest suit, e.g. 'Point of five'. Younger replies 'Good' if he cannot match it, 'Not good' if he can beat it. If equal, he asks 'Counting?', and elder then states the total value of its constituent cards, reckoning Ace 11, courts 10 each, and numerals at face value. Again, younger replies 'Good' if he cannot match it or 'Not good' if he can beat it. If he says 'Equal', neither scores for point; otherwise, the better point-holder scores 1 per constituent card.

*Declaring sequences.* Elder, if he wishes to score for sequences, now states the length of his longest, e.g. 'sequence of four'. Younger replies 'Good' if he cannot match it, 'Not good' if he can beat it. If equal, he asks 'To?', and elder then states the top card of the sequence. Again, younger replies 'Good' if he cannot match it or 'Not good' if he his top card is higher. If he says 'Equal', neither scores for point. Otherwise, the holder of the best sequence scores for it and any other sequence he can declare. Sequences of three and four score 3 and 4 respectively, of five to eight 15 to 18 respectively. (Sequences of three to eight are called, respectively, tierce, quart, quint, sixième, septième, huitième. *Quart* is pronounced *cart.* The traditional way of declaring a sequence is 'I have a tierce', or whatever it may be. If younger has an equally long sequence and seeks clarification, reply 'Tierce (quart, etc) major' if it is headed by the Ace, 'minor' if by the King, otherwise 'to the Queen', and so on.)

*Declaring sets.* Elder, if he wishes to score for sets, now announces his highest-ranking quatorze or trio, e.g. 'Fourteen Queens' (*sic*), 'Three Tens', or whatever. A higher-ranking set beats a lower, but any quatorze beats a trio. Younger replies 'Good' or 'Not good', as the case may be. Whoever has the best set scores for it and any other he may hold. Trios score 3 points each, quatorzes 14.

*Leading.* All such declarations having been made, elder plays a card face up to the table, saying, and scoring, 'One for leading'. Before younger responds, however, the scores so far announced verbally may be noted down, together with any bonus scorable for *pique* or *repique*.

*Pique, repique.* If either player reaches a score of 30 or more for declarations before the other has scored anything at all in the deal, he adds a bonus of 60 for repique. Here it must be noted that scores accrue strictly in this order: blank, point, sequence, set. If, therefore, *either* player scores for blank or point, the other cannot score repique for reaching 30 on sequences or sets. Conversely, scoring for sets alone offers no protection from repique if the other player reaches 30 while scoring for sequences. (Some say that declaring equality for point or sequence prevents the opponent from claiming repique, but this contravenes the Portland Club Laws.)

Pique is similar, but scored only by elder. If elder, by adding to his declarations points made in the play of tricks, reaches 30 before younger has scored anything at all in the deal, he thereby qualifies for an additional 30 for pique.

*Tricks.* Tricks are played at no trump. Suit must be followed if possible, otherwise any card may be played. The trick is taken by the higher card of the suit led, and the winner of each trick leads to the next. Score 1 for winning a trick to which you led, or 2 for winning a trick led by your opponent. A convenient way of recording this is to store 1-point tricks face down and 2-point tricks face up on the table. (*The trick-scoring rule is usually stated '1 for leading to a trick, 1 for capturing the lead, and 1 for the last trick'. My wording amounts to the same thing.*)

For winning a majority of tricks, i.e. seven or more, score an additional 10 'for cards'. For winning all 12 tricks, score 10 for cards plus 30 for *capot*.

*Game score.* Scores are cumulated at the end of each deal ready for the next. The player with the greater score at the end of six deals reckons, for game, 100 points, plus his own score, minus his opponent's. If, however, the loser failed to reach 100, he is 'rubiconed', and the winner then reckons 100, plus his own score, *plus* his opponent's.

## Sample deal

Let's follow a sample hand played by – for the sake of argument – Napoleon and Josephine.

Josephine deals, making Napoleon elder hand, and the cards are:

Nap: ♠A K J ♡A Q J 8 ♣J 8 7 ♢9 8
Jos: ♠T 7 ♡T 9 7 ♣K Q T ♢A Q J T

Napoleon has up to five exchanges, and hopes to draw more hearts and the 'fourteenth' Jack. He therefore discards ♠K and the two low clubs and diamonds.

Josephine must keep her fourteen Tens and discards ♠7 ♡9 ♡7. After the draw, the hands are:

Nap: ♠A J 9 8 ♡A K Q J 8 ♣J 9 ♢K
Jos: ♠Q T ♡T ♣A K Q T ♢A Q J T 7

Declarations proceed as follows:
*Nap* Point of five.
*Jos* (*also having a point of five*) Worth?
*Nap* 49.
*Jos* (*with 48*) Good.
*Nap* In hearts. And a quart major. (*Meaning a sequence of four to the Ace.*)
*Jos* Good.
*Nap* That's five for point, four for the sequence nine . . . (*Looks for*

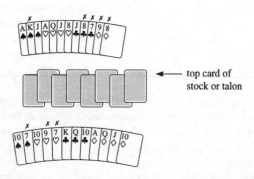

← top card of
stock or talon

**Figure 3: Piquet** Napoleon, as elder hand, can discard and draw five cards. Wishing to keep his point in hearts and to draw the fourth Jack, he discards those marked with a cross. This leaves three for Josephine, whose main aim is to retain the diamond point and four Tens.

*another sequence to count, but fails to find any. His next call is some-
what tentative.*) Three Jacks?

*Jos* Not good.

*Nap* (*leading* ♡ *A*) And one's ten.

*Jos* I count fourteen Tens and three Queens, seventeen.

Tricks are played as follows, each announcing their score upon winning a trick.

| Nap | Jos | | |
|-----|-----|-----|-----|
| ♡A | ♡T | (1) | *Nap* Eleven. |
| ♡K | ◇7 | (1) | *Nap* (*playing all his hearts simultaneously*) Twelve, thirteen, fourteen, fifteen. |
| ♡Q | ◇T | (1) | |
| ♡J | ◇J | (1) | |
| ♡8 | ◇Q | (1) | *Jos* (*repeating her score*) Seventeen. |
| ◇K | ◇A | (2) | |
| ♣9 | ♣A | (1) | *Jos* Nineteen. (*Lays out all her clubs*) |
| ♣J | ♣K | (1) | Twenty, twenty-one, twenty-two, twenty-three |
| ♠8 | ♣Q | (1) | |
| ♠9 | ♣T | (1) | |
| ♠A | ♠Q | (2) | *Nap* Seventeen. |
| ♠J | ♠T | (1) | *Nap* Eighteen, and ten for cards twenty eight. *Jos* Twenty three. |

If this hand is played over it will be found that Napoleon would only
have divided the cards, failing to score ten for the majority, if he had
led spades after his run of hearts. As it is he just comes out ahead of
Josephine with an average elder score of 28, whereas Josephine has
more than younger usually expects to score and will hope to push ahead
as elder on the next deal.

## Notes on play

The difference in strategy as between dealer and non-dealer is more
marked in Piquet than in any other two-hand game save perhaps Cribbage. Elder (non-dealer) starts with all the advantages, being entitled
to five of the eight cards of the stock, having the lead and so determining
the point of attack, and being alone able to score for pique. Younger's
draw of usually only three cards is rarely sufficient to rescue a bad
hand from disaster, while only he can find himself in the position of
holding all eight cards of a suit and yet lose every trick. As if further
proof were needed, statistics show that elder scores nearly twice as

much as younger, on average. It follows that elder is in a position to take chances and should play an attacking hand, while younger should see to his defence first and not take chances that might weaken them.

To start, then, elder should always seek to exchange his full entitlement of five cards, for to take fewer is to waste his overwhelming advantage and to give younger considerably more room to manoeuvre. If he takes only four cards instead of five, he has reduced his advantage by 20 per cent but increased younger's by 33 per cent. Cards taken in excess of those he feels necessary to his hand are not wasted, as they are not only denied to younger but also remain unknown to him.

As elder hand, which five cards should you throw out? This is a problem that beginners find hard to solve, as they tend to feel that only non-combinable and non-trick-winning Nines, Eights and Sevens should be discarded, and if they have only three or four such cards will prefer to take fewer than their entitlement. What you should do, however, is to look at it the other way: decide which cards you must retain for the best chances of combining, and throw out the rest.

Of those to retain, the most important are usually those of your potential point – the suit of which you hold the greatest number of cards, or, if equal, that with the highest pip-values or best chances of turning into a sequence. The point in this hand, for example, is hearts:

♠A K J T ♡Q J T 9 ♣A Q ♢K 9

since either of two cards (King or Eight) will convert it to a sequence of five, called a *quint*, which is twice as many chances as the solitary Queen that will make a quint in spades. The quint is particularly worth going for as it would be 'good against the cards' – meaning that it is obvious from your own cards that younger could not possibly draw an equal or better sequence. The discards from this hand, therefore, are ♠J ♠T ♣Q ♢K ♢9.

Discards are also made with a view to completing a quatorze, and problems can arise because this combination tends to cut across the discard requirements relevant to point or sequence. The hand above was not complicated by this factor because it contained two each of the valid ranks, thus ensuring that younger cannot score so much as a trio, but not offering strong enough chances of filling a quatorze to allow this hope to influence the discards. Furthermore, the potential quint would have been, if realised, good against the cards.

But this superficially similar hand is far from easy:

♠A K J T ♡J T 9 8 ♣A K 7 ♢K

Again, there are virtually twice as many chances of making a quint or better in hearts (5 to 4 against, or 44%) as a quint in spades (3 to 1 against, or 25%). This time, however, it is not good against the cards, as younger might fill, or even have been dealt, an equal or better sequence in diamonds. Furthermore, you have three Kings and would prefer to keep them with a view to drawing the fourth, especially as younger may wind up with fourteen Queens. Since it is vital to restrict younger's entitlement to not more than three cards, you are faced with two possible ways of discarding from this hand.

1.  Keep the heart sequence and the Kings, neither of which is at present good against the cards, and discard ♠A ♠J ♠T ♣A ♣7.

2.  Keep the Kings and the potential spade quint, discarding the hearts and bottom club and drawing to ♠A K J T ♣A K ◇K.

(A third possibility is to forget the Kings and keep both spades and hearts in the hope of making two quints and repique, but the chances of doing so are too remote since only four cards can be exchanged.)

The chances of drawing the fourteenth King are the same in both cases. In the first case there is a 1 in 4 chance of making the quint; in the second there are 4 in 9. But although the latter gives better odds, it would lose if younger had a *sixième* (sequence of six cards) in diamonds and might tie if he has a quint, whereas the quint major (to the Ace) in the former would be good against a diamond quint.

Further, if younger gets only five diamonds instead of six, the retention of spades here stands a better chance of scoring for point because the cards held are higher in value (as it stands, worth 31 against only 27). On the whole, then, case **2** is the safer holding against younger's possibilities, even though case **1** gives better chances on the face of it.

To summarise, elder should nearly always exchange up to his maximum of five cards, unless the hand dealt is so strong as to contain a quint or quatorze and the chance of (re)pique or capot. The longest suit should be kept intact for point, or, if suits are of equal lengths, then that with the highest count or longest sequence should be retained. A trio should be kept intact with a view to the quatorze, except that a trio of Tens or Jacks may be broken if the cards show that younger may hold a higher ranking quatorze and there are other pressures for discarding from them. If it becomes essential to choose between keeping the point or the trio, go for the point. Having classified cards into those that must be kept for combinations and those that need not, prefer to discard unneeded Aces and Kings rather than discard fewer than five, unless this spoils the chance of capot. If discarding requires it, do not hesitate to unguard Kings or Queens. Discard from as few different suits as possible. Unless it contains a card needed for a combination, it is often as well to throw out the whole of a suit as part of it, and sometimes even better.

As younger hand, your approach is quite different. Having normally only three cards to exchange, you have considerably less opportunity to draw to high combinations. The question of tricks is also of greater importance, since – to take an extreme case – you can be capoted though holding a handful of high cards, if they are of suits in which elder is void. Whereas elder can usually expect to win the cards (take more tricks) with an average hand and proper play, younger must usually discard and fight to at least divide them (six each).

Your first concern, then, after looking for carte blanche, is to ensure adequate coverage in all suits to avoid the danger of capot. A hand such as this;

♠A K J 9 8 7 ◇J T 9 ♣Q 9 ◇8

will lose every trick if elder, as is likely, has no spade in hand. Here it is vital, before thinking about combinations, to cover the three weak suits by discarding spades. Even the lowly ◇8 must be retained, to act as a guard in case the King is drawn. Of course, the probability of drawing one guard in each of the three suits is extremely low, but at least two should be drawn to defend against capot. Even then, it may be hard to find the right discards to elder's winning leads. Quite apart from tricks, the potential combinations are not worth much. From the cards, there is every chance that elder will hold seven diamonds, and even six clubs would be worth more than your six spades. (Assess this quickly by noting that your spade suit lacks cards worth 20 in combined face value, whereas his six clubs would lack only 19, *i.e.* the Q+9 held by yourself.) And if you drew ♠Q for a quart major, he is likely to hold at least a quint in diamonds.

This hand, however, is an extreme case of weakness for tricks, and is introduced only to point out that a good-looking hand at first sight must be looked at very closely before any discarding decisions are made. As far as combinations are concerned, judge your discards in much the same way as for elder hand. Two points must be noted, though. First, do not aim for a particular combination if it means unguarding a suit or losing a vital trick. And second, although it is best for elder to exchange his full entitlement of five cards, as younger you should not hesitate to take only two or even one if it means throwing good cards after bad. In this case (unlike elder's situation) any cards you leave remain out of play instead of going into your oponent's hand.

To summarise: as younger, discard defensively with a view to retaining coverage in sufficient suits to avoid capot. Do not take all cards available if this means throwing out guards or trick-winners, and do not waste good cards in going after high combinations which are not good against the cards. Other things being equal, always keep your point suit, as it is your best and cheapest defence against pique/repique.

The next important part of the game is not the playing of tricks but the announcement of combinations. Practised players often enter the play with a pretty shrewd idea of their opponent's holding, gleaned from what he has announced in declarations together with an estimate of which of the other cards are more likely to be out of his hand than in it. For this reason it is important not to say more about your holding than you really need in order to establish whether or not your declaration is 'good'. Suppose, as elder, you hold:

♠Q J T 9 ♡A Q J T ♣A K T ◇T

You call a point of four; younger asks its value, and replies 'not good' to your 40. Your next declaration is 'fourteen Tens', with not a word about the sequence. Why? Because if your point of four is not good at 40, younger must have a point of four worth 41, and from your own holding you can see this to be ◇A K Q J. Your sequence of four is bound to be not good, so to mention it at all would only be to give him gratuitous information about your hand. Again, if as elder you held fourteen Kings after exchanging five cards, but had not seen hair nor hide of an Ace, there would be no point in announcing them unless younger took fewer than three cards, as he would certainly not have thrown an Ace with Kings against him.

Similar considerations apply to younger. Suppose you hold:

♠A Q J T 7 ♡87 ♣Q J T ◇K 9

Your discards were two diamonds and a club. Elder calls a point of five. Without hesitation, you should immediately announce 'good'. Since his point can only be in hearts, it must be worth at least 49 to your 48 in spades, and there is no point in giving away free information.

It is because so many of the opposing cards are known by the time tricks are played that it has been said, in reference to this part of the game, that 'in Piquet, there are no surprises' – which is not quite true, but worth bearing in mind. Elder should normally lead his point suit from the top down, unless headed by a tenace (A–Q or, more especially, K–J); younger, when no longer able to follow, will start discarding from the bottom of his point, unless he is confident of gaining the lead and winning tricks with the whole of his point. A time for elder not to lead his point is when it lacks the top card and there is pique to be made by leading non-point winner – for example, from

♠K Q J T 8 ♡A K Q ♣A K ♢K Q

elder has point equal, a quart good plus tierce major making 7, fourteen Kings 21 and a trio of Queens 24, plus 1 for leading 25. He leads hearts and clubs, reaching 30 in tricks and adding 30 for pique.

In defending against elder's point lead, younger must do everything to avoid unguarding suits, even to the extent of throwing out winners from his own point. For example, suppose younger holds:

♠Q 8 ♡Q J 9 ♣K 7 ♢A K J T 8

Elder has counted point six and three Aces, and then leads his six spades. Younger must throw diamonds from the bottom up after playing his two spades, for if his sixth card is a heart or club he may well be capoted. If possible, of course, younger should keep his point and throw low cards from other suits if this can be done without losing the guard.

The addition of the rubicon has added much interest and excitement to the strategy of the game by sometimes making it vital to play to the score. If your opponent is well in the lead by the sixth deal, while you are still short of the rubicon, you are faced with a nice problem: whether to go all out to reach it, taking chances and playing boldly if need be, or, instead, to go for as few points as possible, by seeking equalities in combinations and playing to divide the cards. (If you are rubiconed, remember, your opponent adds your own score to his, plus 100 for game.)

If elder is trailing at the last deal and feels unable to reach 100, he will do best to sink everything he holds, even if (*especially* if!) this includes a quint or quatorze – in other words, declare nothing and let younger count whatever he holds as 'good'. There is no point in trying to equalise. As elder, you may be convinced that younger has point five and quint major as well as yourself, but if you declare either of them, younger will simply announce 'good' and let you make the score, since it will ultimately be credited to his own account. In trying to divide the cards, elder must not allow younger to manoeuvre him into taking the majority by 'suicide' play to tricks. Younger does not mind who wins the cards, so long as they are not divided.

If the positions are reversed, younger is somewhat better placed for declaring equalities, since elder has to announce first, and younger can sink as much as may be necessary to equalise. For example, suppose you hold a point consisting of K–Q–J–T–7, worth 47. Elder declares a point of four. You ask its value; he replies 'thirty nine'. You announce 'equal', sinking nine from your face value, and neither scores. Elder next announces a tierce to the Queen. Again, you equalise. By sinking the King, you also have a tierce to the Queen.

(Some players only allow whole cards to be sunk, thus making it illegal to sink nine from K–Q–J–T–7 since that value does not correspond to a card held. This nice point, not covered by the Portland Club Laws, should perhaps be agreed beforehand.)

It is easy to see the value of sinking for the purpose of keeping one's score low when certain of being rubiconed, but there are other circumstances in which advantage may be gained from it, or, indeed, when all depends upon it. Here is an extreme example, provided by Cavendish – who pointedly adds 'It is useless to practise this stratagem against an indifferent player who does not count your hand'. In other words, you can't bluff a fool. Elder holds:

♠A K Q J 9 8 7 ♡K ♣A K ◇A K

After equalising on point (younger having seven hearts), elder is in a position to call fourteen Kings. But this would give his hand away. If younger knows he has the singleton ♡K, he will play everything except his red Ace and be assured of taking at least one trick. Elder therefore sinks one King, knowing his trio of Aces and Kings to be good against the cards, because he himself discarded a Ten and can see that younger cannot hold a quatorze. Younger asks him which King he does not count, and elder (of course) replies 'hearts', which younger may believe or not, as he wishes. This puts younger in the unenviable position of choosing whether to throw all his hearts to elder's lead of spades in order to retain a guard in clubs or diamonds, or to hold back ♡A until the last trick in case elder has not discarded the King. By sinking, elder drops 11 points (counting 3 instead of 14 for Kings); against this, however, he has a good chance of making capot – except, as Cavendish says, 'against a very acute or very stupid player'. There are, of course, circumstances in which, as younger, one would sink an unguarded King in order to avoid being capoted.

# 6

## ════ SIXTY-SIX ════
## AND COUNTING

### *For those quick on the draw*

Sixty-six, a popular Continental game, is one of the most delightful two-handers and deserves a wider following. Originating in 17th-century Germany and alternatively called by the French name *Mariage*, it is still greatly enjoyed in Austria under the name *Schnapsen*. A similar game called **Tute** is played in Spanish-speaking countries, and will be found at the end of the chapter by way of variation.

As some people find Sixty-Six rather complex at first attempt, try leading up to it gently via the simpler game of Elfern and its progressive variations.

## ════════ Elfern ════════

This old German game, which I also call *Elevenses*, is said to be still popular with children. It could be ancestral to Sixty-Six, and I think it likely that so-called German Whist – which does not appear to be a genuine German game – is based upon it. The name means 'making eleven'.

*Cards*. Use a 32-card pack ranking A K Q J T 9 8 7 in each suit. Deal six cards each and stack the rest face down.

*Object.* To win, in tricks, a majority – at least 11 – of the 20 honours. The honours are all the Aces, Kings, Queens, Jacks, and Tens.

*Play.* Non-dealer leads to the first trick. There is no trump, and suit need not be followed. The trick is taken by the higher card of the suit led, and the winner of each trick leads to the next. Before doing so, the winner draws the top card of the stock and the loser draws the next, so long as any remain. When the stock is empty a new rule comes into force – namely, that in the play of the last six tricks it is obligatory for the second player to follow suit if possible.

*Score.* Score a single win for capturing 11–14 honours, a double for 15–19, a treble for all twenty.

*Variant 1.* Elfern becomes more interesting with the addition of trumps. After the deal, the top card is turned face up and slipped half under the stock to indicate the trump suit. It will eventually be drawn by the loser of the tenth trick. A trick can now be taken by playing a higher card of the suit led or by trumping a non-trump lead. In the last six tricks the second player must, if possible, play a trump when unable to follow suit to the card led.

*Variant 2.* It becomes even more interesting if the honours are given point-values as follows:

|        |       |          |             |
|--------|-------|----------|-------------|
| each   | Ace   | counts 11 | card-points |
|        | King  | counts  4 |             |
|        | Queen | counts  3 |             |
|        | Jack  | counts  2 |             |
|        | Ten   | counts 10 |             |

The total number of card-points is now 120. Score a single for capturing cards totalling 61–90 points, a double for 91 to 120, a treble for winning every trick regardless of points.

This card-point system is common to a wide range of games played throughout central Europe. If you get used to it early on, you will be able to pass with ease to such great card games as Sixty-Six, Skat, Belote, Pinochle, and Klaberjass.

# Sixty-Six

*Cards.* Twenty-four, ranking A T K Q J 9 in each suit. Note the high position of the Ten. Deal six each in two batches of three and stack the rest face down. Turn the top card of the stock for trump and slip it half under the pack so as to remain identifiable. Whoever holds the Nine of trumps may exchange it for the trump turn-up so long as it remains beneath the stock. The exchange may be made at any time.

*Object.* The aim is to be the first to reach 66 by counting as follows:

For capturing in tricks:

| | |
|---|---|
| each Ace | 11 |
| each Ten | 10 |
| each King | 4 |
| each Queen | 3 |
| each Jack | 2 |

For holding and showing:

| | |
|---|---|
| trump marriage (K+Q) | 40 |
| non-trump marriage | 20 |

For winning the last trick: 10

The significance of 66 is that, disregarding marriages, it is one more than half the total number of points available in play, since 30 for the card-points in each suit plus 10 for last makes 130.

Throughout play, you must count and remember the total number of points you have gained so far, as the deal is not necessarily won by the first player to reach 66 but by the first to claim (correctly) to have done so. The additional hefty scores for marriages make it possible for both players to pass this total, hence the importance of announcing it.

*Play.* Non-dealer leads to the first trick and the winner of each trick leads to the next. Any card may be led, and, so long as cards remain in stock, any card may be played second – it is not obligatory to follow suit or trump. The trick is taken by the higher card of the suit led, or by the higher trump if any are played. The winner of each trick draws the top card of the stock and waits for the other player to draw the next before leading.

*Marriages.* If at any time you hold a King and Queen of the same suit, whether dealt or drawn from stock, you may declare and score for the marriage upon leading to a trick. You do this by showing both cards, announcing 'and 40' if it is in trumps or 'and 20' otherwise, and leaving one partner on the table as the lead to the trick. Since you may only do this upon leading, it follows that, as Dealer, you will have to win a trick before you can declare a marriage.

*Endgame.* The first half ends when the loser of the sixth trick draws the trump turn-up, which will be the Nine if it has been exchanged. The last six tricks are played to different rules. You may lead any card,

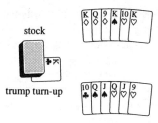

**Figure 4: Sixty-Six** The turned King makes clubs trump. North will start by showing the diamond marriage, announcing '20 to come', and leaving the Queen on the table as the opening lead. North's 20 does not come into effect until he has actually won a trick. South, having nothing to declare and seeing no reason cash the trump Ten so early in the game, will pass this by throwing a worthless card (Nine) from his longest suit. North then draws from stock and will lead again when South has also drawn.

but the second to play must now follow suit if possible and win the trick if possible. If unable to follow suit you must trump if possible. Marriages may still be declared. For winning the last (twelfth) trick, count an extra 10 'for last'.

*Shut-out.* If, before the stock runs out, you think you can reach 66 from the cards left in hand, you may shut the stock by turning the trump turn-up face down. You may do this before or after drawing a sixth card, but, of course, if you do draw a sixth you must allow the other player to do so as well. The last tricks are played in the same way as described above (follow suit, head the trick, trump if unable to follow), except that '10 for last' does not apply, as this is credited strictly for winning the twelfth trick, and there will not have been that many played.

*Score.* The first player to claim correctly to have reached 66 scores 1 game point, or 2 if the other player has not reached 33 (*schneider*), or 3 if the other has not won a single trick (*schwarz*). The latter applies even if non-dealer declared a marriage upon leading to the first trick but failed to win that or any subsequent trick.

If one player incorrectly claims to have reached 66, the other scores 2 game points, or 3 for having taken no trick.

If one player shuts the stock and fails to win, the other scores 2 game points.

If both make 65, or neither claims to have reached 66 by end of play, the game point is held up and goes to the winner of the next deal.

*Game.* Play up to 7 game points.

*Variant.* The Austrian game of Schnapsen varies only in being played with 20 cards. As the Nines are omitted, it is the Jack that may be exchanged for the trump turn-up.

*Notes.* For a game based on so few cards and simple material, Sixty-Six offers extraordinary scope for tactical and strategic skill.

The most important strategic requirement is to decide whether and when to shut the stock and foreclose the game. Between experts, few games are played out to the bitter end. The time to foreclose is when you have a majority of the trumps remaining in play, including the Ace and Ten (unless either has already gone), and can be sure of reaching at least 60 from the winners in your own hand. You can reckon on gaining an average 2–3 card-points from each losing card played by your opponent, but don't expect to capture an Ace or Ten that you have not yet seen in play, as it could well be lying in the undrawn stock.

Before the shut-out, or the last six tricks, an average safe lead is the Nine or Jack of a plain suit, especially if you hold the Ten, as your lead will probably force the Ace out and leave your Ten high. If, however, you hold the Ace, keep it for as long as the Ten remains unseen, as you may thereby manage to catch it with the Ace in the play of the last six.

Don't lead plain-suit Aces in the first half of the game unless you want them trumped in order to weaken your opponent's trump holding. You might do this, for example, if you know you have three trumps each and want to enter the end-game with a majority of trumps. More often, it can be a good move when you yourself are weak or void in trumps and want to prevent the other player from enjoying as clear run of trumps in the end-play. If you find yourself short of trumps and holding such a long suit that it is unlikely your opponent can follow, lead low from that suit as often as possible. Either you will pick up points from castaways thrown to them, or you will force out trumps with little loss to yourself.

Obviously, you will keep single Kings and Queens in hope of marrying them. But if your opponent plays to a trick the partner of a King or Queen in your own hand, you will know there is no point in keeping it and thus be given a spare discard or good lead.

Sixty-Six calls for much concentration to be played successfully. Always be aware of how many of the six trumps you have, and how many have been played to tricks, so that by the time the last six are played you will know pretty well what the trump division is between you and play accordingly. It is a tremendous advantage to go into the last six with one trump more than your opponent.

Keep track of Aces and Tens, so that you will know what the chances are of your capturing a Ten with an Ace, and how to avoid losing a Ten to an Ace. Keep track of Kings and Queens, so that you will know whether or not it is safe to discard an unwed marriage partner.

Finally, keep count not only of your own point-score to date but also of your opponent's. This takes practice, and you will probably have to start by just concentrating on your own.

# Tute

This cross between Sixty-Six and Bezique is popular in Spanish-speaking countries and is played with the 40-card pack lacking Eights, Nines and Tens. It is said to be of Italian origin, the name deriving from *tutti*, meaning 'all' or 'everyone'. (Both syllables are pronounced.)

*Cards.* The cards rank from high to low in each suit as follows, and individual high cards have point-scores as indicated:

| rank | A | 3 | K | Q | J | 7 | 6 | 5 | 4 | 2 |
|------|----|----|---|---|---|---|---|---|---|---|
| value | 11 | 10 | 4 | 3 | 2 | – | – | – | – | – |

You may prefer to replace Threes with Tens.

*Deal.* Each player receives 8 cards dealt in batches of 3–2–3. Stack the rest face down, then turn the top card face up and slip it half under the stock to indicate the trumps.

*Taking the turn-up.* If the turn-up is a counting card (Jack or higher), it may be taken at any time in exchange for the trump Seven, whether this has been dealt or is subsequently drawn from stock. If the turn-up is the Seven, whether turned up itself or exchanged for the turn-up, it may be taken at any time in exchange for the Two of trumps.

*Object.* The aim is to reach 101 points or more for counting-cards captured in tricks, or to collect all four Kings or Queens and so declare a *tute*. A tute wins the game outright, but if this does not happen it may take two deals for one player to reach 101.

*Play.* Non-dealer leads to the first trick.

The second player must follow suit only if a trump is led. If not, he may follow, trump or discard as preferred. If unable to follow when a trump is led, he must prove it by laying his hand of cards face up on the table, and must then leave it exposed until he draws a trump from stock.

The trick is taken by the higher card of the suit led or by the higher trump if any are played. The winner of each trick leads to the next after drawing the top card of stock and waiting for his opponent to draw the next.

*Declarations.* Upon leading to a trick (*not* when following), a player may show and score for a marriage or a *tute*. A marriage is a King and Queen of the same suit, and adds 20 to his card-points, or 40 if in trumps. Only one marriage may be declared at a time: if two are held, another trick must be won before the second can be called.

A *tute* is all four Kings or all four Queens, and wins the game outright without further play. Play also ceases if one player announces that he has reached 101 points for cards taken in tricks. This wins the game if correct, otherwise loses.

*Last eight.* When the last card – the turn-up – has been drawn from stock, the rules change. A marriage or *tute* may no longer be declared. The second to a trick must now follow suit if possible and win the trick if possible. If unable to follow suit, he must trump if possible. If one player wins all eight tricks, he announces 'Capote!' (three syllables) and wins the game. If not, a bonus of 10 is credited to the winner of the last trick.

# 7

## —— KLABERJASS ——

### *A game of many facets*

Klaberjass originated in the Low Countries during the 19th century and has become, by adoption, an essentially Jewish game. In this capacity it has spread far afield and acquired a number of different names. **Belote**, for example, which has long replaced Piquet as France's major national game, is but a slightly modified form of the Klaberjass thought to have been imported into the country by immigrant diamond workers and dealers around the time of the First World War. Damon Runyon's Broadway characters of the 1930s are often found playing 'Klob', or, more rarely 'Kalabriasz', and in that same period Ely Culbertson, famed Bridge guru, tried to promote a cross between it and Bridge which he named 'Jojotte' after his wife Josephine. In Britain it is known as **Klobiosh**, **Clob** or **Clobby**, and I have encountered it under the name **Bella** from one of its principal features. Various forms of it are also widely played in Eastern Europe, especially Hungary.

The name Klaberjass (the J is pronounced Y) means 'club Jack', probably because this was the highest single card at some early stage of development. Nowadays the top card is the Jack of trumps, whatever its actual suit may be, and it is merely known as *Jass*. It may look complicated at first sight, but well repays the effort of learning. It is easier to grasp if you already have experience of Sixty-Six (see previous chapter) of which it represents one line of development. A different line of development led to Bezique and Pinochle, which you will find in the following chapter.

# Klaberjass

*Cards.* Standard 32-card pack.

*Deal.* Whoever cuts the lower card (A K Q J T 9 8 7) deals first, and the deal alternates thereafter until one player reaches a score of 500, which ends the game. Deal six cards each in two batches of three. Place the remainder face down to form a stock. Turn the top card face up and place it beside the stock. The suit of this card is the preferred suit for trumps, but will not necessarily be accepted as such.

*Object.* After the bidding each player will receive three more cards and play nine tricks. Whoever accepts or nominates the trump suit (the 'maker') thereby undertakes to win the greater number of points for tricks and melds. Trick-points are scored by capturing certain cards with point-values, as shown below. A meld is a sequence of three or more cards in the same suit, or the King and Queen of trumps, known as *bella*.

*Rank and value of cards.* In non-trump suits cards rank A T K Q J 9 8 7 – note the high position of the Ten. In trumps, the highest card is the Jack, or Jass, second-highest Nine, known as *Menel* (accent on the second syllable), then Ace and so on down to the Seven. Cards also have point-values, credited to the player winning them in tricks, as follows:

| | | | |
|---|---|---|---|
| Jass | 20 | | *Jack of trumps* |
| Menel | 14 | | *Nine of trumps* |
| Ace | 11 | each | |
| Ten | 10 | each | |
| King | 4 | each | |
| Queen | 3 | each | |
| Jack | 2 | each | *except in trumps* |
| Nine | 0 | | *except in trumps* |
| Eight | 0 | | |
| Seven | 0 | | |

*Melds.* A sequence of three cards in the same suit counts 20, a sequence of four or more counts 50. The sequential order of cards is A K Q J T 9 8 7 in every suit. (Thus Q–J–T is a sequence of three even though the ranks may not be adjacent in trick-taking power.) The King and Queen of trumps together (*bella*) score 20. Melds are not counted until both players have nine cards, and only the player with the best sequence may score for sequences.

*Bidding.* The rank and value of cards and melds have been described first because bidding can only be carried out on the assessment of one's chances of winning more points than the opponent. It is to be noted that the total value of all the scoring cards in the pack is 152, though not all will be in play, and that the winning of the last trick carries a bonus of 10.

Elder hand starts the bidding by announcing one of three things:

- *Accept.* In which case he accepts the preferred suit as trumps and becomes the maker.
- *Schmeiss* (pronounced *shmice*). This is a proposal to abandon the deal. If younger accepts it, the hands are thrown in and there is a new deal. If he refuses, elder is obliged to accept the preferred suit as trump and so become the maker.
- *Pass.* This is a refusal to become the maker with the preferred suit as trump. Now younger has the same choices: he may accept, schmeiss, or pass. If he passes, elder may either nominate another suit as trump, thereby becoming the maker, or pass. In the latter event, younger may also nominate a suit or pass. If both pass this time, the hands are abandoned and a new deal made.

*Play.* When one player has become the maker, the dealer deals another batch of three cards to each player from the top of the stock, so that each has nine. Then he takes the bottom card of the stock and places it face up on the top. This card is for information only and has no part in the play. (The purpose of this curious manoeuvre is to ensure that neither player has had the unfair advantage of being the only one to see the bottom card, which may be accidentally or otherwise observed during the deal.)

*Dix*, pronounced *deece*, is the Seven of trumps if the preferred trump was accepted. If either player has this card he may exchange if for the turned trump-card at any time before the first trick is led. This privilege cannot apply if a different suit was entrumped.

*Scoring melds.* Before elder leads to the first trick, scores are made for sequences if either player holds any. Only the player who holds the best sequence may score, and he is thereby entitled to score for as many as he shows. (The relevant cards must be revealed.) The best sequence is the one of greatest length; if equal in length, the one with the highest card; if still equal, the one in the trump suit. If neither is in trumps, that of elder hand prevails. Note that the dix may be exchanged either before or after melds are declared, depending on whether the Seven or the card taken is required for a sequence.

(Whether or not it is permissible to count the Seven in a sequence of 7–8–9 and then change it for (say) a turned Ace to make and also score another sequence of A–K–Q is a point on which I can find no authority, but I suggest that this should be disallowed.) Bella, if held, is not yet declared.

*Tricks.* Elder leads to the first trick and the winner of each trick leads to the next. It is obligatory to follow suit, and if a trump is led, the second must play a higher trump if he can. A player unable to follow suit is obliged to trump if he can. (In short: you must try to win the trick if the lead is of trumps or a suit in which you are void.)

*Bella.* If either player holds the King and Queen of trumps he may score 20 by announcing 'bella' upon playing the second of them to a trick.

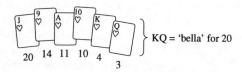

**Figure 5: Klaberjass (1)** A hand of top trumps if hearts are turned. In addition to the individual card-points, this player will add 20 for *bella* and 50 for the six-card sequence.

*Last trick.* Whoever wins the last trick (sometimes known as *stich*, pronounced *stish*) scores 10 points for it.

*Score.* Each player announces the total he has made for cards captured in tricks, stich, melds and bella (if any). If the maker has more than his opponent, each counts towards game exactly the amount he has made. If the maker has less, he is said to have 'gone bête' (pronounced and sometimes spelt *bate*); he scores nothing, but his opponent counts towards game the combined total made by both players in that deal. If both have taken the same amount, the maker is 'half bête': he scores nothing, and his opponent scores only the amount he himself has made. The game ends when either player, at the end of a deal, has reached or exceeded a previously agreed total, usually 500.

*Variants.* Among the variations and additional rules followed in different countries and localities, the following may be adopted in whole or part.

● The bid of schmeiss is a comparatively recent addition to the game and may be ignored by purists, though most American and British players like it.

- In making trumps, first preference is always on clubs and second on the suit of the card turned, if different. This variant is recommended, as it increases demands on good judgement and is in keeping with the name of the game – which, as we have seen, means 'Jack of clubs'.

- If the suit of first preference has been rejected by both players, either may make a bid of no trump (*sans atout*), which takes precedence over a bid in suit and may be used to overcall it. In this case there is no Jass or Menel, cards rank A T K Q J 9 8 7 in every suit, and each player's final score for the deal is doubled – which makes it attractive to bid no trump on a safe hand, but expensive to go bête on a bad one. If one player bids no trump, the other can overcall him by bidding 'grand' (*tout atout*). In this case there is a Jass and Menel in every suit – in other words, cards rank J 9 A T K Q 8 7 in each suit, and all Jacks are worth 20 and all Nines 14. Otherwise it is played as no trump and also scores double. Grand may only be bid to overcall a previous bid of no trump.

- In the event of equality for best sequence, the result is a tie and neither may score, instead of declaring elder's to be better by virtue of his position. This is not recommended, as sequences are rare enough already without making them even harder to score.

- Sometimes a sequence of five or more is valued at 100 points instead of 50 (which is retained for a sequence of four). But such sequences occur so rarely that it hardly seems worth the bother.

- One source refers to a bonus of 40 for winning all the tricks. It seems reasonable to recognise some sort of bonus for this feat, though the figure quoted would appear to be lifted straight out of Piquet.

- In the game of **Belote** (in which there is no bid of schmeiss) additional melds may be scored. Sequences of three count 20, of four 50, and of five or more 100. Also, whoever has the best four of a kind (a *carré* or quartet) may score for any and all quartets he may show, valued thus: four Jacks 200, Nines 150, Aces, Tens, Kings or Queens 100, lower ranks not counting. Game is usually at least 1000 points.

- If, during the course of play, either player considers that he has reached the target score on melds and/or counting cards so far captured in tricks, he may claim 'out' and end the game immediately

– provided that he has already won at least one trick (Belote rule). If he is wrong, he loses the game. Otherwise he wins, even if his opponent has a higher total.

## Notes on play

Nearly all points are scored for cards won in tricks plus 10 for stich. A whole game may pass without the appearance of a bella or of more than two or three small sequences, and these therefore hardly need to be taken into account in the bidding, unless you are dealt one to start with.

Although the theoretical maximum number of trick-points is 162, it is impossible for all the value-cards to be in play in one deal. In practice, the average number of points in play per deal lies between 100 and 120, of which the maker, if he wins, should expect to score 80–90 against the loser's 20–30. If the game were played with a compulsory trump and no opportunity to pass, each player would expect to take an average of 50–60 points per deal. Since you are called upon to bid on only two thirds of your final hand, you ought to hold 30–40 points in high prospective trumps and supporting Ace-Tens before accepting the preferred suit or nominating another.

It is possible to bid successfully on a hand containing as little as a singleton Jass and two Aces or an Ace-Ten. But this does not mean that all hands are playable. The more expert players become, the more hands they tend to throw in. It does not take more than a few rounds of the game to discover how easily some weak-looking hands win while others, apparently quite promising, fall at the first fence. It is easy enough to recognise a strong hand when you see one, but takes practice to know whether or not to pass or play on something less clear cut. Beginners, I think, should play boldly. You will learn much more from bidding and losing than from passing and never knowing.

In assessing the hand look first for the dix (Seven) of the turned card, unless the latter is an Eight, which is not worth having. In any prospective trump suit it is imperative to hold either the Jack or an accompanied Nine, with preferably an Ace or Ten for company. Do not play a trump suit containing the Ace or Ace-Ten as highest cards, except in the unlikely circumstance of their being accompanied by at least two others of the suit, as there is too great a chance of losing one or more big ones to Jass or Menel in your opponent's hand. Nor be tempted into entrumping a suit just because you have been dealt the King and Queen, worth 20 for bella. If you have a mediocre hand including bella, or a sequence in any suit, the extra value may be just enough to make up either for weaknesses in the hand, or a stout opposition. But never bank on being dealt the marriage partner to a King or Queen already in hand, or a specific card required for a sequence. The odds are more than 7 to 1 against.

A two-card prospective trump including Jass or Menel is sufficient if adequately supported in plain suits, and the mathematical odds favour the appearance of a third in the last part of the deal.

In non-trumps the best holding is an unaccompanied Ace or Ace-Ten, and there is even a goodish chance (4 to 3 in favour) of winning a trick with an ace-less Ten provided that the suit is not held so long as to risk being trumped. A long plain suit, say four or more, is not good for tricks unless it contains low cards which can be used to weaken the opposing trumps – bearing in mind the obligation to trump a suit in which one is void. A void suit in the prospective bidder's hand is a mixed blessing for the same reason. It must, for safety, be accompanied by long trumps, otherwise it will be used to weaken the trump holding.

Younger hand may always bid with greater boldness than elder, since elder's pass is suggestive of weakness. Younger is also in a better position to schmeiss on a hand which is not good for a straightforward acceptance of the turned suit but in which that suit is the only one that stands any chance of succeeding. The fact that elder has passed may justify this move. Elder himself should be very wary of schmeissing, except as a bluff on a good hand, which of course runs the danger of not being called. Otherwise the danger is that younger will accept the schmeiss and prove to hold a fistful of trumps himself.

If you have the lead as maker, your normal strategy on a reasonable hand will be to draw trumps first, partly to test the situation and partly to clear the way for Aces and Tens in plain suits. With a short trump suit or one headed by a tenace (Jack, Ace or Nine, Ten) it is preferable to lead a short plain suit with solid top cards. If you feel that your opponent might hold too many trumps, force them out by leading worthless cards from a long plain suit.

When leading trumps, it is worth starting with the Jack if there is a chance of seizing the Ace or Ten thereby, but (of course) it is dangerous to lead the Nine, Ace or Ten if you lack anything higher. Much of the interest of the game derives from the peculiar positions – third and fourth highest – of the highscoring Ace and Ten of trumps.

With an average holding of two cards in each suit, it is desirable to win with Aces and Tens as soon as the opportunity arises. If (say) an

Eight is led into your Ace/King, it is best to assure yourself of the Ace while you can, rather than hold it back in the hope of catching the Ten with it.

## Sample deals

*First deal.* Our two players are Abel and Baker, of whom the latter deals as follows and turns up ♡A:

Abel ♠K ♡9 7 ♣T J ◇A
Baker ♠7 ♡J T 8 ♣Q 8 7

As elder, Abel holds the Menel of the turned suit and can take the Ace by way of the dix. His hand is worth 35 in cards worth counting, and he accepts the turned suit. After three more cards are dealt, and ♠8 turned for information, the hands are:

Abel ♠A K ♡9 A ♣A T J ◇A 9
Baker ♠7 ♡J T 8 ♣K Q 8 7 ◇T

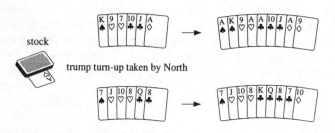

stock

trump turn-up taken by North

**Figure 6: Klaberjass (2)** North accepts the turned heart as trumps, holding *menel* (Nine) and *dix* (Seven), which latter may be exchanged for the turned Ace. After an additional deal of three, North is strong in side suits and South in trumps, including the unbeatable *jass* for 20. It proves a close-run game (see text).

Neither player has improved his trump holding, and it is interesting to note that Baker was dealt three trumps including the Jass. With a short trump suit headed only by the second highest, Abel leads clubs in the hope of retrieving his Ace and Ten before drawing trumps. He takes 21 points on the first two tricks, but then loses his Jack to Baker's King (worth a point more than taking it with the Queen). Given the initiative, Baker now plans to make the most of his comparatively long trumps. He starts aggressively with the Jass, drawing ♡A for 31 points and the certain knowledge that Abel has only the Menel in hand, which he next forces out by leading ♡8. Now void of trumps, Abel plays his Aces, gaining 32 card-points in the process, and continues with ♢9. This Baker trumps with his Ten, and concludes with ♣Q, drawing ♠K plus 10 for the last trick. Abel has just succeeded in his bid, taking 67 to Baker's 64. The latter was lucky to hold not only more trumps than his opponent, but also more cards in the same long suit.

*Second deal.* Abel turns up ♠T, having dealt:

Baker   ♠K 9 7 ♡A K ♢T
Abel    ♠J 8 ♡T 9 8 ♣A

Baker has three trumps and access to bella by means of the dix. He therefore accepts the turned suit, in which, it will be noted, Abel holds the top card. The information card, after completion of the hands to the following, is ♢K:

Baker   ♠9 K Q ♡A K ♣T K ♢T 9
Abel    ♠J 8 ♡T 9 8 ♣A 8 ♢Q 8

After hearing Abel declare his sequence in hearts for 20, Baker leads. He must allow his clubs and diamonds to be led into, as either Ten could fall needlessly to an Ace if led. He therefore decides to force out any high trumps by means of ♠Q, and is fortunate enough to bring the Jass down, leaving his Menel in charge. He can be sure that the Ace and Ten are not in play, otherwise Abel would have played one of them and held back the Jass for better things, such as catching the Menel or winning the stich. Abel continues with ♢8, which is taken by the Ten. The maker now returns ♠K, announcing 'bella' and scoring 20. This draws ♠8, which Baker can be certain is the last trump in his adversary's hand. The remaining tricks are played like bat and ball. Baker wins his game, scoring 49 in tricks plus 10 for stich and 20 for bella, 79 in all, to Abel 53 in tricks plus 20 for the sequence, 73 in all. The round totals after two deals are A 140, B 143. And it's anybody's game.

# 8

## BEZIQUE AND PINOCHLE

### *Romance on the cards*

Another offspring of Sixty-Six, Bezique developed in the clubs and coffee-houses of Paris in the 1840s and by the end of the century had become a world-wide classic. It has been played in many different forms, and in America gave rise to Pinochle in all its varieties. Although no longer played as a club or tournament game, it maintains a devoted following among all true card-lovers. Indeed, as it has long since been abandoned as a serious gambling game, Bezique could nowadays be well described as a game for lovers. Much is made of 'marriages' between Kings and Queens, and the name of the game itself (only fancifully derived from besico, supposedly Spanish for 'little kiss'), denotes an irregular liaison between a Queen and Jack of different suits.

The form of the game described below is for two players using two 32-card packs shuffled together. Other versions are recorded, for various numbers of players and involving greater numbers of cards, but are not now much in evidence. Who, really, is going to keep out of circulation eight or even six 32-card packs shuffled together for the rare occasions on which they have the time and inclination to embark on such exotic monstrosities? At most, it will be worth appending to this chapter a note on the almost identical game of two-handed Pinochle, and a description of the single-pack ancestor of Bezique known as Cinq Cents.

# Bezique

*Equipment.* Two 32-card packs shuffled together, consisting of A K Q J T 9 8 7 in each suit. It does not matter if they are of different back designs or colours, so long as they are of the same dimensions. Scores are made continually throughout the game, and can be kept on paper, though some sort of mechanical scorer is useful. Patent Bezique markers, of the same design as Whist and Piquet markers, are now antiques, but dial-type scorers are still produced from time to time. Even a Cribbage board will do. All Bezique scores are in tens, so twice round the crib board at 10 per hole gives a maximum of 1210 points, enough to be getting on with.

*Rank.* In each suit, cards rank: A T K Q J 9 8 7. Note the position of the Ten. It counts higher than King both in play and in cutting for the deal.

*Deal.* Whoever cuts the higher-ranking card may choose whether or not to deal first. Deal eight cards each in batches of three, then two, then three. Turn up the next card – the seventeenth – and lay it to one side between the two players. The suit of this card is the trump suit for the current deal and, if it is a Seven, the dealer immediately scores 10 for it. Place the undealt cards face down across this card to form the stock, so that the turn-up projects from beneath it.

*Object.* The winner is the first player to reach 1000 points, which may take one or several deals. Points are scored for capturing *brisques* (Aces and Tens) in tricks, counting 10 points each, and, through drawing and discarding, acquiring certain combinations of cards scoring anything from 20 to 500 points each.

*Tricks.* Non-dealer leads to the first trick. The second player need not follow suit, but may play any card he chooses. A trick is won with the higher card of the suit led, or the higher trump if any are played. If identical cards are played, the first beats the second. The winner of a trick lays the won cards before him (not necessarily face down), shows and scores for any scoring combination he may hold in his hand, then draws the top card of stock to restore his hand to eight. The trick-loser draws the next card of the stock, and the trick-winner then leads to the next trick. This continues until the stock is exhausted, when the rules of play change. The purpose of winning a trick may be to capture any brisque it contains, though brisques (Aces and Tens) are not actually counted into the score until the end of the hand, and do not add up to much. The main advantage of winning a trick is that only the winner may declare a scoring combination. The loser may hold one, but he can do nothing about it until he wins a trick.

*Scoring combinations.* Upon winning a trick, a player may declare and score for any one (not more) of the following combinations, by removing its constituent cards from his hand and laying them face up on the table before him. Such cards remain on the table, but continue to count as part of his hand – *ie*, in subsequent tricks, he may play either from the hand or from a combination-card on the table before him.

| | |
|---|---:|
| *Sequence* (A T K Q J of trumps) | 250 |
| *Royal marriage* (K–Q of trumps) | 40 |
| *Common marriage* (K–Q of plain suit) | 20 |
| *Hundred Aces* (any four Aces) | 100 |
| *Eighty Kings* (any four Kings) | 80 |
| *Sixty Queens* (any four Queens) | 60 |
| *Forty Jacks* (any four Jacks) | 40 |
| *Bezique* (♠Q-◇J) | 40 |
| *Double bezique* (♠Q–◇J–♠Q–◇J) | 500 |

Special rules govern the formation and re-formation of such combinations. The basic principle is that a card which has already been used as part of a scoring combination (and is therefore still lying on the table) may be used again as part of a different type of combination, but not of the same. Cards won in tricks remain out of play and cannot be used to form combinations.

*Examples of re-use*: If a marriage has been declared in spades, three more Queens might be added on the next turn to score Sixty Queens, and ◇J on the turn after to score bezique, so long as the ♠Q remains on the table throughout and is not played to a trick. If a royal marriage is declared for 40, then so long as both cards remain on the table it is permissible to add A–T–J of trumps and score 250 for the sequence.

*Restrictions on re-use*: If a marriage has been declared in spades, neither card may be remarried by the addition of another King or Queen (but another spade marriage may be scored by declaring the other King *and* Queen). Once a quartet (of Aces, Kings, Queens or Jacks) has been declared, none of its cards may be added to form another quartet, though it is permissible (if improbable) to declare another four of a kind straight from the hand to the table. It is also not permitted to declare a sequence for 250 and subsequently claim the royal marriage contained within it – as shown above, you must score the lower first and then the higher. Similarly, it is not permissible to score 500 for double bezique and subsequently count each constituent bezique for 40, but it is correct to declare, while winning three tricks, single bezique once, single bezique twice, and then double bezique, so long as all four bezique cards are on the table when double is declared.

It is sometimes stated that a combination is scorable only if at least one of its cards is played directly from the hand. This is not so. For example, it is proper to declare Kings for 80, Queens for 60 at the next opportunity, and then, so long as the appropriate cards remain on the table, a marriage upon winning each of the next four tricks. Or suppose Kings have been declared for 80, and two have been played out, leaving ♡K ♠K on the table. At a later turn, it is permissible to play ♠Q–♢J from the hand and announce 'bezique for 40, and a marriage to score', subsequently counting the ♠K–♠Q upon winning another trick.

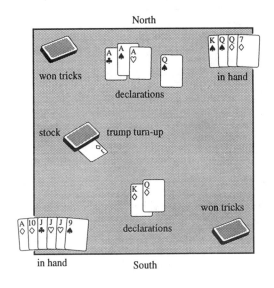

**Figure 7: Bezique** A game in progress. North has evidently scored '100 Aces' earlier on and since played one to a trick. Rules of play forbid the same combination to be re-formed and scored again by the addition of another Ace. Similarly, North's ♠Q on the table is left over from either a marriage for 20 or a bezique for 40. Drawing another Queen would enable the addition of three Queens from hand to that on the table to score '60 Queens'. If North has just won a trick, the ♢7 may now be exchanged for the turned Jack, enabling it to be added to the ♠Q for bezique.

South, who has scored 20 for a diamond marriage, would also very much like to get the turned Jack. It could be combined with the marriage and the Ace-Ten in hand to yield 250 for the trump sequence, and then, on a later trick, the other three Jacks in hand could be added to it for '40 Jacks'.

*Seven of trumps*. A player who holds a Seven of trumps may declare it at any time – usually upon playing it to a trick – and score 10 points for it. Alternatively, he may, upon winning a trick, declare it for 10 and exchange it for the turn-up. This, however, counts as a declaration, and prevents him from declaring any other combination at the same time. (There are conflicting rules on the use of the trump Seven. This one is a recommended compromise.)

*End-game*. When the loser of the 24th trick has taken the turn-up into his hand, and there are no more cards in stock, the rules of play change. Each takes into hand any cards he has left on the table, and the last trick-winner leads to the first of the last eight tricks. The second to a trick must follow suit if he can and must win the trick if he can. If unable to follow, he must trump if he can. No combinations may be declared after the last card has been drawn. The winner of the last trick scores 10 points for it.

*Score*. Each player sorts through his won cards, counting 10 points for each Ace and Ten captured (unless one player has reached 1000 points, in which case brisques are not counted). This total is then added to his total for combinations and the result recorded. As many more deals are played as are necessary, until at least one player has reached 1000 points, the winner being the player with the higher total. If the loser has failed to reach 500, the winner counts double the margin of victory.

## Notes on play

It is generally not worth winning a trick unless it contains a brisque or you have something to declare. Indeed, other things being equal, it is preferable to lose a trick and play second to the next one, as this gives you more latitude – for example, you know whether or not you can safely win it with a brisque, whereas you will avoid leading one for fear of losing it. On the other hand, situations often arise in which you suspect that your opponent has a valuable declaration to make, in which case you may attempt to keep winning tricks until the stock is exhausted in order to prevent him from declaring it. Bearing in mind that the same will be done against you, try to keep back trumps, especially high ones, to ensure the ability to declare.

It is obvious that good cards to throw to worthless tricks, or lead to those in which you have no interest, are Sevens, Eights and Nines. Often, however, you find yourself with none in your hand, which seems to consist of part-combinations and valuable cards. In this case treat Jacks as dispensable, as Forty Jacks is not a very high scoring combination and not worth spoiling the hand for. Keep hold of a diamond Jack, however, so long as there is the possibility of making bezique. Also be prepared to play a Ten if you can win the trick by doing so, as Tens cannot form part of scoring combinations except in trumps and are therefore not worth keeping from this point of view.

When it comes to breaking up part-combinations, you must weigh the value of each against the probability of making it, to which end you will be guided by what you can see among your opponent's declarations and what has already been played to tricks. For example, if he has declared a marriage in spades and you hold both Jacks of diamonds, it is impossible to make double bezique, and so one more Jack becomes available for discarding – unless, of course, you have seen so few of the eight Jacks to date that there seems a fair chance of forming a Jack quartet.

Cards still lying on the table after being declared are suitable candidates for playing to tricks, on the principle that you give your opponent less information about the state of your hand by playing a card he knows you have rather than one he hasn't seen. Marriage partners and quartetted Jacks are particularly good candidates for this purpose. At the same time, however, it is important to retain those which stand a fair chance of being re-used in other combinations, and those which belong to the trump suit and may therefore be needed for trick-winning. In particular, never break up (by playing a card from) a single bezique so long as the possibility remains of forming a second and scoring the double, as double bezique is the most valuable combination in the pack and will nearly always win the game.

Given a choice of combinations, it is naturally better to score the more valuable ones first. But there is an exception to this rule, in that given a sequence, you may score 40 for the royal marriage first and then 250 for the sequence for a total of 290, but if you count the higher combination first you are restricted to 250, as the marriage may not then be scored. The same applies to beziques: you may declare, on three successive turns, a single, a single and a double, for a total of 580, but you cannot score for a single after counting the double. In these cases you score more for starting with the lower combination and working upwards. If, however, it seems unlikely that you will have time to make these scores the long way, in view of the number of tricks left to play and the state of your own hand, it may be better to score the higher combination first and forgo the lower.

In the last eight tricks, the ideal is to play worthless cards of a suit in which your opponent is void, in order to weaken his trumps. Experienced players will know what cards their opponent holds and play accordingly. Experience, in fact, is essential to success at Bezique, as it is a game of judgement rather than analysis. The practised player soon develops an instinctive feel for the state of his opponent's hand, and will know when he can safely lose tricks and when he must keep winning in order to prevent a high combination to be scored against him.

# Pinochle

Pinochle is the American form of the German game Binokel, itself still played in Europe and derived from the French Binocle. More elaborate varieties of Pinochle subsequently developed in the United States, but most have now fallen out of use.

Two-hand Pinochle is virtually identical with Bezique, as described above. The only significant difference is that the doubled pack is reduced to 48 cards by stripping out the Sevens and Eights. It will come as no surprise to learn that the Queen-Jack combination is called pinochle instead of bezique.

# Cinq Cents

Several games are known as Cinq Cents, from the target score of 500 points to which they are played. This one is an early form of Bezique played with a single instead of a double 32-card pack. As it amounts to an almost exact cross between Bezique and Sixty-Six, I will save space by assuming a knowledge of both games and concentrating on the differences.

Deal eight cards each in batches of 3–2–3. Turn the next for trumps and slip it half under the stock. Whoever gets the Seven of trumps may exchange it for the turn-up, so long as the latter has not yet been taken, and scores 10 points for so doing. Cards rank and count as follows: Ace 11, Ten 10, King 4, Queen 3, Jack 2, Nine-Eight-Seven 0 each. These points accrue as soon as the cards are won in a trick, and players are permitted to keep track of their accumulating scores in writing or on mechanical markers as play proceeds.

Tricks are played as at Bezique and Sixty-Six, there being no need to follow suit until the stock is exhausted. In the play of the last six tricks the second player must follow suit and win the trick if possible, and, if unable to follow, must play a trump if possible.

Either player, having dawn from stock and being about to lead (not follow) to a trick, may declare and score for one (not more) of the following melds:

| | |
|---|---|
| Sequence (ATKQJ) | 250 in trumps |
| | 120 if not trumps |
| Four Aces | 100 |
| Four Tens | 80 |
| Four Kings | 60 |
| Four Queens | 40 |
| Four Jacks | 20 |
| Marriage (KQ) | 40 in trumps |
| | 20 if not trumps |
| Mariage de besi | 40♠Q+♢J |

(Some accounts have quartets scoring as follows: Aces 100, Tens 90, Kings 80, Queens 60, Jacks 40. This may be preferred for more closely resembling the schedule of two-pack Bezique.)

Melds cannot be claimed in retrospect once a card has been led.

The players deal alternately, adding their scores up as they go along. The game is won by the first player to state, correctly, that he has reached or exceeded a total of 500, even if his opponent proves to have a greater score but has failed to announce it. A false claim, of course, loses the game.

If it is found at the end of a deal that both players have reached 500 without declaring, the game is won by the player with the higher score, or, if equal, by the winner of the last (16th) trick.

# 9

## CRIBBAGE

### *Old Englysshe pubbe game*

Not only is Cribbage one of the oldest and longest popular card games played in England, it is also the only one that appears to be of entirely English invention. It is traditionally credited to the poet-soldier Sir John Suckling (1609–42), but, while there is no doubt that he was an enthusiastic Cribber, there is nothing to prove that he had any hand in developing it from its known ancestor, the 16th-century game of Noddy. Crib was much favoured by the court and aristocracy until well into 'good King Charles's golden day', but in this capacity was superseded by the more intellectual Ombre (ironically now defunct), and went down-market. This has done nothing to reduce its continuing popularity, its status confirmed by the fact that it is the only game legally playable in public houses without special licence, and nowadays increased by its particular susceptibility to computerisation. A remarkably stable game, the only significant change it has undergone since Suckling's time has been an increase in the number of cards dealt from five to six – a change that was regarded with suspicion as an innovation in the late 19th century. The great thing about Cribbage is that so much variety derives from such basically simple material that it can be played fast and chattily, and never palls.

*Players*. Two. There are versions for three players and for four in partnerships, but two is original and best and should be stuck to.

*Cards.* Crib is played with a 52-card pack ranking from low to high A 2 3 4 5 6 7 8 9 T J Q K. Ace counts as 1 for all purposes and does not follow on from the King. Numeral cards count at face value, court cards 10 each.

*Game.* A game is won by the first player to reach 121 points, play ceasing the moment this happens. If the loser fails to reach 91 he is *lurched*, or *in the lurch*, and loses double; but as this rarely occurs between experienced players it is rather theoretical. Because scores are made in continuous dribs and drabs throughout play, it is more convenient to record them mechanically than to keep a written tally. The traditional scoring device (it goes back to the 16th century and was originally called a Noddy board) is illustrated in figure 8 and must be well known even to non-players. How to use it is explained in the caption.

*Deal.* The deal alternates, the first being made by the player cutting the higher card (King highest, not Ace). The dealer is said to be 'in the box', and has several advantages which should normally result in his making the higher score in his own deal. Deal six cards each face down in ones, starting with non-dealer, and stack the rest face down to one side.

*Laying away.* Each player examines his hand and discards two cards face down to form a four-card *crib*. The crib belongs to the dealer, who will score for any combinations it may contain at end of play, but it must remain face down and unlooked at while play proceeds. Each player's aim is to retain four cards that will be of most use in the play and will score best for the combinations to be described in a moment. As to the crib, it is of course the dealer's object to lay aside cards that will help him score for combinations, and non-dealer's aim to contribute cards he hopes to be useless for this purpose.

*Scoring combinations.* The combinations and their scores (and their traditional names in brackets) are as follows:

> *Fifteen.* Two or more cards totalling 15 (e.g. 9–6, K–5, A–6–8, A–2–3–4–5 etc) score 2 points.
>
> *Pair.* Two matched cards (e.g. 2–2, Q–Q) score 2 points.
>
> *Three alike (prial).* Three matched cards (e.g. 4–4–4, J–J–J) score 6 points.
>
> *Four alike (double pair royal).* Four matched cards (e.g. 8–8–8–8) score 12 points.
>
> *Run.* Three or more cards in sequence (e.g. A–2–3, 9–T–J–Q) score 1 per constituent card.
>
> *Flush.* A hand of four cards all of the same suit scores 4.

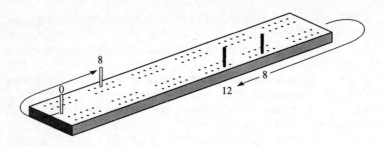

**Figure 8: Cribbage (1)** Using the 61-hole Crib board. Each player starts from zero at each short edge and records scores by moving two pegs alternately 'up the outside' (from 1 to 30) and 'down the inside' from 31 to 60. Two such circuits are played in the standard game to 121 points. As illustrated here, White has evidently pegged nothing in play and 8 in hand, while Red must have made 8 in play and hand followed by 4 in the box.

Note that any individual card may be counted as many times as it forms part of a distinct combination. For example, 7–7–7 scores 6 because it consists of three distinct pairs of two cards, scoring 2 each. The combination 8–7–7–7 would score, besides 6 for the Sevens, another 6 for the three different fifteens that can be made by attaching each Seven in turn to the Eight.

*The turn-up.* When both have discarded to the crib, non-dealer cuts the pack (without revealing the bottom card of the top half), and dealer takes the top card of the bottom half and places it face up on top. If the turn-up is a Jack, dealer scores 2 'for his heels'.

*The count.* Non-dealer leads to the first count by placing any card face up before him and announcing its value, e.g. 'One' if an Ace, 'Ten' if a court, etc. Dealer responds by playing a card face up before himself and announcing the combined value of the first two cards. If these form a combination – fifteen or a pair – he scores 2 immediately.

This continues, with each playing alternately, announcing the new total value of all cards so far played, and scoring for any combination (other than a flush) which the card just played makes in conjunction with those immediately preceding it in unbroken succession.

Neither player may bring the count beyond 31, but each must play if able to do so without busting. A player making 31 exactly scores 2 and the count ends. A player who runs out of cards, or who cannot add a card without busting, says 'Go'. If the other also cannot legally play, the first scores '1 for the go'. Otherwise, the second continues adding cards and scoring for combinations until he too either runs out of cards or cannot play without busting. In either case he scores 1 for the go, or 2 for making 31 exactly.

If either player has a card or cards left in hand, the cards played to the first count are turned face down, and a second count is started by the opponent of the player who scored a go. Play continues as before, a third count being started if necessary. When one player runs out of the cards, the other continues playing alone, scoring for combinations and 'goes' as they may occur, until he also runs out.

If either player reaches 121 in course of play, the game ends. If not, continue as follows.

*Counting the hands.* The two players then pick up the four cards they each played to the count(s) and score for combinations contained within their hands. For this purpose, the turn-up is reckoned as part of each player's hand, so each scores for five cards instead of four.

Non-dealer turns his cards up and scores first, counting for each and every combination that can be made from the five cards concerned. A run may therefore be three, four or five cards long, and scores as many points. A four-card flush in hand scores 4, or 5 if it matches the suit of the turn-up. Finally, if non-dealer's original four-card hand includes the Jack of the same suit as the turn-up, he scores an extra '1 for his nob'.

For the sake of discipline, and to ensure that players keep track of their own and the other's rightful score, combinations should be reckoned in this order: fifteens, pairs, runs, flushes, and his nob. Scores are announced cumulatively as the player goes along. For example, suppose the hand is ♠5 ♡5 ♣6 ◇J and the turn-up ◇7. The player declares 'Fifteen 2, fifteen 4, pair 6, seven-eight-nine, ten-eleven-twelve, and one's thirteen.' (Note that the two Fives, besides scoring 2 for a pair together, each makes a fifteen with the Jack, and each a three-card run of 5–6–7. The final 'one' is for 'his nob'.)

If non-dealer has not reached 121, dealer then turns his hand up and scores in exactly the same way. If he does not thereby reach 121, he finally turns the crib face up and scores also for it in its capacity as a five-card hand, including the turn-up. This is scored in the same way, except that a four-card flush does not count: a flush must include the card of the turn-up as well, when a score of 5 may be claimed. Note, too, that if the turn-up is a Jack, neither player can claim 'one for his nob', as this is precluded by the dealer's original score of 'two for his heels'.

*Points of order.* The correct procedure for making the turn-up is as follows. Non-dealer lifts off the top of the pack a packet of cards numbering not fewer than six and leaving not fewer than six on the bottom half. To prevent the bottom card of the top half from being seen, they should not be tilted or lifted any higher than necessary to enable Dealer to take out the next card down. They are then placed squarely on top of the bottom half before the turn-up is place on top of them by Dealer.

Disputes sometimes occur about the validity of combinations scored during the count. They often arise from the difficulty of perceiving the sequence of cards played because although successive cards are to be regarded as forming a consecutive line, they are in fact played in two separate piles, one in front of each player. Here is an example of the sort of play which is permissible, but easily missed.

North: $4^4$    $6^{17}$    $4^{26}$    $3^{31}$
South:       $7^{11}$    $5^{22}$    $2^{28}$

South's second card, a Five, enables him to score 4 for completing the sequence 4–5–6–7. North's second Four gives him 4 points, as it completes a similar sequence with the three immediately preceding cards. South's Two nets nothing, as it makes no sequence, but North's final Three scores for completing the sequence 2–3–4–5–6–7.

A sequence is not scorable, however, if broken by a pair. For example:

North: $4^4$    $6^{15}$    $7^{28}$
South:    $5^9$    $6^{21}$

North's second card scores 'fifteen 2, and three-four-five (for the run)'. South's Six gives him 2 for the pair of Sixes. This prevents North from claiming a run for his Seven, as the immediately preceding cards were not 6–5 but 6–6–5. This restriction applies only to the count, however, not to the hand. Thus a hand consisting of 7–6–6–5 would score 2 for the pair plus 6 for two runs of three.

The following point of play is true even if it seems illogical. North leads 6, South plays 2, North adds 6. North does not score 2 for his pair of Sixes, as the second is separated from the first by South's Two. If, however, North leads 6, South plays 6 (scoring 2 for the pair) and North adds a third 6, he now scores 6 for the prial, i.e. 2 for each pair. In this case his second Six is regarded as linked to his first by means of South's Six. South could then add the fourth and score 12.

*Strategy.* There are fifteen different ways of discarding two from a hand of six cards, and the knack of Crib lies in always choosing the best two. To add to the interest, the best two to throw from any given hand usually differs according to whether you or the other player is in the box. Let's deal a few and see what happens. South deals, and North gets:

♡3 ♠4 ♣5 ♣7 ♣10 ♣Q

Thinking only of his own score, North could keep:

(a)  4–5–10–Q, yielding two fifteens for 4 and hoping for a turned Three or Six to add 3 for a run; or
(b)  the club flush for 4; or
(c)  3–4–5–7 for 5, i.e. fifteen 2 and a run of 3, to which a 6 turned up would add another fifteen 2 and extend the run to 5, total 9.

Against these must be set the value to South's crib of the resultant discards.

Case (a) puts 3–7 in the crib. These are sufficiently spaced to make a 5-card run unlikely, albeit possible, and should not be rejected on grounds of matching suit, as only a 5-card flush counts in the crib and the chances of making it are remote. The only danger is that 3 and 7 make 10, and dealers are highly prone to laying away Fives. Case (a), therefore, gains 4 points, with a remote possibility of 7, less a probable fifteen for 2, net gain 2.

Case (b) leaves 4–5 in the crib, with high chances for South of making one or more fifteens and possibly a three-card run. Result: North's 4 for the flush stands to be reduced by a fifteen 2 and a possible 3-card run, leaving a net gain of 2, if any.

Case (c) counts 5, or 9 if a Six is turned, but gives South two cards worth 10, with the consequent danger of his making two fifteens for 4, net gain 1 or possibly 5 if lucky.

An alternative is to forgo the chance of a long sequence by keeping the Ten and discarding the Seven. This retains the fifteen 2 and run of three for 5, leaving South only one chance of making a fifteen 2, and North a net gain of 3. Mathematically, this looks like the best bet. Note that 3–4–5–Q would produce the same score, but, as a discard to the crib, the Ten is sufficiently close to the Seven to threaten a possible run of four. Note, too, that if North were dealer, Ten and Queen would undoubtedly be the best discards, being good for fifteens and requiring only a Jack to make a run of three.

Now let's look at South's hand.

♡A ♢5 ♠9 ♡10 ♡J ♠K

Rather nice, and not too problematical. As it stands, it contains four fifteens (including A–5–9) for 8, and a run of three, making 11. Something, however, will have to go. We can see that a discard of Jack and King would go nicely with the Queen contributed by North. But the obvious discard requirement is to keep the run of three and two fifteens for 7, and discard Ace, King, to the crib – which will not, remember, constitute a run of three, as Ace always counts low.

Let's now make a turn-up, and, just for fun, assume it is ♡5. The play is not very interesting – all I got out of it was 2 for South, 1 each for a 'go' – but the hand scores are worth a look.

Counting the turn-up, North has:

♣3 ♡4 ♡5 ♠5 ♣10

and scores: Fifteen 2, fifteen 4, pair 6, 7–8–9, 10–11–12 (for the runs).

South has:

♦5 ♡5 ♠9 ♡10 ♡J

and scores: Fifteen 2, fifteen 4, fifteen 6, fifteen 8, pair 10, 11–12–13 (for the run), and 1 (for his nob) 14.

The crib is unusually meagre –

♡A ♡5 ♣7 ♠Q ♠K

– with a mere 4 for the two fifteens.

To sum up, both players will generally want to keep the four cards that give them the best score, and good discards for the Dealer are Fives, pairs, two cards in sequence, and a Ten if accompanied by a Five. Non-dealer, however, should avoid throwing precisely these cards and anything higher than Nine. Perhaps his ideal discard is Ace, Eight, as they are too far apart for a run, and do not total 10. If, as Non-dealer, you must discard high, prefer a King or a Queen, as they offer less chance of a run.

In playing to the count, the leader will obviously avoid a Five, Ten or court card. A card lower than Five is a good lead, as the next player cannot immediately make it fifteen. Once past fifteen, the worst thing you can do is to let the other player go out with a pair to 31. For example, you don't, if you have any choice, play a Ten to a count of 21, Nine to 22, and so on.

Interesting points of strategy occur when both players are approaching the 121 mark. Dealer has the advantage of scoring for both hand and crib, but this is often less useful than Non-dealer's advantage of counting his hand first. So, if you are within a few points of 121, concentrate on discarding to a hand that will yield points in the play-off, and, if you are Non-dealer, don't worry about throwing 'good' cards to the crib if they leave you enough points in hand to count you out first.

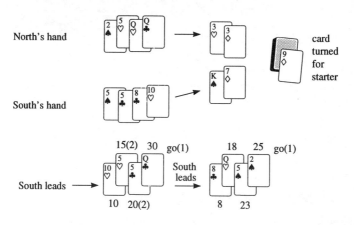

**Figure 9: Cribbage (2)** North deals and is 'in the box'. It would be nice to discard the Queens and have a Four turned, as the hand would then count 2 for the pair of Threes and 8 for two runs of four, total 10 plus at least 2 in the box. Alternatively, a Ten or court turned up would yield fifteen 2, fifteen 4 (for each 2–3–1 combination), fifteen 6 (for 5–10), and a pair 8. Safer, however, is to throw the Threes, retaining the two fifteens and a pair for 6. South has several fifteens, including the 7–8. He would like to keep the pair of Fives and the King, Ten, giving four fifteens for 8 and a pair makes 10. But this would necessitate throwing a fifteen (7–8) to North's box, with the danger of giving North a sequence as well. He therefore makes the safest discard of King, Seven. South then cuts and North turns a Nine as the starter.

South leads his Ten to the first sequence, in which North pegs 2 for the fifteen and 1 for the go, and South 2 for the pair. The only score made in the second sequence is North's 1 for the go.

South counts his hand: fifteen 2, fifteen 4, pair 6, Eight-Nine-Ten 9.

North's hand counts fifteen 2, fifteen 4, pair 6. He then turns his box and counts fifteen 2 (for the Nine and two Threes), pair 4.

Thus at the end of the first deal North has pegged 4 in play, 6 in hand and 4 in box, total 14, to south's 2 in play and 9 in hand, total 11.

South, had he dealt these hands, might have put the 7–8 in his own box. North's best result from a difficult hand would have arisen from the rather unpromising discard of 3–5. Depending on the play, the outcome could be 3 in play and 6 in hand for 9, to South's 0 in play, 10 in hand and 7 in the box for 17.

# 10

## —— GIN RUMMY ——

### *From the great days of Broadway*

Although Gin first appeared in the early 1900s (some credit its development to Bridge tutor Elwood T Baker, who later achieved posthumous fame as an unexplained murder victim – an irate partner, perhaps?), it wasn't until the 1930s that it struck gold in the annals of popular culture by revealing itself to be the game of the great movie stars, as you may readily see if you set your video to record the films of this period. There's a simple explanation for this. Gin is easy to learn and fast to play, requires no fiddly in-deal scoring, can be performed on mental auto-pilot, and can be picked up and dropped out of at a moment's notice between takes or while indulging in walking on-and-off parts on Broadway. We have already noted the frequent occurrence of Klob or Klaberjass in the writings of Damon Runyon, but it is worth remarking that his characters are far more frequently encountered playing Gin.

So what is it, exactly? Well, exactly, it is not greatly different from the earliest known form of Rummy, which can be traced back to the mid-19th century Mexican game of Conquian. Conquian was a simple win-or-lose game for a fixed stake, and if Elwood T Baker can be credited with anything, it is most probably with the refined scoring system, which made it more interesting to play for money, and gave an edge to players who could think and calculate just that little bit faster than their opponents. The great thing about Gin is that everyone thinks they can play it well, so, if they lose, they can blame it on card distribution. Those who really can play it well keep quiet about it, and just pocket their winnings.

Gin is the classic two-player member of the Rummy family. As in all Rummy games, the object is to collect cards which 'go together', either being of the same rank, like ♠7 ♡7 ♣7, or forming a sequence in the same suit, such as ♣7 ♣8 ♣9. Such a matching collection is called a *meld*.

Any cards left in one's hand at the end of a deal which fail to form a meld of three or more are called *deadwood*, and incur penalties equivalent to their combined face values. The method by which cards are collected for this purpose will probably be well known even to non card-players. At each turn you draw a card from a stockpile and throw out an unwanted card to a discard pile, and keep doing so until all the cards you hold can be arranged in matching sets, or melds. It is a method which is to be found in essence in the game of Mah Jong, and which has been borrowed as part of the mechanics of many modern table games. One could even claim to recognise it in Monopoly, by noting that you may not build upon a property until you have formed it into part of a 'meld' of three properties of the same colour.

Gin Rummy is very easy to learn and the rules are clear, simple, and fairly well standardised.

## The game

*Cards.* One standard 52-card pack.

*Game.* The game is won by the first player to reach 100 points, which normally takes several deals.

*Rank and value of cards.* Cards rank A 2 3 4 5 6 7 8 9 T J Q K and are worth their face value, with Ace 1 and court cards 10 each.

*Deal.* Whoever cuts the higher card chooses whether to deal first. Thereafter the winner of one hand deals to the next, and the winner of a game deals first to the next. It is important that the cards be thoroughly shuffled before play, dealer having the right to shuffle last. Deal ten cards each, one at a time. Place the remainder face down to form a stock. Take the top card of the stock and lay it face up beside it to form the first 'upcard'. This will form the base of a gradually constituted waste pile of faced cards, the topmost of which is always known as the upcard.

*To start.* Nondealer may start by exchanging the upcard for any card in his hand. If he refuses, dealer has the same privilege. If either player does so, that constitutes his first turn and the game continues from there. If both refuse it, nondealer must start the game by drawing the top card of the stock, adding it to his hand, and discarding any card face up on the original upcard to continue the waste pile.

*Play.* Thereafter, each player in turn must draw and add to his hand either the unknown top card of the stock, or the faced upcard surmounting the waste pile. In either case he completes his turn by making one discard face up to the waste pile. It is *not* permissible to draw the upcard and discard it on the same turn.

*Object.* The object is to collect cards which together form one or more melds, a meld consisting of either (a) three or four cards of the same rank, or (b) a sequence of three or more cards in the same suit. (For this purpose, Ace and King are not consecutive.) A hand consisting entirely of melds, with no deadwood, is described as 'gin' and carries a bonus. But a player may end the game as soon as the total value of his unmatched cards is 10 or less, at which point the player with the lower value of deadwood wins. During play, melds are not revealed but retained secretly in the hand.

*Knocking.* When a player is satisfied with the low value of his deadwood, he ends the game by (theoretically) knocking on the table after he has drawn an eleventh card and before making his final discard. It is now the practice to indicate closure of the game by laying the final discard face down on the waste pile, an action still referred to as knocking. The knocker then spreads his hand of cards face up on the table, arranged in melds and with any deadwood clearly separated from them. His opponent then does the same, but also has the privilege of 'laying off' any cards of his own deadwood which may be matched with any of the knocker's melds, in order to reduce the penalty value of his deadwood. This privilege does not apply, however, if the knocker has a gin hand (no deadwood).

*End of stock.* The two last cards of the stock may not be taken. If neither player has knocked by the time they are reached, the result is a no-score draw, and the same dealer deals again.

*Score.* Each player keeps his score cumulatively, the winner of a hand adding his score for the hand to his previous total and writing down the combined amount in order to make clear when 100 has been reached or exceeded.

If the knocker has the lower count for deadwood, he scores the difference between the two deadwood values. If he went gin, he adds a bonus of 25.

If the opponent has an equal or lower value of deadwood, he scores the difference (if any) plus a bonus of 25 for *undercut*. But he cannot undercut a gin hand, for which the knocker still counts 25, nor may he himself score the bonus for gin, whether he had it already (in which case he should have knocked) or acquired it by laying off.

*Game score.* As soon as either player has reached or exceeded 100 points, the game ends and a line is drawn beneath both totals, beneath which various bonuses are recorded. First, the winner records a bonus of 100 for game; next, he adds a 25-point 'box' bonus for each hand that he won. Finally, if he won every hand he adds a bonus for 'shut-out'. This is equivalent to twice the basic amount he scored plus another 100 for game. (In some circles, the box bonuses are also doubled.

Other bonus systems may be encountered, but the one described here is usual American practice.) The difference between the two final totals is the margin of victory.

*Hollywood scoring system.* For those who can't get enough of it, this is a method of playing three games simultaneously (or more if preferred, following the same principle). Three sets of double columns are drawn up, each double column headed by the initials of the players. When a player wins his first hand, his score is recorded in the first set only. When he wins his second, it is recorded in the first and second sets. His third, and so on, is recorded in all three, unless and until any of them has been ruled off with a win. As soon as a player reaches 100 in any of the three sets of columns, that set is ruled off and bonuses noted in the usual way. Play continues until all games have been completed and scored.

*Oklahoma variant.* In this version the maximum count of deadwood with which you may knock is not necessarily 10, but is determined by the value of the initial upcard. For instance, if it is a Six you must have six or less to knock; if a King, ten. It is usually agreed that if the first upcard is an Ace, you must have a gin hand to go out. The variant may be recommended for the variety it adds to the game.

## Notes on play

Gin is a game of observation, inference and memory, in that order. Each player's management of his own hand is a somewhat mechanical affair in the sense that for any given situation there is a fairly calculable best move. It is because there is a 'best' move that observation is the foremost aspect of skill required. You *observe* what your opponent is discarding and which of your discards he is drawing; from that, *infer* the structure of his hand on the assumption that he is either making the best moves or acting in accordance with a personal style of play to which you have become accustomed; and thereafter *remember* all the cards that have gone and the changing contents of your opponent's hand as the play proceeds.

As to the play of your own hand, the first thing to note is the inadvisability of going all out for gin. The bonus of 25 is not sufficient to compensate for the times when you should have knocked instead of waiting around for glory, and thereby found yourself more knocked against than knocking. And, worse still, being undercut for your pains. A typical game ends about half to two thirds of the way through the pack, so if you get a knocking hand much earlier than that do not hesitate to go down for all you can get.

It is generally better to draw the stock card than the upcard. The more upcards you draw, the more of your hand is known to the other side, and the more of the rest of it can be deduced. You are also taking cards of no use to your opponent, when by drawing the next card of stock you may well be preventing him from going gin. The best exception to the rule is when you need the upcard to convert two matching cards into a meld of three, thus eliminating three pieces of deadwood (including the discard), or, of course, when it enables you to knock immediately. It may also be useful to expand a meld, especially if you thereby eliminate a high unmatched card; but this should be done with caution rather than as a matter of course, as it can do more harm than good. If, for example, you hold

♠K ♡K ♣K, ♢7 8 9, ♠5, ♢5, ♡2, ♣2

it is not worth taking ♢T as the upcard, as you must then throw one of a pair and so halve the number of draws that will enable you to knock. One other conceivable reason for taking the up card might be to reduce your deadwood when you suspect an imminent knocking from the other side of the table. The lower the rank he discarded, the worse the danger would appear to be.

Because it is desirable to throw high cards instead of low ones, in order to keep your deadwood down, it is also reasonable to retain high-ranking pairs and two-card sequences acquired early in the game, in the hope that your opponent will discard a matching third in exchange for a lower-valued draw. But this should not be kept up too long. When to give up such expectations and start reducing deadwood is a matter for fine judgement.

Keeping track of discards is fundamental to the play. Suppose your opponent throws ♣J. The easy assumption is that he is 'not collecting Jacks', so you discard ♡J at the next opportunity – and are surprised to see him pounce on it. Too late you spot the ruse. He might have held ♡9 ♡T ♣J and thrown the Jack to draw one of the proper suit for the sequence. Even more cunningly, and perhaps at greater risk (depending on how well he knew the contents of your hand) he might have discarded from ♠J ♢J ♣J. Why, then, should he run a risk to bluff the fourth out of you? Because he thereby not only re-forms his meld, but also prevents you from laying off a Jack when he goes out on the next turn, and perhaps undercutting him.

Of course, what's sauce for the gander is sauce for the goose, and you are at liberty to practise such stratagems yourself. And here's another. Suppose he throws a Jack and you have two Jacks. You are tempted to take it immediately and complete a meld. But resist! He might have been playing from a pair. If so, leave it. He will be bound to throw the other Jack, and then you can take it and be certain that he cannot lay off against that meld of yours and be in a position to undercut. For this to work, you must be pretty sure that he was playing from a pair to start with, and that he is not retaining the other Jack as part of a sequence. If all the Tens and Queens have gone, there is no danger of the latter; and if you have held your Jacks for some time, there is a fair chance that his discard was made from two. If it does go wrong, there is still the chance that either you will draw the other Jack or he will draw and discard it before too great damage is done. Unless he knows every card in your hand, he would be unlikely to draw it and keep it.

So much depends upon observation and remembrance of the contents of the waste pile that you must clearly be very careful in your choice of discard. The first card *not* to throw out is the one you have just drawn from stock and are still holding in your hand: if it really is useless, don't let him know. Hang on to it for a turn or two before getting rid of it. On general principles, as we have seen, it is desirable to throw out a high unmatched card in order to reduce deadwood. The time not to do so is when you suspect that it may be of use to your opponent. In particular, he may be deliberately forcing a card out of you by one of the bluffing stratagems described above, in which case you must hold it back for a turn or two. Check this by matching your proposed discard against the current upcard. The less relation it bears to it, by rank and suit, the better. One player of my acquaintance insists that the ideal discard is different in suit from, but adjacent in rank to, the existing upcard.

It is possible to select a discard in such a way as to elicit useful information. Suppose you have to split up ♠K ♡K, ♠Q ♣Q. In this case throw ♠K. If it is picked up you will know he has the other Kings (in which case you keep yours to lay off if necessary), since your own holding of the Queen shows that he cannot need it for the sequence.

In arranging your melds after knocking, prefer to attach a card to a set of four rather than a sequence if it could equally well go with either. In this way you certainly prevent your opponent from laying off against it, whereas with a sequence there is the danger that he may hold (and therefore lay off) an odd card that attaches to one end of it.

In brief, play your own hand with methodical accuracy, and devote all your thinking to the constitution of the waste pile and the probable structure of your opponent's hand. Above all, remain flexible. Don't select a hoped-for meld at the start of play and concentrate upon it fixedly: circumstances may require you to change plans at any time.

# 11

## ══════ CASSINO ══════
## AND SCOPA

### *Italian fishing games*

Many English-language card-game books describe a two-hander called Cassino, which is not (I think) much played in Britain, but has always had more of a following in America. Especially, that is, in those parts originally favoured by the Italian element of the population, for Cassino belongs to an unusual family of card games which is essentially Italian. The chief member of the family is Scopa for two, or Scopone for four, both of which are still played vigorously enough to be classed, along with Briscola and Tressette, as Italy's major national card games. The more elaborate Cassino, so far as I am aware, is no longer current in the old country, and in any case was always stronger in America, where it seems to have acquired most of its elaborations.

The family of games that these two represent is quite unlike any other, as it involves neither playing tricks nor collecting melds, which are the commonest mechanisms of Western card games. The basic idea in this case involves capturing cards from the table by playing matching cards from the hand. Such games are common in China, where they are generically known as 'Fishing'. They first appeared in Europe in the 18th century and are now mostly played, in numerous forms and varieties, in south-eastern Europe – in, besides Italy, the Balkans, Greece and Turkey.

Although Cassino is usually represented in American books as a children's game, I found it rather tricky to learn at first acquaintance.

Given that experience, I recommend beginners to start with the simpler and more classical form of the game, whose name means 'scoop' or 'sweep'.

# Scopa

*Cards.* Scopa is played with the 40-card Italian pack, which can be approximated by stripping out the Eights, Nines and Tens from a 52-card pack.

*Deal.* Shuffle the cards thoroughly and deal three cards to each player, one at a time, then four cards face up to the table. These four are known as 'table cards', as opposed to 'hand' cards. Stack the rest face down to one side. When both players have played their three hand cards, three more each are dealt from stock. Play continues until none remain in stock and both have played out their last three cards.

*Object.* Each in turn plays a card from the hand in an attempt to capture one or more table cards by matching. In each deal a point is scored for taking the majority of cards, for taking the majority of diamonds, for taking the ◇7, (called *sette bello*) in particular, and for a factor called *primiera*, which cannot be properly explained until we come to the scoring. Points are also scored for making 'sweeps'. A sweep is the capture of all the table cards in one turn. The overall objective is to reach a score of 11 points over as many deals as it takes.

*Play.* Starting with non-dealer, each in turn plays one card from the hand face up to the table. If it makes a match with one or more of the table cards (as described below), those cards are captured and are placed face down, together with the capturing card, in front of the winner. If not, the hand card is simply 'trailed' – i.e. it becomes a table card and is left in place to be captured in its turn.

Playing a card from the hand entitles you to capture one or more table cards in either of the following ways:

*Pairing.* You may capture an Ace with an Ace, a Two with a Two, a King with a King, and so on. Only one table card may be paired in one turn.

*Totalling.* You may with one card capture two or more cards whose face values total that of the capturing card. For this purpose Ace counts 1, Two to Seven count face value, followed by Jack 8, Queen 9, and King 10. For example, if the table cards are 4–A–3–Q and you hold 5–

6–J, you could play the Five to capture 4+A, or (better still) the Jack to capture 4+A+3.

You may only capture by totalling, however, if the capturing card does not pair with a table card. For example, if the table cards were 4–A–3–J instead of 4–A–3–Q, and you played the Jack, you would be forced to capture the Jack by pairing. This does not mean you are obliged to pair just because you can. Here you could instead retain the Jack and capture A+4 with the Five.

*Sweep*. If you capture all the table cards in one go you will score, at end of play, for a 'sweep'. You could do this, for example, if the table cards were A–2–2–5 and you played a King. To indicate a sweep you leave the capturing card – the King – face up among your won cards instead of face down. Of course, there may be more or fewer than four table cards at any point in the game. If there is only one card on the table, and you take it by pairing, you get the benefit of a sweep.

A further benefit, in addition to the score, is that it forces your opponent to trail, since there will be nothing left to capture. If you then capture the trailed card by pairing, you win another sweep, and so on. This can sometimes prove devastating!

*Ending*. The game ends when both players have run out of cards and none remain in stock. The player of the last card captures all the cards remaining on the table and adds them to his winnings. This does not count as a sweep, even if, technically, it fulfils the conditions of one.

*Score*. Points are scored strictly in the following order, and the game is won as soon as either player reaches 11, including any points scored in previous deals:

1 for taking most cards. If 20 each, neither scores.

1 for taking most diamonds. If 5 each, neither scores.

1 for taking the *sette bello* ($\diamondsuit$7).

1 for *primiera*, as explained below.

1 per sweep, as recorded by faced cards.

To determine the point for *primiera*, each player extracts from his won cards the highest-scoring card he holds in each suit, counting on the following basis: Seven 21, Six 18, Ace 16, Five 15, Four 14, Three 13, Two 12, K–Q–J 10 each. The point is scored by the player whose four cards make the highest total. A player who has failed to take any card in one or more suits cannot score for point. If both took at least one of each suit, and the combined values are equal, neither scores for *primiera*.

*Note*. There is a theoretical rule that you must capture if you can, and may not voluntarily trail. This rule is of questionable value. For one thing, there is no way of policing it, and, for another, there is so rarely any advantage to be gained by trailing deliberately that it is only likely to be done in quest of a tactical coup, and such applications of skill ought to be encouraged rather than penalised. More sensible is the rule that you *must* capture if you play a card that *can* capture, as it imposes restrictions on trailing which in themselves give scope for skill.

# —————— **Cassino** ——————

*Cards*. Fifty-two. For the purpose of making totals, numerals Ace to Ten count 1–10 respectively. Court cards have no counting value.

*Deal*. After agreeing who goes first and then shuffling and cutting, deal two cards face down to your opponent, two to the table, two to yourself, and the same again. Each player takes his four cards into hand, and the four table cards are turned face up and arranged in a row. The rest of the pack is put face down to one side to form a stock.

*Object*. The object at each turn is to capture one or more table cards by matching it (them) in certain prescribed ways with a card played from the hand. If the card played from hand cannot properly match, it is left on the table and so increases the number of cards available for capture. If the card from hand captures all cards on the table, it is called *sweep* and scores a bonus. Each player lays his captured and capturing cards face down in a pile, and at the end of the game scores:

   3 for taking more cards than the opponent
   1 for taking more spades than the opponent
   2 for taking ♢T, known as Big Cassino
   1 for taking ♠2, known as Little Cassino
   1 for each Ace captured
   1 for each sweep made

In brief, the object is to capture as many cards as possible, especially Aces, spades, and the Ten of diamonds.

*Play*. Each player at each turn plays a card from the hand face up to the table, and may or may not capture as explained below. When neither has any cards left, the same dealer deals four more (in pairs) to each player from the top of the stock, but no more to the table. When the last round is being dealt, the dealer must announce that it is the last.

In playing a card to the table, a player may do one of the following:

- Capture by pairing, combining or both.
- Build pairs or totals for subsequent capture.
- Increase such builds, whether made by himself or his opponent.
- Trail (none of the above).

*Capturing ('Taking in')*. A court card played from the hand may capture one table card of the same rank by pairing: a King captures a King, and so on.

Numeral cards also capture by pairing, but can capture as many of the same rank as may be available: an Ace can capture one or more Aces, and so on.

Numeral cards, furthermore, can capture by combining. That is, two or more single cards on the table may be captured by playing from hand a card equal to their combined values. For example, a Ten can capture an Ace and a Nine, or two Fives, or two Threes and a Four, and so on.

One numeral card may make as many captures as it can in one turn by pairing and/or combining. But table cards which have been grouped together in builds, as described below, can be captured only as builds, not as individual cards.

*Building*. Numeral cards (not courts) can be played from the hand in conjunction with cards on the table to form builds for capture on subsequent turns. This may be done by pairing or combining.

*A pairing example*: If you hold two Fives and there is a Five on the table, you can play one from hand upon the one on the table (announcing 'Building Fives'), then capture both by pairing on your next turn – unless, that is, your opponent held the fourth Five and himself captured them on his intervening turn.

*A combining example*: If there were a Five on the table and you held a Three and an Eight, you could on one turn play the Three upon the Five (announcing 'Building eight'), and on your next turn use your Eight to capture the build, along with any other captures that may be open to it.

It is obligatory to announce what build is being made, as this could otherwise cause confusion. For instance, if one player plays a Five upon a Five and announces 'Building Fives', that build can be captured only by a Five; but if he announces 'Building ten', it can be captured only by a Ten.

You may only make a build if you are able to capture or increase it on your next turn.

North

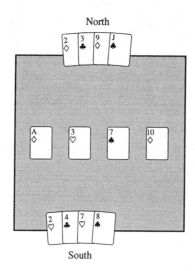

South

**Figure 10: Cassino** From this position North could capture the table Three by pairing, but would do better to play the Two to the table Ace, announce 'Building threes', and add the table Three to the Ace-Two. On the next turn it would then be possible to capture the Ace-Two and Three with the Three from hand.

South could add hand Four to table Three, announce 'Building sevens', and subsequently play hand Seven to capture the table Three-Four and Seven.

*Increasing builds.* A pairing build can be increased by the addition of another card of the same rank. For example, if you held three Fives and there was one on the table, you could build one on your first turn, add another on your second, then capture them all on your third.

A combined-total build may be increased by the addition of another card from hand, provided that you hold a card that can be used to capture it on the next turn. For example: Opponent plays a Two to a Three, announces 'Building five', thereby indicating that he can capture it on his next turn with a Five from the hand. You, holding an Ace and a Six, add the Ace to that build and announce 'Building six', hoping that he himself cannot immediately capture with a Six, or increase it further.

It is not permitted to increase a multiple build. For example, if one player builds fours with a Four, a Three and an Ace, the other may not add a Two and announce 'Building ten'. He could do so, however, if the other had declared that combination to represent eight instead of fours when he built it.

A build may be increased only by the addition of a card from the hand, not with one already on the table.

*Trailing.* If a player cannot or will not take in, build or increase, he 'trails' by playing any card face up to the table, thereby adding to the cards available for capture. But a player may not trail if any build he made is still on the table.

*Sweeps.* If a player sweeps the board by capturing all the table cards with a single card from his hand, he is credited with making a sweep. To indicate this fact, he should place the card he captured with face up (instead of down) on his pile of won cards. At the end of the game, sweeps can then be counted by scoring for each face up card. After a sweep, the opponent can only trail.

*End of game.* The game ends when there are no cards in stock and both have played out their cards from the hand. Any cards left on the table at the end of play are credited to the player who last made a capture. This does not in itself count as a sweep, though it is possible for the last move of a game to be a valid sweep in the usual way.

*Score.* Each player sorts through his cards and scores according to the table. If there is a tie for 'cards' neither scores for that feature. Each deal is regarded as a complete game when two play.

# 12

# — SPITE AND MALICE —

## *A game of competitive impatience*

This fast and furious game seems to be a modern development of such competitive patiences as **Russian Bank** (Crapette) and **Racing Demon** (Race Canfield, or Pounce), and the name – very descriptive, as will be seen – may be older than the game, as I have heard it apply to Racing Demon. I nearly avoided referring to it as a form of competitive patience, as there are some card-players who dislike the one-player activity and get put off by the word itself. So let us be quite clear from the outset that this is not a simple case of each player having a game of patience and seeing which one comes out first. This is a real two-player game offering every opportunity for the exercise of – well, spite and malice. In the long run, it will always be won by the more spiteful and malicious of the two.

### The game

*Cards.* Two full packs are used. They should be of the same size and format, but of differing back designs or colours, and are not to be shuffled together at the outset. One of these packs should contain the standard 52 cards, the other a total of 56 cards by the addition of four Jokers. Ideally, the four Jokers should be of the same back design/ colour and thus indistinguishable from the rest of their pack. In practice, since most packs contain only two Jokers or at most three, it doesn't matter too much if two Jokers are used from the other pack. This works out better than dispensing with one Joker if a three-Joker pack is used.

    *Deal.* Both packs must be very thoroughly shuffled before play. The importance of this cannot be over-emphasised, as poor shuffling ruins

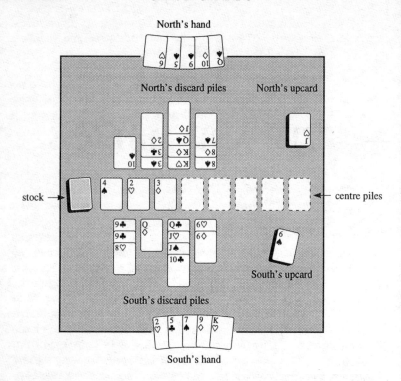

**Figure 11: Spite and Malice** Whoever plays next can complete a centre pile up to a King. South can play (to the ♠4) Five from hand, the upcard Six, Seven from hand, Eight to Queen from discards, and King from hand. North can play Five-Six from hand, Seven-Eight from discards, Nine-Ten from hand, and J-Q-K from discards. However, since the object is to get rid of one's riddance pile, North would probably play the upcard Jack followed by the Queen from hand, stopping there for lack of access to a King.

If North plays first, South is denied this possibility because the table Three is then inseparably attached to the Ace. Similarly, if South plays first, North will no longer find the Three available for capture.

the game. The 52-card pack is divided evenly, each player receiving 26 cards face down. Five cards each are dealt from the second pack, the rest of which is placed face down to one side to form a stock. Each player squares up his 26-card pack, placing it to his right (or left if he is left-handed), and turning the top card of it face up. This pile of cards is his personal pack, and will be referred to here simply as his 'pack', the central pile being known as the 'stock'. The other five cards he takes up as his playing hand.

*Object.* Each player's object is to be the first to get rid of his pack by playing out all 26 cards to the table, one by one as the opportunity arises. The first to do so automatically ends the game and scores 1 point for each card left in his opponent's pack. This is the sole object: there is no score for doing anything else.

*Rank of cards.* Cards rank A 2 3 4 5 6 7 8 9 T J Q K. Suits have no significance in the play. Jokers are wild. The holder of a Joker may declare it to represent any rank he pleases and play it as if it were a card of that rank.

*Play.* The first move is made by the player whose pack has the higher-ranking upcard. (If the upcards are of the same rank, each player shuffles his pack and turns up the top card again.) A move consists of transferring a card from one place to another, and a turn may consist of as many moves as the player is able and willing to make. Few moves are compulsory, and the decision whether to move or not is sometimes a tricky point of strategy. It sometimes happens that one player is unable to move at his turn, or unwilling to do so, in which case the other may take a number of turns in succession.

If the first player holds an Ace he may play it to the centre of the table. Upon this he may play a Two if he has one, upon the Two a Three, and so on, such cards coming either from his hand or from the top of his pack. Each time he plays a card from the top of his pack, he immediately faces the one beneath. Throughout play, any Ace played to the centre of the table forms the base of a pile of cards which is gradually to be built up in sequence as far as the King, regardless of suit. The only way in which either player may reduce his pack is by playing off the upcard to one of these centre piles at the appropriate point. We will call these centre piles 'stacks'. (Patience games lack an adequate word for this feature. 'Foundation' is inaccurate, and 'centre pile' long-winded.)

If the starter has no Ace, or is unwilling to play one, or is otherwise unable to proceed further, he may finish his play by discarding one card face up to the table in front of him. He may not make more than one discard, but is not obliged to make any. He completes his turn by drawing from the top of the stock as many as he needs to restore his hand to five.

It is then the turn of the second player. If his upcard is an Ace he is obliged to start a stack with it; if it is a Two, he is obliged to stack it upon an Ace if one is available; if it is anything else, he is not obliged to stack it (but will be advised to do so if he can). Apart from that, he may start and add to as many stacks as he is able and willing to, and may complete his turn by making one discard before drawing from the stock to restore his hand to five.

Play continues in this way, but with the following added feature. Each player may start up to four discard piles altogether, and may make subsequent discards to any of his own piles, provided that the card it is played upon is of the same rank or one rank higher. (Example: If the first card of a pile is a King, subsequent discards may run: Q J J J T 9 9 8, and so on.) It is never permissible to discard an Ace. The top card of a discard pile is always available for playing to a stack.

Whenever a player succeeds in playing all five cards from his hand, he is entitled to another turn immediately upon drawing five more cards from stock.

Other rules governing play are as follows.

*Replenishing stock.* No more cards may be added to a stack when it has been built up to the King. Whenever the stock is depleted to fewer than 12 cards, it is replenished by taking all the stacks that have been built up to the King and shuffling them in with the stock. Since some of these cards will be those played off the personal packs, the number of cards available from stock gradually increases during the play. If no stacks have been completed by the time the stock is exhausted, all the stacks that have been started are gathered up, shuffled, and turned to form the new stock. (The importance of thorough shuffling at these points cannot be over-emphasised. The best way of carrying it out is to put the stacks together, deal a row of six or seven cards face down, then another row on top of that, and so on until they are all out. Then pick up the piles in random order, shuffle them once or twice, and place the whole pile beneath the few cards remaining in stock.)

*Compulsory/optional play.* The following moves, when possible, are compulsory. If a player's upcard is an Ace he must use it to start a stack. If an Ace is available on the table, waiting to be built upon, the player in turn must cover it if his upcard is a Two, or if a Two is visible among his discards (though in this case he *may* cover it from the hand instead). If a player is unable to play, he must pass his turn without compensation. If he is unwilling to play, he may say 'pass' and allow his opponent an extra turn as often as he likes. If both players pass, the first to do so must then play an Ace or a Two from his hand if he can, and his opponent must then do likewise. For this purpose, however, it is not compulsory to play a Joker as such if no Ace or Two is held. If both players are still unable or unwilling to play further, *all* cards in hand and on the table (except the private packs) are gathered up and shuffled together. The new stock is turned down, five more cards are dealt to each, and play begins again as if from scratch.

*Jokers.* When a Joker is discarded, its holder need not specify which rank it represents until he needs to do so. For example, if the top card of a discard pile is a Nine, and two Jokers are added to it, they may be followed by a Nine, Eight, Seven or Six. A Joker may not be discarded upon a Two. (This rule, which causes no hardship, is here recommended to overcome inconsistencies and points of argument that might otherwise arise. The need to invoke it rarely occurs.) No matter what a Joker represents when it lies on a discard pile, it may be played to a stack at any time, or used as an Ace to start a new one.

*Score*. Play ceases as soon as one player has played his last up-card, and he scores 1 point for every card left unplayed from his opponent's pack. As there is a natural tendency to play at least three games to a session, here are some suggestions for spicing up the game score:

- A rubber is won by the first player to win two games, and a bonus of 10 is added for the rubber.
- Three games are played, and the margin of victory is the difference between the two totals; but if the second and third games are won by the same player his total is doubled (unless this results in a tie).
- Three games are played, and the winner of a game scores the number of cards in his opponent's pack multiplied by the face value of his upcard (counting numerals at face value, courts 10 each and Ace 11).
- Three games are played, and the winner of a game scores 100 plus the total face value of all cards remaining in his opponant's pack (counting as above).
- The Hollywood scoring system devised for Gin Rummy may be used – see page 83.

Other elements of variety might be introduced by permitting a player to resign, in which case his opponent scores the difference between the total of cards left in the two packs, or by offering 'double or quits' as in the game of Le Truc (p. 28). The first possibility should be governed by some sort of control against indiscriminate resignation, *e.g.* by allowing the winner a minimum score of 10.

### Notes on play

You may find the game gets off to a slow start. This is quite normal, and it will invariably pick up speed later. What often happens is that neither player is dealt an Ace or a Joker, and for several turns the only thing each can do is make a discard and draw one from stock. Even this may get held up. One, for example, may find himself unable to discard after a few turns, in which case he has no choice but to wait until the other has changed the situation by inaugurating a stack. Or again, if one player's upcard is low, say a Three, the other may well hold back the play of an Ace until he can play A–2–3 and so block that opening. Although it is undeniably disadvantageous (not to say annoying) for one player to be stuck this early in the game, allowing the other to play off perhaps half a dozen or more upcards, the possible swings of fortune are such as to give him a fair chance of catching up later.

It is worth noting that, as Aces get played off, the number of potential stacks increases from the original eight (Aces and Jokers) to a maximum of twelve. At a later stage in the game a position is usually reached from which there are so many stacks at different stages of construction that one may be able to play off anything up to ten upcards in succession. It may also be useful to know that at the very start of play there is a slightly better than 1 in 6 chance of drawing any given rank or a Joker, a figure liable to considerable fluctuation as play progresses. It is therefore a marked advantage to be able to play out all five cards from the hand, as you have an immediate second turn with about a 5-in-6 chance of drawing a desired card. Not only should you never miss an opportunity to play out all five, but also you should often refrain from play if there is a chance of reaching this position. For example, holding A–2–3–5–9, you may prefer to discard the Nine and hope to draw a Four (or Joker) rather than play A–2–3 for a new stack. Of course, this principle may be unwise to follow in certain positions. But it quite often happens that a player manages to clear his hand two or three times in succession, and this will always do him more good than harm.

Given the choice, you should prefer to play to a stack

- from the top of your pack, or, if not possible,
- from your hand, and only then
- from your discards.

Since the whole object of the game is to empty your pack, while nothing else counts, you should never miss an opportunity to play the upcard, remembering to turn the next one *immediately*, in case it will also go. It is worth playing from your pack even if it gives your opponent an opening too. Perhaps the only time this does not apply is when it gives him a certain play-off and he is considerably in the lead. But whenever you are in the lead, or there is not much in it, always play the upcard when you can.

With the choice of playing from hand or discards, it is usually desirable in principle to play from the hand, as this enables you to draw from stock and so keep up a constant throughput of varying cards. Sometimes, of course, you must play from the discards in order to run through a sequence, and it is usually better to play from the discards in order to get rid of a kink – *i.e.* two or more consecutive cards of the same rank preventing access to other cards beneath them. For example, with a pile consisting of 9–8–7–6–5–5 it would be better to play a Five from the table than from the hand, unless perhaps you could otherwise clear the hand and have another turn. (Incidentally, in my circle we spread each discard pile to form a column of overlapping cards so that all are visible, in which case the word 'pile' is not strictly accurate. If they are kept as piles so that underlying cards are not visible, the skill of the game becomes that of memory rather than calculation. Which is preferable is a matter of taste.)

With no choice but to play a discard to a stack, do not bother to do so unless it brings some advantage. It may, for example, enable you to continue with a card from hand or even the upcard, or empty a discard pile to make room for a new one, or build a stack up to the same rank as that of your opponent's upcard, or perhaps raise several stacks to the same level where this looks as if it will hinder him more than yourself. But don't build a stack up to the King just because you can, nor higher than you need in order to block your adversary. Otherwise you may, after next playing your upcard, turn a rank which *could* have been played had you not previously blocked it by purposeless building.

The true test of skill in Spite and Malice lies in the management of discard piles. Never discard without carefully considering the likely consequences: one bad move can hold you up for a long time. The important thing to remember is that you are not obliged to discard, and it is sometimes better to refrain from doing so, especially to avoid creating a kink. A tricky situation often arises in which the only available move involves making a doubtful discard; the question is then whether to make it for the sake of drawing from stock, or to leave it and perhaps allow your opponent several consecutive turns. You just have to play it by ear.

If the game is a long time in starting, with neither player able (or willing) to stack an Ace, do not worry about using up all four of your depots. Later, however, it is desirable to restrict them to three for as long as possible, in order to leave space for the eventual transfer of a card or cards vital to your game. A positive example would be if you held A–3–4–5–K and your upcard were a Six, in which case you would open a column with the Five and hope to pick up a Two as you built downwards. A negative example would be if you suddenly found yourself drawing third or fourth cards of the same (and useless) rank, in which case you would have to use up that space as a dumping ground for them.

We have already noted that kinks consisting of several consecutive cards of the same rank can be a distinct hindrance to your game, and should therefore be avoided as much as possible. This only applies, of course, where kinks are obscuring access to other cards, and it follows that a run of identical cards can be quite safely played at the base of a discard pile, since they obscure nothing. A good rank to start a pile with is therefore one of which you hold two or three, as you are guaranteed a discard – and a draw from stock – for several turns to come without spoiling your game. If you lack duplicates, it is best to open a pile with the top card of a sequence. For example, holding 2–5–6–7–Q, drop the Seven first, as it assures you of three consecutive discards and draws. Note that it is not important to start all piles with the highest rank possible. Four Kings, for example, are better discarded as the base of one pile than as the bases of four. The ideal arrangement is to run four piles from different bases – say K, J, 8, 5 – so as to maximise your chances of discarding any given rank.

Having started a descending sequence, try to avoid creating a kink by the play of a duplicate. If one duplicate becomes necessary, forming a single kink, do not worry too much as a subsequent play-off as far as the first will unblock the sequence for a later move. But it is usually disastrous to play two or more duplicates in mid-sequence, causing a double or multiple kink, as you will then have to devote as much energy to unkinking it as to playing your upcards, which is self-defeating. The higher-ranking the duplicates are, the more difficult it is to get rid of them. At a pinch, you can allow a run of Twos or perhaps Threes, as it is rarely profitable for either player (hence your opponent) to consti-pate his hand by holding back Aces and Twos, since the former cannot be discarded and the latter must be played off if no other move is open to either player.

It is useful to stop a sequence at the card next in rank above your own upcard. Suppose that you are trying to play off a Six, that you hold 2–3–6–J–Q, that you have three current discard piles of which one runs T T T 9 8 7, and that you are unable to discard except to the empty depot. In this case you will discard your Six (in hand) not to the Seven but to the spare depot. If you subsequently find yourself able to play off your Six, and then turn up 8, 9, T, J, Q or K, you will be able to play that off with the aid of your sequence, which you would not have been able to do had you blocked it with the Six. This is a good example of the need for a spare discard pile, and hence of the value of clearing out a discard pile whenever you can do so without incurring any tactical disadvantage.

Jokers require careful management too. It is certainly an advantage to be able to discard one without specifying which rank it represents, and then be able to stack it as any other rank you please. Personally, however, I go to every length to avoid wasting a Joker on a discard pile. In my view the primary purpose of a Joker is to enable the upcard to be played. Keep Jokers in your hand for as long as you can, and use them only (and immediately) as part of a sequence leading to the play of your upcard. One other reasonable use of a Joker is to enable you to play out all five cards from hand and draw five more for another turn, though I would not myself use *two* Jokers for this purpose.

A Joker on a discard pile is a drawback for two reasons. First, your opponent can see it, and will adjust his play accordingly, thus lessening its power. Second, you may be forced to cover it with another discard, and once this is done there follows a period during which you might as well not have it at all. Another good way of wasting a Joker is to count it as an Ace and stack it for no other reason than that there was nothing else to do.

Despite all these thoughts about playing off your own upcard, don't forget that at least half your game lies in preventing your opponent from doing the same. Never make a move without examining his upcard, the uppermost stack-cards, the cards which you can see to be available to him in his own discard columns, and the possible cards he holds. Or, as more often applies, the ranks he possibly lacks from his hand. For instance, if his upcard is a Seven, and he keeps discarding and drawing when one of the stacks goes up to Five, then it is evident that he lacks a Six and a Joker from his hand. You, therefore, will avoid stacking a Six until you can cover it with a Seven, and will lose no opportunity to build any stack up to the Seven – perhaps even using a Joker for the purpose if the situation is critical. If several piles are stacked to the Four or Five, and you have low cards to get rid of, it is often worth building up lower stacks to the same rank. If he is going to be able to play anyway once he has drawn a Six, he might as well have half a dozen stacks open to him as two or three.

If his upcard is high – let's say a King – and all the stacks are fairly low, look carefully at his discards and note how many ranks he needs in hand to be able to run up a sequence to the King. For instance, he may have visible access to 6, 7, 8 and T, J. In this case, you would avoid building up to a Five as there is a fair chance that he holds a Nine and Queen (or Joker), but you might build up to a Four, banking on his not holding all three missing ranks.

To summarise, the most important requirements of the game are to keep your eyes open and your wits about you, and never to play a single card without a thorough appraisal of the consequences likely to proceed from it.

# 13

## SOLO

### *Whist for individualists*

Solo Whist crossed the Channel from Belgium in the late 19th century and soon became naturalised as one of the most popular of British card games. In its early days there was almost a moment at which it rivalled Bridge as a potential successor to partnership Whist in clubs, homes and 'polite society'. In the event, Bridge won out, but Solo went on to secure an alternative niche as a game of home and hearth, of public house, and, up to the death of the railway system in the 1960s, as the quintessential commuter game. Incidentally, it should not be thought of as an adaptation or perversion of partnership Whist. It is a game in its own right and with its own pedigree, which may be traced back, via Boston Whist, to the classic French game of Quadrille.

As a social activity, Solo differs from Bridge in a number of significant and related respects. These all stem from, and reinforce, the fact that Solo has no overall game structure. As each deal is complete in itself, the result can be settled up immediately in cash or hard score, players can cut in and out of a game without disturbing its flow, and a game can last for as many deals as there remain four people round the table, even though (as well befits a commuter game) they may not be the same four that started the session going. For all these reasons, it is by nature a far less formal game than Bridge – chatting and ragging is not merely permitted but virtually required as an integral part of the proceedings. A more unfortunate consequence of all these circumstances is the fact that Solo is regarded by some as a rough and ready gambling game, and so not credited with the attention and respect it deserves as a game of skill.

Solo also has the rare merit of being one of the few trick games designed for four players in which the participants play for themselves and not in fixed partnerships. This makes it ideal for those who dislike partnership games and prefer to play on their own account, beholden to no-one for their mistakes or their bouts of creative experimentation.

A variant called **Auction Solo**, devised under the influence of Auction Bridge, will be found at the end of this chapter.

# Solo

*Cards*. Fifty-two.

*Deal*. The turn to deal and play passes clockwise around the table. Shuffle the cards thoroughly at start of play, but not between deals until a slam or abondance has been played and won. Deal twelve cards to each player in batches of three at a time, followed by a single card to make thirteen. The final single card, which belongs to Dealer, is dealt face up to the table and not taken into hand until after the auction. Its purpose is to fix a suit of first priority for trumps.

*Auction*. A round of bidding ensues to determine whether the contract to be played will be a partnership one or a solo against three opponents. The player at Dealer's left bids first, and each subsequent player must either pass or make a higher bid than any gone before. From lowest to highest, the bids are:

- Proposal ('Prop'): An offer to win eight tricks with the aid of anyone willing to form a partnership, with the turned suit as trump.
- Acceptance ('Cop'): An offer to partner the player who made a proposal, provided no higher bid has supervened.

The following are all higher and all independent (non-partnership) bids:

- Misère ('Mis'): An offer to lose every trick, playing at no trump.
- Solo: An offer to win at least five tricks, with the turned suit as trump.
- Abondance ('a bunny', 'a bundle'): An offer to win at least nine

tricks, with a trump suit other than that of the turned card.

- Royal abondance: An offer to win at least nine tricks with the turned suit as trump. This is actually announced as 'Abondance': at this stage it is only necessary to specify 'Royal' in order to overcall an earlier player's bid of abondance.
- Misère ouverte ('Spread'): An offer to lose every trick, playing at no trump, and with one's hand of cards exposed on the table.
- Abondance declarée ('Slam'): An offer to win all 13 tricks, playing at no trump but with the advantage of the opening lead. (Some schools allow slam with a personal trump suit, which may be overcalled by slam with the turned suit as trump. If this is followed, the soloist does not need the advantage of leading to the first trick.)

A contract is established when a bid is followed by three consecutive passes. The dealer then takes the turn-up into hand.

If the first player passes, and a subsequent player makes a proposal which no-one accepts or overcalls, the first player (only) is permitted to accept the proposal, but not to make a higher bid.

If the only bid made is a proposal, and no-one accepts it, the proposer may raise his bid to a solo.

Otherwise, if all four players pass, the cards are carefully stacked without being shuffled and the next dealer deals them out. (Alternatively, some form of 'general misère' may be played. In the simplest form, all play at no trump and the winner of the last trick loses an agreed amount.)

*Play.* Tricks are played as at Whist. The opening lead is (normally) made by the player at Dealer's left. Follow suit if possible, otherwise play any card. The trick is taken by the highest card of the suit led or by the highest trump if any are played. The winner of one trick leads to the next.

Particular contracts have particular rules as follows.

PROP AND COP: Partners do not change positions or go out of their way to play alternately. If they are sitting next to each other, they play consecutively.

MISÈRE: If the soloist wins a trick he loses the contract without further play.

ABONDANCE: In some schools, the soloist is not required to name trumps until the first trick has been played and won.

SPREAD MISÈRE: The soloist's hand is laid face up on the table only after the first trick has been played and won.

SLAM: If playing at no trump, the soloist leads to the first trick, regardless of position.

Note that, following a successful abondance or slam, the cards are thoroughly shuffled before the next deal.

*Hard score*. Typical pay-offs are as follows.

Prop and cop wins a basic 10p plus 2p per overtrick. One opponent pays this to one partner, the other opponent to the other partner. If lost, each partner pays an opponent 10p, plus 2p per undertrick.

Solo pays the same as prop and cop, but to the soloist by each opponent, or, if lost, to each opponent by the soloist.

For abondance, the rate is 30p for the contract, plus 3p per over- or under-trick.

Misère wins or loses a flat 20p, spread misère 40p, a slam 60p.

A general misère, if played, requires the loser to pay 10p to each opponent.

Some schools keep a separate kitty for slams and abondances. Everyone contributes an agreed amount to the kitty at start of play and after it has been won. The player of a slam or abondance wins the kitty if successful, or, if not, increases it by the amount of his original contribution.

*Soft score*. Notional scores may be kept in writing. I recommend the following schedule, in which scores are made only by bidders – plus if successful, minus if not.

Prop and cop: each partner scores 1 per trick taken between them. Solo: 10 basic plus 1 per overtrick. Abondance: 20 basic plus 5 per overtrick. The penalty for losing any of these is a flat 10 per undertrick.

Misère, spread, slam: win or lose 20, 40, 50, respectively.

## Notes on play

Solo Whist is a subtle game in which it is easy to err in either of two directions – that of excessive caution, and that of extreme recklessness. The over-cautious player will never take a chance on a reasonable but not foolproof bid which the more experienced or imaginative player will undertake promptly; the reckless player will undertake too many long-shot hands and come off worst. If all players are cautious, as usually happens with beginners, the game is dull because there are few bids. This danger is best overcome by playing a competitive Misère when all pass, as those who lose by taking the most tricks will thereby learn to recognise strength in hand when they see it. If one player is reckless, the game is dull because he hogs the limelight, preventing

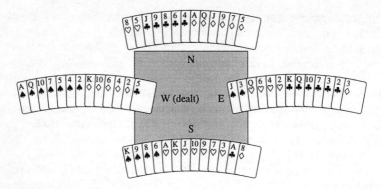

**Figure 12: Solo** Solo is characterised by unbalanced distributions such as that illustrated here, caused by the deliberate lack of shuffling and subsequent dealing of cards in batches of three. North (to lead) has a possible solo if the turned card is a diamond, and East a possible solo (or very dodgy misere) if a club. With hearts turned, South has a certain solo, and even an 'eight-trick abondance' – i.e. one that, if bid, requires a favourable lie and play of both ♡Q and ♠K if nine tricks are to be made. West has a safe solo with spades turned, but is equally well placed for a misere. Vigorous bidding might tempt him to play it ouverte, in the hope that the three lower clubs do not lie one in each hand, and that no-one will be able to lead five diamonds against his dangerous King. (In fact, as the cards lie, North could get this contract down.) Assuming a club turned, the auction might proceed thus: North (riskily) 'prop', East 'cop', South 'a bundle', West 'misere ouverte'. West wins, unless North is lucky enough to hit on the lead of a diamond between Ace and Eight before the soloist's hand is exposed. Had West passed, South's bundle in hearts would almost certainly have fallen one short of the nine.

others from taking a hand with their more reasonable bids, and his frequent losses will be a foregone conclusion. (What makes any game exciting is the fight, not the defeat.) Since dullness can therefore be caused by one reckless player, though not by one cautious player, some argue in favour of playing for money in that the expense incurred discourages reckless overbidding. The point is arguable, in both senses of the word.

Before considering the individual bids that may be made, note first the one important respect in which Solo differs from Bridge, Whist and the majority of other trick-taking games in English card tradition. This lies in the fact that cards are dealt in batches of three with the result that a balanced distribution of cards among the four players is the exception rather than the rule. In Bridge and Whist you normally expect to find the cards of your own hand distributed 4–3–3–3 or 4–4–3–2 among the suits, so that any suit longer than five or shorter than two gives you a hand well worth thinking about. In Solo, a hand of the pattern 7–4–2–0 may well give you a good bid, but should not be regarded as anything out of the ordinary. Whether or not the hand is biddable depends not on the distribution but on the quality of the cards you hold.

With this point in mind it is fairly easy to indicate the difference between a slightly risky bid and an out-and-out long shot. A slightly risky bid is one which you will only lose if the remaining cards are unfavourably distributed against you in your opponents' hands. Such a bid is worth making. A long shot is one which you can only win if the remaining cards are distributed among the others in your favour. Such a bid is not worth making.

When you are not the caller, remember that you are playing as a member of a partnership of three, and not just for the pleasure of making as many tricks as you can yourself (or losing them, in the case of a misère). It is always to the advantage of the caller's opponents – who, in accordance with card tradition, but in defiance of logic, are known as the defenders – to lead through the caller rather than up to him. In other words, the lead to a trick is always best made by the player on the caller's right, so that he has to play second. Caller's preferred position to a trick is either first (leader) or fourth; the others should therefore play as far as possible to deny him this advantage.

When defending a positive (non-misère) bid, lead low through the caller, and try as much as possible to weaken his hand either by leading trumps or by forcing them out of him by leading suits in which he is void. If playing from a sequence (e.g. from Q J T etc.) always take with the lowest but lead with the highest – though, if you hold Ace, King, lead the King. By following these and other principles derived from partnership Whist your co-defenders will be able to deduce useful features of your hand and playing accordingly.

Keeping track of the cards played is important. You need not remember them all, but try at least to count the trumps as they appear, to keep track of the Aces and Kings, and to note when anyone else has a void suit.

## Proposal and acceptance

Some schools do not allow the bids of proposal and acceptance, admitting nothing lower than a solo, possibly on the grounds that 'it is too easy to make'. This view is mistaken. If a particular school does find 'prop and cop' too predictably successful, it means they are playing too cautiously and passing up hands on which more experienced players would go solo. The whole point of aiming for eight tricks between two players is that neither of them adjudges his hand good enough for five on its own.

It is to be generally understood – as a matter of convention, but born of common sense – that the player who proposes has some strength in trumps, though not necessarily enough to justify a solo bid. It follows that a player who accepts need not himself have strength in trumps, but should be able to offer further support, especially in side-suits. If neither partner feels strong enough to lead trumps the bid was probably risky, and the defenders will take advantage of this reluctance, when they spot it, to lead trumps themselves.

Position is of some importance in the bidding, and especially so in respect of 'prop and cop'. The best position from which to accept is as fourth hand, as the fact that the proposal has not been overcalled by a solo bid bodes well for the partnership contract. It is risky to accept eldest hand's proposal as second hand, as the third and fourth to bid may well let the contract stand for the sheer pleasure of defeating it.

As eldest hand (first to bid), do not feel obliged to propose if your cards are only just biddable. If your hand is not strong enough for an independent bid, you may safely pass, since you still retain the opportunity to accept should one of the other players propose – a circumstance which automatically suggests that your hand may be stronger than you think. Alternatively, you may well propose on a hand which may or may not be quite good enough for a solo. If a later player accepts, you have a playable game; if not, and all pass, then you may reasonably consider raising your bid to a solo, knowing that it cannot be overcalled.

Here is a hand on which eldest passed, but subsequently accepted a proposal (spades trump):

$$♠K\ Q\ T\ 4\ ♡K\ 2\ ♣T\ 854\ ♢852$$

The proposer's hand was:

$$♠87653\ ♡A\ ♣A\ 976\ ♢T\ 96$$

This is the sort of combination that makes it criminal to abolish 'prop and cop'!

If you and your partner are sitting side by side, the ideal positioning is for one to be leading to a trick to which the other is playing fourth. As the contracting side, with presumed strength in trumps, you should lead trumps early in order to draw them from your opponents and so establish your side-suits. Against this, however, you should avoid forcing your partner to play trumps if you are weak in them yourself. As in partnership Whist, note what suit your partner leads first, and return it when convenient to do so. Lead from strength – either trumps, or from your strongest suit, whichever you want returned. It is not particularly desirable to lead a singleton.

*Solo.* Solo is a bid to win five tricks in the preferred trump suit. In order to bid it, you need to have a hand that will enable you to win a certain five tricks in the turned trump. This may sound so obvious as to be trivial, but nevertheless in defiance of all probabilities there are players who will quite happily bid solo, in spades, on a hand such as:

♠K Q 9 4 ♡8 ♣A K Q J3 ◇T 9 8

The idea is to make two trumps, one of them on a heart lead after the Eight has gone; at least the top two clubs; and one for luck, in either trumps or clubs. Without the lead, a probable outcome is the win of two trumps as anticipated, the possible win of ♣A when led, and, if very lucky, the possible win of ♣K, for a final result of four or even only three tricks. 'Yes,' says one commentator, who shall be nameless; 'Solo is easy enough; just look for five near-certain tricks.'

At the other extreme, there are players so mesmerised by Aces that they will pass up a perfectly feasible solo bid for lack of them – as, for example, on the following hand, again with spades turned:

♠K J 9 8 7 5 2 ♡5 ♣J 9 4 ◇Q 3

Given the lead, this is a good example of the 'slight risk' which we defined previously as being worth taking. With seven trumps in hand, the holder can afford to lose two of them in the not unreasonable hope that those same two tricks will clear the defenders out of their three top trumps (Ace, Queen and Ten). Correct strategy, therefore, is to lead the King.

Even without the lead, you could safely bid solo (spades, again, for convenience) on:

♠K Q T 8 7 6 ♡K T 9 8 ♣K 4 2 ◇ –

The side-suit Kings should produce two tricks, the void in diamonds brings in a low trump, and the remaining five trumps are good for the outstanding two.

What, in general, are the minimum requirements for a biddable solo?

The first merit is length or strength in trumps, counting as part of this assessment any void or singleton side-suit which can be ruffed with a low one at the appropriate time. On trumps alone, the borderline between a doubtful and a feasible solo is finely drawn. For instance, a holding of A K Q 9 and one lower is risky, whereas A K Q T and one might be expected to succeed without inducing gasps of astonishment.

When holding five trumps, always calculate on the pessimistic assumption that at least one defender may hold five as well. Even a seven-card suit should be headed by nothing less than K J 9.

In side-suits, the chief merit is strength and shortness (not length). The expected failure of the first hand quoted above lies in the undue length of the club suit – A K Q J 3, five in all. The most favourable possible distribution of the outstanding eight is 3–3–2, which means that someone will certainly be trumping by the time you have drawn the odd two with the Ace and King. A more probable distribution is 4–3–1, giving you the Ace but not the King, while there is a strong chance (given the unbalanced distribution of your own hand) of one defender's being void, thus depriving you even of the Ace.

With strength and universal shortness – that is, an unusually even distribution of suits – you may even dispense with strength in trumps. The fact that spades is the turned card does not prevent the following holding from offering a good solo:

♠5 4 3 2 ♡A K 2 ♣A K 2 ♢A 3 2

Of course, it will be beaten if any defender is void in diamonds or holds only one heart or club, but the evenness of the suit distribution in your own hand is good enough to lower the probability of such an event to the acceptable level of 'slight risk'.

Some hands make acceptable solos only if you have the lead; others really require to be led up to. For example, consider the trump holding A K Q T 2 in a hand which does not include a void or easily voidable (singleton) suit. The problem card is the Jack. If you have the lead, you can play out the top trumps in order and without undue optimism hope that the Jack will fall by the time the Queen is out, leaving Ten high and a certain trick with the Two, and giving enough for solo even without side-suit support. Without the lead, the missing Jack is a permanent nuisance. By the time you have voided your short suit you run the danger of ruffing low with the Two and finding it overtaken by a higher trump. On the other hand, a holding that lacks Aces but can place reliance on guarded Kings in short suits will work best if you do not have the lead.

In defending against a solo it is good practice to lead a singleton to the first trick (in which respect the game differs from partnership Whist and also from the play at a 'prop and cop' contract in Solo, where a singleton lead is not to be recommended). With a fairly even distribution, a low trump is also not a bad lead. Otherwise, lead your best card – from not too long a suit – and the highest of a sequence, unless you hold Ace, King, in which case play the King.

*Abondance and royal abondance.* An abondance is a solo, only more so. As before, you must have length and strength in trumps; in addition, you should have a strong, lengthy side-suit and at least one void. Because the dealing system, 3–3–3–1, produces uneven distributions easily, double voids are not uncommon, and a strong two-suited hand is often a must for abondance.

Since the object of the bid is to make at least nine tricks, one way of assessing the hand is to identify the four cards you can afford to lose – and to make sure there are not five of them (otherwise, you make what is known as an 'eight-trick abondance', which comes expensive).

Given two suits of equal length, do not automatically entrump the stronger. Quite often the 'weaker' suit is not merely the better trump candidate, but indeed affords the *only* way of avoiding loss. On this hand, for example –

♠A K Q J T 9 ♡T 8 6 5 3 2 ♣A ♢ –

by all means bid abondance, but nominate hearts as trumps, not the apparently stronger spade suit. The reason is perhaps easiest to see if you examine the hand from the viewpoint of the four losers rather than the nine winners. If you make spades trump, how are you going to avoid losing more than four hearts? With hearts trump, however, you can afford to lose four for the sake of extracting your opponents' trumps and so safely establishing the spade suit. You will make one heart by ruffing a diamond lead, and a second either by a ruff in diamonds or clubs, or by virtue of finding your Ten high when the top trumps have gone.

Defending against an abondance, lead from your longest and strongest suit. Remember that the defenders need five tricks to win, and lose no opportunity to make five as soon as possible – that is, before caller can get in with his trumps and dictate the rest of the play. By all means lead suits in which caller is void, thereby forcing him to trump and so weaken his hand. Sometimes caller will be relying on a 'bum card' for a lucky trick: if you can spot this coming you can defend against it. He may, for instance, lead Ace, King of a side-suit, then switch to another line of attack in pretence of being void. By retaining the odd Queen, Jack or even Ten, instead of discarding at the earliest opportunity, you may well find it winning a low one at the thirteenth trick, led to by caller after extracting all the trumps. Again, if caller is hoping to make a risky King or Queen he may be hoping to do so on a bad lead by the defenders, in which case he will be trying to lose the lead –

which you can give him back by forcing him to trump.

*Declared abondance.* This is a bid to win all thirteen tricks, and as the sort of hand which will enable you to do so is unmistakable there is no point in describing it. Or even playing it; for you only declare abondance on a cast-iron hand, and if it really is cast-iron you simply lay it face up on the table and claim your winnings. If any defender can find a way of beating it then the game must be played, and if he is right you will have learnt a valuable lesson.

It will be worth while explaining why a declared abondance is properly played at no-trump, even though many seem to accept it as a trump game. The reason is, quite simply, that *if* you can make thirteen tricks with a trump suit, then you can make thirteen tricks without a trump suit. 'But surely' (you may say) 'You must declare a trump on a hand with a void, such as –

♠A K Q J T ♡A K Q J ♣A K Q J ◇ –

– otherwise, at no-trump, the hand is beaten if diamonds are led.' Objection overruled. It is precisely to obviate this danger that, for a declared abondance only, caller has the privilege of leading.

*Misère and open misère.* Beginners may be forgiven for imagining that a misère, the winning of no tricks at no-trump, is what you bid when you have no good trick-winners plus a general miscellany of dribs and drabs. Such a hand is one on which you do not bid at all. The misère bid is a positive undertaking to successfully defend yourself against all efforts on the part of your opponents to force you to take a trick. For this purpose you need a very good hand – 'good', that is, from the point of view of beating off such attacks.

Many card-players, especially those who know nothing but Bridge, tend to look down on misère as a sort of jocular substitute round, played when no-one has a good enough hand on which to make a 'real' bid. Nothing could be further from the truth. Both attack and defence at misère call for, and often receive, some of the finest play that can be observed at the card table.

To business: in contemplating a misère, there are two good features to look for. One is low-ranking cards, and the other is a void suit. Note that the length of any suit you hold is irrelevant so long as it contains low cards. For example, in this hand

♠3 2 ♡A Q T 8 6 4 2 ♣7 3 2 ◇ –

the hearts are just as safe from attack as the spades: you cannot be forced to take a trick in either suit. As for low ranks, in a holding of five or more you must have the Two (you may escape without it, but the risk is great); with fewer, you may get away with nothing lower than Three or even Four. If your lowest is the Five, you will be beaten if the Four, Three and Two are evenly distributed among your opponents. Note, too, that a holding of alternating low ranks is just as good as a sequence. In the hand quoted above, for instance, the A Q T 8 6 4 2 of hearts is as strong as would be 8 7 6 5 4 3 2. To prove it, imagine that the Three is led; you play the Two, and your Four is then the lowest of the suit. If the Five is then led, you play the Four and your Six is lowest. And so on.

The advantage of a void is obvious: when it is led, you can throw out your potentially dangerous cards. The recognition of potential dangers can be a subtle affair. Take the hand quoted above. Because the hearts are safe from attack, as we have seen, it contains no dangerous cards, so you need not rush to throw out the Ace or Queen when diamonds are led. Clubs, however, are a different matter, for ♣7 is the most dangerous card in the hand. With three clubs, 6, 5, 4, out against you, you can successfully defend against the lead of only two of them (with 3, 2), and by the time the third is led you may find the other two players void, thus forcing you to take with the Seven. (And do not imagine this to be a case of bad luck – experienced opponents will soon discover your weak suit and exploit it.)

You therefore need the void in diamonds as a means of discarding your dangerous Seven. In general, then, you cannot bid misère with dangerous cards unless you have saving voids to accommodate them, and even then the device may only be expected to work once. Remember, too, to look at things from your opponents' viewpoint. If your hand is good enough for a misère but not good enough for an open misère, then by definition it contains a weakness, and the strategy of your opponents will be to find out where this weakness lies and to exploit it. They need to force you to take only one trick to win; once you have done so, the contract is lost and there is no point in playing further.

In defending against a misère a good lead is any singleton, or, failing that, a middling card from a short suit. Do not play from a long suit, as there is a chance that caller will be void and will immediately throw any dangerous card he may hold. Do not play too low, as you must give your partners an opportunity to get rid of their own high cards in that suit. If you hold a Two, especially in a short suit, you may well hold the means to beat the contract. Save it until the top cards are out, then get the lead and play it – for which purpose retain an Ace or other master card to ensure ability to enter when you judge the time ripe.

## Sample game

*Proposal and acceptance.* East deals, and the exposed card is ◇9:

| | |
|---|---|
| South | ♠K 6 5 ♡Q J 8 6 ♣J 2 ◇J T 8 6 |
| West | ♣A J 9 7 2 ♡4 ♣A K 9 6 ◇4 3 2 |
| North | ♠Q T 8 ♡K 9 3 ♣8 7 5 4 3 ◇K Q |
| East | ♠4 3 ♡A T 7 5 2 ♣Q T ◇A 9 7 5 |

South has nothing, and passes. West, taking a calculated risk, proposes, counting a trick for each Ace, one for a ruff on hearts, and hopefully ♣K to boot. North passes. East accepts, on the assumption that his partner has strong trumps (mistakenly) and the other two Aces (correctly). South leads, and having nothing more noteworthy than over a quarter of the trumps available, plunges immediately into that suit.

| S | W | N | E | |
|---|---|---|---|---|
| ◇J | ◇4 | ◇Q | ◇*A* | |
| ♡6 | ♡4 | ♡3 | ♡*A* | Since South seems happy with trumps, East refrains from leading them. |
| ♡8 | ◇*3* | ♡9 | ♡2 | |
| ♣2 | ♣*K* | ♣3 | ♣T | |
| ♣J | ♣6 | ♣4 | ♣*Q* | West avoids the Ace – he wants East to take over. |
| ♡J | ◇*2* | ♡K | ♡2 | East, properly, leads into his partner's void. West is now out of trumps, but they need only two tricks. |
| ◇*6* | ♣A | ♣5 | ♠ 4 | Waste of an Ace? Not at all – it draws a trump out. |
| ♡*Q* | ♣9 | ♣7 | ♡5 | |
| ♠5 | ♠*A* | ♠8 | ♠3 | |
| ♠6 | ♣K | ♠Q | ◇*5* | |

| | | |
|---|---|---|
| 4 | +4 | = the required eight tricks |

South's trump lead was a danger signal to East: had he continued trumps at the second trick the contract would probably have failed.

*Solo.* Now it is South's deal, and the turn-up is ♡7:

| | |
|---|---|
| South | ♠K Q 2 ♡A K 7 5 2 ♣K 7 5 4 ◇2 |
| West | ♠T 7 6 ♡Q J 9 6 ♣T 9 6 ◇K Q J |
| North | ♠A J 5 ♡T 8 4 3 ♣A J 8 ◇T 6 4 |
| East | ♠9 8 4 3 ♡– ♣Q 3 2 ◇A 9 8 7 5 3 |

West, North and East pass, implying sufficient weakness for South to take a solo upon himself, which he accordingly bids. West leads:

| S | W | N | E |
|---|---|---|---|
| ◇2 | ◇**K** | ◇4 | ◇3 |
| ♡**2** | ◇Q | ◇6 | ◇5 |
| ♡**A** | ♡6 | ♡3 | ♠3 |

South has no side Aces to make and prefers to have his Kings led up to. So he decides to see how the trumps fall, and is aghast to discover East void: if either of the others had five of the other trumps he would be lucky to escape with his life. East throws a spade to conserve his guarded ♣Q and long diamonds.

| ♠Q | ♠6 | ♠**A** | ♠4 |
|---|---|---|---|

South has no choice but to slip into another suit, aiming to clear a King.

| ♡**K** | ♡9 | ♡T | ♠8 |
|---|---|---|---|

A nasty lead. Was South's King a mistake or a necessity? The latter. He must try to make his ♠K.

| ♠**K** | ♠7 | ♠5 | ♠9 |
|---|---|---|---|

Which he now does, for his fourth trick. With four trumps against him in two hands, three of them higher than the Seven, his only chance of another trick lies in the (as yet unseen) club suit. He must force out more trumps to make the clubs safer when they are eventually led. East is void in spades, not so that he can trump (he has none) but because the only possible contribution he can make to South's defeat lies either in retaining his guarded Queen or else in leading diamonds.

| ♡5 | ♡**J** | ♡4 | ◇7 |
|---|---|---|---|
| ♡7 | ♡**Q** | ♡8 | ◇8 |

West leads a trump and the rest fall out. There was no point in retaining the Queen, as South, if he had two trumps, would win anyway.

| ♠2 | ◇**J** | ◇T | ◇**A** |
|---|---|---|---|

This looks like the chance that East has been waiting for.

| ♣4 | ♠T | ♠**J** | ◇**9** |
|---|---|---|---|

Better late than never. Now there are three tricks to play, and all players have three clubs in hand. East to lead, and it all depends on him . . .

| ♣5 | ♣6 | ♣*8* | ♣2? | East has done it wrong! |
|---|---|---|---|---|
| ♣*K* | ♣T | ♣J | ♣Q | |
| ♣7 | ♣9 | ♣*A* | ♣3 | |

| 5 | | | | And South has made his five. |
|---|---|---|---|---|

*Misère.* West deals, and a club is turned:

| South | ♠A J 4 ♡K J ♣J T 8 5 2 ◇Q T 8 |
|---|---|
| West | ♠Q T 9 5 ♡Q 9 6 3 ♣K 9 ◇K 9 2 |
| North | ♠6 3 ♡A T 7 5 2 ♣6 ◇A 7 6 4 3 |
| East | ♠K 8 6 2 ♡8 4 ♣A Q 7 4 3 ◇J 5 |

North, as eldest, bids misère, and the others pass. This is a shaky bid, marginally justified only by the fact that he has the lead and may get away with his singleton Six at the first trick.

| S | W | N | E | |
|---|---|---|---|---|
| ♡5 | ♣*9* | ♣6 | ♣4 | The fates are kind, and besides, if the opponents had all been able to get under, there would have been no tale to tell. West keeps his King of clubs with which to come in later should he get a chance to lead ◇2 or ♡3 with advantage. |
| ♡*K* | ♡6 | ♡5 | ♡8 | A better lead might have been ◇9. |
| ♡J | ♡*Q* | ♡T | ♡4 | |
| ◇Q | ♡*9* | ♡7 | ◇J | East and South discard from their shortest suits. |
| ◇T | ♡*3* | ♡2 | ◇5 | |
| ◇*8* | ◇2 | ◇7! | ♣Q | West, having made a hash of hearts, now leads his winning diamond prematurely. North is right to play high, for he knows that only K, 9, 8 are left in play; if they lie with West he has lost his contract anyway, whereas if any of them lies with South the Seven must be taken. |
| ♠4 | ♠5 | ♠3 | ♠*K* | |
| ♠*J* | ♠9 | ♠6 | ♠2 | |

. . . at which point, North reveals his cards and victory is conceded. This illustrates the sort of misère hand you may get away with if you are lucky: in fact, as the remaining cards lie, it is not easy to find a way of beating the contract.

*Abondance.* North deals, and a heart is turned.

| | |
|---|---|
| South | ♠52 ♡A Q T 5 2 ♣Q 9 ◇Q T 7 5 |
| West | ♠7 4 ♡K 7 6 3 ♣86 ◇A 9 8 6 2 |
| North | ♠A K Q J 9 3 ♡ – ♣A K 4 3 2 ◇J 4 |
| East | ♠T 8 6 ♡J 9 8 4 ♣J T 7 5 ◇K 3 |

Following a prelude of three passes, North bids abondance in spades. His four losers are to be the two diamonds and two of the three low clubs, and the main point of his strategy must be to ensure the win of the third low club. East leads.

| S | W | N | E | |
|---|---|---|---|---|
| ◇5 | ◇2 | ◇4 | ◇**K** | East, having no certain trick, starts to clear his shortest suit and successfully takes his two-to-one chance of winning. |
| ◇7 | ◇**A** | ◇J | ◇3 | Good for East; since caller didn't have the Ace, he can lead his Three, void the suit, and ensure the second of the five tricks his side needs to beat the contract. |
| ◇T | ◇6 | ♠**J** | ♡4 | A good lead – not that South expects to win the trick, but with so many diamonds gone a possible trump by caller may yet be over-trumped. North is considerably put out by it, and feels obliged to trump high. Just as well he did – East is happy to throw a useless card, and could indeed have overtrumped if it had come to the push. |
| ♠2 | ♠4 | ♠**A** | ♠6 | North must now clear trumps with a view to establishing his clubs. |
| ♠5 | ♠7 | ♠**K** | ♠8 | |
| ♡2 | ◇8 | ♠**Q** | ♠T | That takes care of the last opposing trump. Now North plays from ♠9 3, ♣A K 4 3 2, needing five tricks more. |
| ♣**Q** | ♣6 | ♣4 | ♣5 | He attacks the club suit from below . . . |
| ♡**A** | ♡3 | ♠**3** | ♡8 | . . . ruffs a long-awaited heart lead, and continues clubs . . . |
| ♣9 | ♣8 | ♣**A** | ♣7 | |
| ◇Q | ◇9 | ♣**K** | ♣T | That leaves the Jack out against his Three and Two. |
| ♡5 | ♡6 | ♣3 | ♣**J** | |

| | | | | |
|---|---|---|---|---|
| ♡T | ♡7 | ♠*9* | ♡9 | And in he trumps to lead to the last trick . . . |
| ♡Q | ♡K | ♣*2* | ♡J | . . . which it is always a joy to win by the lead of a side-suit Two! |

| | |
|---|---|
| 9 | Abondance succeeds. |

The abondance would not have succeeded if any opponent had held five clubs, which was a risk worth taking. On the assumption that at least one player held four, North made his little club by leading two low ones to force out two high ones, and two high ones to draw out the other two. The whole manoeuvre depended upon his successfully clearing trumps first.

# Auction solo

Auction Solo is substantially the same as basic Solo, but permits a greater degree of competitive bidding, as follows:

Proposal/acceptance
5-trick solo
6-trick solo
7-trick solo
8-trick solo
Misère
9-trick abondance
10-trick abondance
11-trick abondance
12-trick abondance
Open misère
No-trump abondance declared
Trump abondance declared

The 'preferred suit' is established by cutting a second pack rather than by turning up the dealer's last card. Proposal/acceptance and declared abondance in trumps may only be undertaken with the preferred trump. Other solo or abondance bids may be made in any suit, which remains unspecified until the bid has been accepted, but it is possible to overcall any bid by making the same bid in the preferred trump. In other words, the bid 'solo of five' can be overcalled either by 'solo of six' or by 'five in trumps' – meaning in the pre-selected trump.

Different schools vary in which bids they recognise. Proposal/acceptance and a solo of five in one's own suit are often omitted.

In a no-trump abondance declared the bidder leads to the first trick; if there is a trump suit, however, it is made, as usual, by eldest hand.

The value of each game is as follows:

| | | |
|---|---|---|
| Proposal/acceptance | 6 | plus 1 per under/over-trick |
| Solo | 6 | plus 3 per under/over-trick |
| Misère | 12 | |
| Abondance | 18 | plus 3 per under/over-trick |
| Open misère | 24 | |
| Abondance declared | 36 | |

# 14

## WHIST

### *Game for a long drive*

Whist is very English, very old, very simple, and very great. Starting life in the 15th century as a tavern and servants' game, by the late 19th century it had become the number one fashionable game of middle and high society throughout the Western world and its colonial offshoots. At the turn of the 20th, it was in this capacity entirely eclipsed by Bridge. Having since returned to its folksy origins, it is now chiefly played at charitable and social events, typically in the form of Whist 'drives' with individual rather than partnership winners. Its natural habitat is no longer the home or pub but the village hall and the senior citizens' club or social centre.

But it is still a great game, being simplicity itself to learn, and essential to the education of any self-respecting card-player. If it is your intention to learn Bridge, it is essential to start first with partnership Whist. You may then find it helpful to proceed in stages through Dummy Whist, Bid Whist and Contract Whist, all appended to this chapter. Dummy and Bid Whist are useful stepping stones on the way to Bridge, but Contract Whist is rather more, being a pretty good game in its own right.

The form of basic Whist to be described below is classic Rubber Whist, the standard home and club game as it was before overtaken by Bridge on one hand, and by the Progressive 'drive' Whist on the other.

# Rubber Whist

*Players.* Four play in two fixed partnerships. Partners may be determined by drawing cards from a shuffled pack. Whoever draws the highest card has first choice of seats and is partnered by the person drawing the second highest, who sits opposite.

*Cards.* Fifty-two. If two packs are used alternately, one being shuffled while the other is dealt, thorough shuffling is assured without wasting time.

*Object.* A rubber is won by the first side to win two games. A game is won by the first side to score 5 points over as many deals as it takes. (American Whist is played up to 7 points. This is more logical than 5 and is to be preferred.)

*Deal.* Whoever drew the highest card deals first, and the turn to deal and play passes to the left. Deal 13 each in ones. The last card goes face up to the table to establish trumps.

*Play.* The player at Dealer's left leads to the first trick, and the dealer adds the trump turn-up to his hand as soon as it is his own turn to play. Suit must be followed if possible, otherwise any card may be played. A trick is taken by the highest card of the suit led, or by the highest trump if any are played. The winner of each trick leads to the next. All tricks won by a partnership are stored in front of whichever member of it first wins one.

*Revoke.* A player who fails to follow suit though able to to so may correct his play without penalty before the next card is played. If a revoke is discovered later, 3 points are deducted from the current score of the revoker's side, or, if this makes less than zero, are added to the other side's score.

*Score.* Points accrue first for tricks. The side that took most scores 1 point for each trick taken above six.

Honours count after tricks. If one partnership had held, either in one hand or divided between them, all four trump honours (Ace, King, Queen, Jack), they add 4 for honours. If they held any three, they add 2 for honours. Honours are not scored, however, if the side concerned is 1 point short of game, i.e. standing at 4 under English rules. (The Americans dispensed with honours entirely, and modern players may wish to do the same, as they depend entirely on chance and obviously form too large a proportion of the total.)

*Game and rubber.* On winning a second game, a partnership adds 2 points for the rubber. Their margin of victory is the difference between both sides' scores.

## Notes on play

Unless you are exceptionally strong in trumps, your normal strategy as a partnership is to establish and bring home your longest plain suit or suits. To establish a suit means to force out the high cards which your opponents hold in it (preferably by winning them in tricks, though not necessarily) so that those remaining in your hand are the highest left in play. Bringing it home means subsequently leading and winning tricks with those cards without having them trumped.

Let us illustrate the principle at work before examining how to do it. Since there are 13 cards in each suit, each player will be dealt an average of 3¼ of them. Any suit in which you hold four or more is therefore 'long' as far as you are concerned, since you have more than the average number. Those cards of it which are certain to win tricks (disregarding the possibility of trumping for the moment) are described as 'long cards'.

Suppose you have been dealt ♠A K Q 2, spades not being trumps, and the other players have an even three each. How many of these are long cards? At first sight only the top three. But on closer inspection all four, because your lead of

| | |
|---|---|
| Ace draws | 3, 4, 5 |
| then King draws | 6, 7, 8 |
| then Queen draws | 9, T, J |

and now no-one has any of the suit left, so your Two is bound to win if led (and not trumped). You have thus established the suit, and if you can reach a position from which you can lead the Two without having it trumped by an opponent, you will have brought the suit home.

Few holdings are as clear cut as that, of course, and you will generally need the assistance of your partner in bringing home your long suit, while he in turn will need your assistance in bringing home his. Your first task, therefore, is to let each other know what your best suit is. Normally this will be your longest suit. If you hold two long suits, strength (high cards) must be considered as well as length. Thus a holding of A K Q 2 in one suit is better than one of 6 5 4 3 2 in another, even though it is normally better to play a five-card than a four-card suit.

*Opening lead.* The best opportunity you have for declaring your suit is at your first lead to a trick, especially (but not solely) when by virtue of sitting immediately to the dealer's left you are to lead to the first trick of the game.

Lead from your best suit, so that your partner will know which one to return to you when he himself has the lead. And from that suit lead a card which will indicate to him what sort of holding you have in it, so that by deducting his own holding in the suit he will be able to start assembling a picture of where all the key cards are lying.

How can you choose a rank that will convey information to him, and at the same time stand you the best possible chance of either winning the trick immediately or at least forcing out a high card from the opponents with a view to establishing the suit? In response to this need, nineteenth-century experts such as Cavendish worked out a highly complex system of codes and conventions, to which nothing less than a treatise at least the size of this book could be expected to do justice. Because partnership Whist is no longer played with such intensity, and because we are here addressing ourselves to beginners, it will be sufficient to present the simplest account of all, as originally explained in *Foster's Whist Manual* (R. F. Foster, New York, 1890).

Foster prefaced his description with a useful point to remember. It is that the most commonly led card is the King (more than 50 per cent of the time). Therefore, look first for the King, and if you have it be prepared to lead it – but only if you have also a card adjacent to it, that is, either Ace or Queen. The leads in detail are shown in Table 1.

**Table 1**   *Which card to lead from your best plain suit*

| Best suit headed by: | Lead: |
| --- | --- |
| A K or K Q* | King |
| A – Q J, or A x x x x | Ace |
| Q J T etc | Queen |
| K Q J x x | Jack |
| K – J T | Ten |
| Anything else | fourth best |

* Except K Q J x x, which is the Jack lead; x means any low card, so (for example) A x x x x means 'Ace heading a best suit of at least five cards'.

Fourth best means the fourth highest card of your suit, as, for example, the Five from a holding of J 8 7 5 2. The reason for this convention will become apparent later.

Table 1 is all very well, but what happens if your longest suit is trumps? The answer depends much upon the general strength of the hand. If you have a pretty good hand, with (say) five trumps and some high side-suit cards, lead trumps. If not, lead from your best three-card suit.

Conventional (information-giving) trump leads are shown in Table 2. There are two possible leads from a three-card suit. If it is strong (headed by the Ace, King or Queen) lead the lowest of the suit, as your partner will not go far wrong by interpreting this as the lead of fourth best from the above table. If, however, it consists of Q J x, lead the Queen, for reasons which will become obvious upon little reflection. If it is weak, lead the highest – your partner will soon deduce that you are making a 'forced lead' from his own holding in the suit or from the other cards that fall to the trick.

**Table 2** *Conventional trump leads*

| Trump suit headed by: | Lead: |
| --- | --- |
| A K Q J | J then Q |
| A K Q | Q then K |
| A K + at least 5 cards | K then A |
| A K + 4 or fewer | fourth best |

*Following your partner's lead.* When your partner leads to his first trick, he will (unless returning your own suit to you) be playing from his best suit and telling you, from the card he plays, what sort of holding he has in it. His signalling will be a waste of time if you do not use your knowledge of the conventional leads, plus observation of your own cards and those that opponents play to the trick, to build up a picture of how the key cards in that suit lie. For example, if he leads a Ten and you hold the Queen, then you will realise immediately that you have K Q J T between you, and that, as soon as the Ace has been drawn from an opponent, your partner's suit is as good as established. So, before playing your own card to the trick, study his lead and make the necessary deductions. With experience, you will do this without pausing.

If he leads a high card, it is usually best to play your lowest in the suit. But be on the look-out for situations in which it is logically best, or at least a very good risk, to do otherwise. For example, suppose he leads a King and you hold the Ace and Jack. Knowing that he also has the Queen, you should play the Ace, taking the trick, and then lead the Jack, enabling him to win with the Queen. This serves the desirable purpose of leaving him in control of his best suit. If you held on to the Jack, you would then be 'blocking' him from establishing it.

If he leads a low card, indicating weakness, take the trick if you can, and with your best card – do not play clever by attempting to finesse. Again, there are conceivable exceptions, and we may note one in particular to illustrate the meaning of 'finesse'. Suppose he leads a small card, and the opponent on your right does likewise, and you hold the Ace and Queen. It is strictly correct to play the Ace, but perfectly acceptable to play the Queen instead. For if your left opponent now wins with the King, you will have the benefit of having cleared out a high adverse card while still retaining control of the suit (in the shape of the Ace); if not – there being a fair chance that the King is held by the other opponent, or even your partner – you will have made a trick with the Queen and will still retain control of the suit with the Ace. To finesse is to attempt to win a trick with a card lower than necessary. If the Queen does win, the finesse will have succeeded.

It is possible to make some valuable deductions from a low-card (fourth best) lead, and to take useful advantage of them. Foster's 'rule of eleven' is well worth applying in particular. The rule says: deduct from eleven the number of pips on the card led, and that will tell you how many higher cards lie against the leader; deduct the number of higher cards held by yourself, and that will tell you how many are held between the opponents'. Let us see it in action.

Suppose your partner leads a Seven, and second hand plays low. Seven from eleven is four, so there are four cards higher than Seven which are *not* held by your partner. Suppose you have two of them – say, Queen and Nine. Then your opponents between them hold two of the following ranks: A K J T 8. They surely hold the Ace or King, if not both, otherwise your partner would have led the King (see Table 1); equally, they cannot hold the Ace and the Eight, otherwise he would have held a suit headed by K J T and accordingly led the Ten. And so on. In this particular case you would refrain from attempting to finesse with the Queen, as there is too strong a probability that it will fall to Ace or King from the left.

If your right-hand opponent fails to follow suit to your partner's lead, don't panic – just play low and await developments.

If you hold a top sequence in the suit your partner leads, take with the lowest, in accordance with the general principle of always winning a trick as cheaply as possible.

*Returning your partner's lead.* If your partner led to a trick before you did, and you subsequently win a trick, then you in turn have your first lead and are immediately faced with the question whether to declare your own suit by leading from it – in accordance with the same conventions applicable to the opening lead – or to return your partner's suit.

Sometimes you can more or less do both. For instance, if your best suit is headed by A K you can lead the King and then follow with your partner's suit. The fact that the King won is enough to let him know that you also have the Ace. Thus you will have gained a trick, conveyed useful information, and kept command of your own suit, which is now known to both of you.

On principle, it is better to show your own suit before returning his, even if you lack the Ace and are likely to lose the lead; otherwise, at a later stage in the game when he has exhausted his own suit, he will have no idea what to lead for the best. You certainly must show your suit if you have reason to believe that he was making a forced lead, for to lead into such weakness would be to play into your opponents' hands. On the other hand, if you have no good suit of your own, and he has not made a forced lead from a weak three-card suit, return his immediately.

What should you lead when returning his suit? The rule is: if you have two left in the suit play the higher of them; if more, play the lowest. Why? If you have two, and play high before low, your partner will know by convention that you have none left in the suit. Furthermore, if your higher card is significantly high – say Ten or better – then by playing it you remove the risk of blocking his suit and so preventing him from establishing it. If, however, you have three or more, you must have been dealt the suit long to start with (having already released one to the trick he led in it). In this case the suit is good for both of you, and the need to unblock is less urgent – though you can still do so by playing high to a subsequent trick as required.

If your partner led from trumps, return your lowest.

*Playing second to a trick.* Play low, unless you know for certain that you can win the trick. Do not try to compete for it: this is the job of your partner, who will have the advantage of playing last and knowing what he has to beat, whereas you would be playing speculatively. If, however, there has as yet been no sign of the Ace, and you hold the King and Queen, by all means attempt a finesse by playing the Queen: you will either win the trick, which is good, or be left with the commanding card, which is also good. There are those who would play the King when holding neither Ace nor Queen. This is a risk that may or may not be worth taking.

If you are void in the suit and do not know whether or not your partner is able to win the trick, should you ruff it or not, on the off-chance? This depends on your trump holding. If it is weak, then the best use you can make of your small trumps is to attempt all reasonable ruffs; if strong, pass it up. You can afford to lose the trick if you have strength in trumps for later play, where trumps come into their own, while, by discarding from a side-suit, you not only get rid of a useless card but also convey potentially useful information to your partner about the rest of your hand.

*Playing third to a trick.* In this position you are either leading your own suit or returning your partner's, as previously described. You should attempt to win the trick if your partner is not already doing so.

*Playing fourth to a trick.* In this position your only job is to take the trick if your partner has not already won it, and the only logical requirement for you is to play the lowest you can for either purpose. Be it noted that the rule about winning a trick as cheaply as possible applies even when you are playing from a sequence. For instance, if you are playing fourth to a trick containing (improbably) the Two, Three and Four of a suit, and you hold (say) Seven, Eight and Nine, play the Seven. It is true that any card of a sequence is as good as any of its fellows for trick-taking purposes, but for the purposes of conveying information, the fact that you are known to be playing the lowest can be of considerable significance to your partner.

*Discarding.* When you are void and prefer not to trump, choose carefully which suit to discard from. It is not right to look merely for the lowest-ranking card regardless of suit, and it is positively wrong to discard from your longest suit or the one you are trying to establish. Prefer to throw the lowest card from your weakest suit. But consider this example: you have the choice of discarding from A Q 2 in one suit or T 9 3 in another. Here it is better to throw the Two, for reasons which you should be able to work out for yourself.

*Trumps.* If you have five or more trumps, lead them, unless they are all very low and you have a well-headed plain suit. Do not lead trumps if you have only four, although if they include two honours and you have no other clear lead, you may be justified in leading trumps (low).

If you have such strength but do not have the lead, you may still find an opportunity to call for them by the way in which you play to other tricks. The call for trumps – a signal known as the Blue Peter – consists in playing an unnecessarily high card in a given suit, and then following it with one lower at the suit's next appearance. We have already seen something similar at work in the situation where, holding two only of your partner's suit, you return the higher of them first: when you play the second, you thereby indicate that you are void in the suit, and are in a position to trump if it comes round again. The fact that you are not necessarily void in the suit being used for the Blue Peter does not militate against its communicative value: the fact that your partner sees you play high then low should alert him to the fact that you are ready to play in trumps.

There is also the question of forcing trumps, which means leading a suit in which you know somebody else is void. You should always force if you know that your opponents are strong in trumps, for, if effective, this reduces the power left against the establishment of your own suits as well as against your own trumps when trump tricks are led. If the opponents refuse to be drawn, keep on forcing until they dare not do otherwise than to ruff.

You may also force your partner, but only if you are strong in trumps yourself.

# Dummy Whist

This is basically the same as Whist but with the following significant difference.

When the first card has been led to the first trick, Dealer's partner lays his hand of cards face up on the table. They should be arranged in four columns, one for each suit, with the trump suit at his right, and with the cards of each suit ranking in order from highest (near him) to lowest (pointing towards Dealer).

The open hand is the Dummy. Its owner takes no active part in the play but leaves it all to Dealer. Dealer plays from dummy as well as from his own hand. Upon winning a trick, he leads to the next from whichever of the two hands furnished the previous winning card. The fact that every live player can see two hands, his own and the dummy, means, of course, that more information is available as to the lie of cards and therefore more skill can be exercised in calculating how best to win tricks. The owner of the dummy hand may not do or say anything to assist or advise his partner in the play, but is permitted to draw attention to a revoke, or any other irregularity such as leading from the wrong hand after winning a trick.

---
# Bid Whist
---

This represents another step on the route from Whist to Bridge, and is worth embarking on as part of the learning process. There is no universally acknowledged standard form of the game, and the following way of playing it is as good as any other.

Play as basic partnership Whist but with these differences.

After the deal, each player in turn, starting with the dealer, either says 'No bid' or bids for his partnership to take a minimum number of tricks using a given suit as trump. The bid consists of a number of tricks over six and a suit. The lowest bid is 'one club', an offer to win at least seven tricks with clubs as trump. The next in turn can overcall by bidding the same number of tricks in a higher suit, or a higher number of tricks in any suit. For this purpose, the suits rank in ascending order clubs, diamonds, hearts, spades. Thus one club may be overcalled by one of any other suit, one diamond by one heart or spade, one heart by one spade, and one spade only by a higher number. Each in turn must make a higher bid than the previous one, or else pass. Passing does not prevent a player from subsequently overcalling another player's bid.

The auction continues until a bid has been followed by three consecutive passes. That bid is thereby made a 'contract'. For example, the auction might proceed:

| North | East | South | West |
|-------|------|-------|------|
| 1◇    | 1♠   | 2♣    | NB   |
| 2◇    | 2♠   | NB    | NB   |
| NB    |      |       |      |

In this case the contract is two spades, and East–West must win at least eight tricks with spades as trump in order to score.

The opening lead is made by the player sitting left of the last bidder, and play proceeds as at ordinary Whist.

If successful, the declaring side scores 1 point for each trick taken above six. If not, the opposing side scores 1 point per undertrick (i.e. per trick short of the number bid).

Game may be set at 7 or 10 points, and the rubber is won by the first side to win two games.

# Contract Whist

This cross between Bid Whist and Contract Bridge was devised by Hubert Phillips in the 1930s. It forms an excellent stepping-stone from Whist to Bridge, amounting, in effect, to Contract Bridge with simplified scoring and without a dummy. The fact that all four play with hands concealed increases the need for accuracy in bidding and play. This makes it a sound and demanding exercise for regular Bridge-players, besides being an excellent game in its own right.

The basic format is that of Whist, but with the following significant features.

*Game structure.* The scoresheet is divided into an upper and a lower half by a line drawn horizontally across the middle. Scores made for tricks contracted and won are recorded below the line in a downward direction. Scores made for overtricks or for defeating a contract are recorded above the line in an upward direction. The first side to reach 10 points below the line wins a game. Another line is then drawn, below which each side starts from zero again. If the other side wins the next game a second line is drawn and a third game played. Play ceases when one side wins the rubber by winning its second game.

*Auction.* Each in turn, beginning with the dealer, must either pass or make a higher bid than any that has gone before. Passing does not prevent a player from bidding again later. A bid is the number of tricks above six which the bidder proposes his side to win, and the trump suit, if any, proposed for this purpose. In ascending value, the bids are one club, one diamond, one heart, one spade, one no trump, followed by two clubs, two diamonds, etc, and so upwards to the maximum possible bid of seven no trump, which requires the winning of all 13 tricks.

A player may announce 'Double' if the previous bid was made by an opponent. This threatens to double the score whatever the outcome, being made in the doubler's belief that he and his partner can beat the contract. If one player doubles, a member of the opposing side can 'redouble' provided no other bid has intervened. A double or redouble is automatically cancelled if followed by another bid.

The auction ends when a bid, double or redouble is followed by three consecutive passes. The last-named bid becomes the contract. The opening lead is made by the left-hand opponent of the contracting player who *first* bid the suit made trump, or first bid no trump if such it be.

*Score.* If successful, the declaring side scores below the line 3 points for each trick contracted and won, or 4 each at no trump. Any overtricks score 2 points above the line regardless of trump. (Example: Bid three clubs, win ten tricks, score 9 below and 2 above the line. Bid two no trump, win ten tricks, score 8 below and 4 above the line.)

A doubled or redoubled contract scores double or quadruple below the line, i.e. 6 or 12 per trick, or 8 or 16 at no trump. A successful contract if doubled or redoubled scores a further 5 or 10 points above the line, plus 5 or 10 per overtrick.

For defeating a contract, the non-declaring side scores above the line 10 per undertrick, or 20 if doubled or 40 if redoubled.

The first side to win two games adds 50 for the rubber. All above-and below-line scores are then totalled, and the difference between both sides totals is the margin of victory.

# 15

# ———— BRIDGE ————

## *The king of card games*

Bridge – properly known as **Contract Bridge** to distinguish it from previous incarnations – is too well known as the king of card games to require any further comment on its status. You may find it more helpful, if approaching it for the first time, to take note of what the game's most notable features are and how they have developed. I believe you will find the game easier to learn if you understand *why* certain things about it are the way they are and not some other way.

Bridge arose in the 19th century from various experiments made at different times and in different countries to increase the depth and variety of partnership Whist. One line of development concerned trump selection. In Whist, trumps were randomly fixed by turning the last card. But experience of classic games like Boston, Preference and Solo Whist had shown that more fun and skill attached to the idea of letting players bid for the right to choose trumps in return for undertaking to win a greater number of tricks than anyone else. These were essentially solo games, however, and the problem was to find a way of incorporating it into the fixed partnership format of Whist. It resulted in various forms of Bid Whist, of which the most advanced example was represented by the Russian game of Vint.

A second line of development resulted in another defining feature of Bridge, namely, 'dummy' play. When Whist-players found themselves short of a fourth at the table they preferred to adapt Whist for three rather than turn to an essentially three-hand game such as Ombre or

Preference. A good way of doing this was to deal one of the hands face up and have the player sitting opposite it to play from the exposed hand as well as from his own. French players in particular were so impressed by the additional skill factor this introduced that they tended to retain it even when there were four at a table. This resulted in Dummy Whist, in French *le Mort*, or 'dead' hand.

A third feature was that of scoring above and below the line. Many Whist players felt that scoring points for 'honours', i.e. being dealt particularly favourable cards, introduced too great an element of luck into what they considered essentially a game of skill. Rather than defy tradition by dropping honours altogether, some players took to drawing a line half way down the scoresheet and scoring points for tricks below it and points for honours above. The game could only be won by reaching a target number of points 'below the line', i.e. by means of trick-play. A bonus was then awarded for reaching this target first, and only afterwards were the honour scores taken into account, their usual effect being to determine the size of the win rather than who had won.

Bridge was the first and only game to combine these three defining features in one format. Exactly who first played it and how the name arose is unclear. Anecdotal evidence suggests a Levantine location (reports mention Athens, Constantinople, Cairo) and a French-speaking culture. Whatever the details, the fact is that Bridge is not recorded before the 1880s, but by 1900 had completely ousted Whist as the foremost intellectual card game of Western society.

In original Bridge, or Bridge-Whist, there was no true bidding. The dealer merely examined his hand and announced a trump suit or declared 'no trumps', or else, if undecided or faced with an indifferent hand, passed this privilege across to his partner, who was then obliged to exercise it. This procedure was sometimes called 'bridging', but it is unclear whether that term accounted for the name of the game or was inspired by it.

Shortly after 1900, Bridge-Whist was superseded by Auction Bridge. In this version, all four could bid, each in turn doing so either by increasing the number of tricks they contracted to win, or by naming a higher-scoring trump suit. By 1915, the French were playing a more advanced version called Plafond, in which scores were made below the line only for the number of tricks the declarers actually contracted to win. Any overtricks they may have taken did not count towards winning the game but were merely recorded as bonuses above the line.

The modern game, an extension of Plafond properly known as Contract Bridge, was developed in the late 1920s by the American millionaire Harold S Vanderbilt, and promoted as a home game by means of a world-wide publicity campaign waged by the American eccentric Ely Culbertson. Its distinctive feature is an elaborate but highly refined scoring system, involving increased bonuses for slams and the so-called 'vulnerability' factor, whereby a side that has won one game towards the rubber is subject to increased bonuses and penalties in certain circumstances.

From this account it should be clear why you should not approach Bridge entirely from scratch. If you have no card-playing experience you should first learn a simple two-hand trick game such as German Whist. You should then progress to partnership Whist for the fundamentals of partnership trick-play, and thereafter Dummy Whist and Bid Whist in order to concentrate on the distinctive features implied by their names. You can then proceed to Bridge with a confident grasp of its various fundamentals. Experience of Solo Whist and Contract Whist, though not essential, would be very useful, and both have the further merit of being excellent games in their own right.

The last thing you need to know before playing Bridge is which format of the game you intend to follow. For home and informal play there are two possibilities: Rubber Bridge and Four-deal Bridge, or Chicago. A rubber is the best of three games, and a game is won by the first side to reach 100 points below the line over as many deals as it takes. As a rubber may take anything from 10 minutes to over an hour to complete, traditional Rubber Bridge is best if there are just four of you.

Chicago, on the other hand, consists of exactly four deals and therefore consistently lasts about 20–30 minutes. This makes it more suitable if you have enough players for two or more tables and wish to change partners or opponents after each game, or if you have an odd number of players so that one or more are sitting out at any one time.

The third format, Duplicate Bridge, requires at least eight players and an umpire, and is really a club or tournament game. The basic idea is that a team consists of at least four players, two of whom play as partners at different tables. The game is so arranged that the hands dealt to a partnership at one table are noted down and reproduced at the other table, but there dealt to the members of the opposing team. The effect of this is to cancel out the 'luck of the deal' so far as any one team is concerned, thus producing (theoretically) a win for the team that played, overall, with the greatest skill.

*General idea.* Four players, sitting crosswise in partnerships, each receive 13 cards from a well-shuffled 52-card pack. An auction is held to determine what contract shall be played. A contract is an undertaking made by one partnership to win a stated number of odd tricks in return for naming the trump suit, or specifying 'no trump' if preferred. Odd tricks are tricks in excess of six. Thus a bid of 'one club' is an offer to win at least seven of the 13 tricks played provided clubs are made trump, and a bid of 'seven no trump' an offer to win all thirteen without a trump suit.

When no-one will bid any higher, the last-named bid becomes the 'contract'. The player who first named the contracted trump suit is the 'declarer', and the members of the opposing partnership are called the 'defenders' (illogically, as they are not so much *defending* anything as *attacking* the contract). Declarer's partner, after the opening lead, lays his hand of cards face up on the table as a dummy, and Declarer plays from both hands.

If successful, Declarer's side scores 'below the line' (towards game) for the number of odd tricks contracted and won. Any overtricks earn 'premiums' (bonuses) above the line. Premiums for honours and slams also go above the line. If unsuccessful, the defenders make appropriate scores above the line, i.e. not counting towards game.

A game is won by the first side to reach 100 points below the line. This can only be done by winning a contract, not beating one. The rubber is won by the first side to win two games, and carries an additional premium which is larger if the losing side failed to win one game. A side that has won one game is described as 'vulnerable', and is subject to certain extra premiums for success or extra penalties for failure. The effect of vulnerability, if not its purpose, is to discourage a side that has won a game from deliberately seeking high but unsound contracts for the sole purpose of preventing the other from winning a game.

As befits its social status, Bridge tends to be played with great formality and is accordingly equipped with a multiplicity of procedural niceties amounting almost to ritual. The beginner should learn these from the outset in order to avoid potential embarrassment when playing in formal situations – in other words, as a form of social self defence.

*Preliminaries.* Bridge is played with a single 52-card pack, but it is customary to use two such packs distinguishable from each other by the colour or design on the reverse. Both are shuffled, one is spread out face down on the table and each player draws a card from it. The two drawing the highest cards become partners (unless partnerships were agreed in advance), the highest having first choice of seats, right of first deal, and choice of which pack to deal from. For the purpose of drawing and playing, cards rank high-low A K Q J T 9 8 7 6 5 4 3 2 in each suit. Of drawn cards equal in rank, spades beat hearts beat diamonds beat clubs.

*Shuffle and deal.* On the first deal, the player at Dealer's left 'makes' (shuffles) the pack to be dealt from while Dealer's partner makes the other. The pack when made is set face down at the maker's right, as his right-hand opponent will be next to deal. Dealer takes the shuffled pack from his left and sets it face down for his right-hand opponent to cut. Having completed the cut, Dealer distributes the cards face down one at a time in clockwise rotation starting with the player at his left and finishing with himself.

*The auction.* Each in turn, Dealer first, must do one of the following:

- Pass, by saying 'No bid'. This does not of itself prevent a player from bidding later.
- Make a bid, which must be higher than any previous bid. The lowest bid is 'one club'. A higher bid is made by increasing the number of tricks bid or offering the same number but in a higher suit. For this purpose suits rank upwards thus: clubs, diamonds, hearts, spades, no trump. Thus 'one club' can be overcalled by 'one' anything else, but 'one no trump' only by raising the level to 'two' or more. The highest possible bid is 'seven no trump'.
- Announce 'Double' if the previous bid was made by an opponent. This offers (or threatens) to double whatever score is won or lost if the last-stated bid is established as the contract.
- Announce 'Redouble' if the previous announcement was an opponent's 'Double'. This offers (or threatens) to quadruple the scoring value of the proposed contract.

A double or redouble is automatically cancelled if followed by another bid, whether or not in the same suit as the one doubled.

The auction ends when a bid, or a double or redouble, has been followed by three consecutive passes.

The last-named bid becomes the contract, and its suit, if any, is trump. The member of the contracting side who first named the trump suit (or none) in the auction is the Declarer.

If all four pass immediately, the cards are thrown in and the next deal made by the next player in turn to do so.

*Play.* Declarer's left-hand opponent leads to the first trick by playing any card face up to the table. Declarer's partner then lays his hand of cards face up on the table in four columns, one for each suit, each running from high to low towards the Declarer, and spread just sufficiently to enable each card to be identified. The trump suit (or clubs, if none) should be placed at dummy's right, i.e. Dealer's left as he faces it.

Declarer plays second to the trick from dummy and fourth from his own hand. Normal rules of trick-taking apply. Follow suit if possible, otherwise you may play any card. A trick is taken by the highest card of the suit led, or by the highest trump if any are played, and the winner of each trick leads to the next.

Declarer, upon winning a trick, leads from whichever of his side's two hands furnished the winning card. His partner not only takes no active part in the play but may not communicate anything to Declarer by way of advice, suggestion, criticism, query, appeal, horror, apoplexy etc. The most he may do is call attention to errors of procedure, such as Declarer's failing to follow suit from dummy when able to do so, or leading from the wrong hand upon winning a trick.

The defenders keep all their won tricks together, customarily in front of the partner of the first defender to win one.

*Revoke.* A player who fails to follow suit though able to do so may correct his mistake at any time before the trick has been quitted (turned down), after which any subsequent players may also reply. A card played in error and retracted is left face up on the table and must be played to any trick to which it is legally playable upon demand of either defender, or, if not so called, led to a trick at the first opportunity. If a revoke is established after a trick has been quitted, but before scores have been written down, the offending side must concede two of its won tricks to the opposition, who count them as if they had themselves won them in play.

*Score.* One member of each partnership keeps a scoresheet ruled into two columns, one for each side, and divided into an upper and a lower half by a horizontal line. Scores are recorded below the line for tricks contracted and made, and above the line for overtricks, bonuses and penalties.

All scores are recorded individually, not cumulatively. When one side's below-line scores total 100 or more (as can readily be seen 'by inspection'), a second horizontal line is drawn beneath their last score and across both columns. A new game begins, with both sides scoring below this line as before. The side that has won one game is now 'vulnerable', and subject to certain increased rewards and penalties. Another line is drawn when a second game has been won. If it is won by the same side, the rubber ends, and the side with two games gets a bonus before scores are totalled. If not, a third game is played, both sides now being vulnerable, and the rubber ends when either side has won its second game. This carries a smaller bonus.

The rubber ended, each side totals all the scores made above and below the line in its column. The difference between the two side's totals is the margin of victory. The rubber bonus is usually (but not inevitably) sufficient to ensure that the side that won two games wins overall, regardless of above-line scores. Slam bonuses, however, are so great that the scores they attract above the line are capable of outweighing a rubber bonus made by the opposing side.

Details of scoring are presented in the table opposite. The following notes explain and amplify it.

If the contract succeeds, the declaring side scores below the line a number of points for each trick bid and won. For example, if the contract was 'two' and they made three, they score only for two below. The actual score per trick depends on which suit was trump, if any, and is affected by doubling or redoubling. Note that a successful contract of three no trump suffices for game, the score being 40+30+30 (=100). Any overtricks they may make are scored above the line. In normal circumstances (undoubled) they score at the same rate as those scored below the line. If doubled or redoubled, however, they each score 100 or 200 respectively, and twice this if the declarers were vulnerable. In addition, any successful contract that was doubled scores a flat bonus of 50, or 100 if redoubled, 'for the insult'.

A successful small slam (contract of six) carries a flat bonus of 500, increased to 750 if made when vulnerable. A grand slam (contract of seven) scores twice these amounts. They are not in themselves affected by doubling or redoubling. Note that slam bonuses accrue only if bid: if you bid five and win six, you don't score for the small slam. By way of compensation, there is no extra penalty for failing a slam bid: one trick down is one trick down, regardless of the size of the contract.

If the contract goes down (fails), the defenders score above the line in respect of each trick by which the declarers fell short of their contract. The actual amount per trick does not depend on the trump situation, but does vary according to doubling and vulnerability. The rarely occurring bonus for the fourth and each subsequent undertrick applies only in the case of a doubled or redoubled contract, and is additional

**Table of scores at Contract Bridge (right)**
*tv = normal trick value (20 in minor suit, 30 in major or NT), D = if contract doubled, R = if contract redoubled, vulnerable = as applying to declarers, not defenders*

## Contract made

*Declarers score below the line per trick bid and made:*

| | | | | |
|---|---|---|---|---|
| if minor suit trump | (♣◇) | 20 | 40D | 80R |
| if major suit trump | (♠♡) | 30 | 60D | 120R |
| at NT, first trick | | 40 | 80D | 160R |
| . . . , thereafter | | 30 | 60D | 120R |

*Declarers score above the line for:*

| | | |
|---|---|---|
| each overtrick made | tv | 100D 200R *not vulnerable* |
| or. . . . . . . .. | tv | 200D 400R *if vulnerable* |
| making doubled contract | – | 50D 100R *vulnerable or not* |
| making small slam | | 500, or 750   *if vulnerable* |
| making grand slam | | 1000, or 1500 *if vulnerable* |

## Contract failed

*Defenders score above the line:*

| | | |
|---|---|---|
| for first undertrick | 50 | 100D 200R *not vulnerable* |
| or. . . . . . .. | 100 | 200D 400R *if vulnerable* |
| per additional undertrick | 50 | 200D 400R *not vulnerable* |
| or. . . . . . .. | 100 | 300D 600R *if vulnerable* |
| bonus for 4th and each | 0 | 100D 200R *vulnerable or not* |
| subsequent undertrick, | | |

## Honours, regardless of contract success or failure

*Scored above the line by either side holding in one hand:*

| | | |
|---|---|---|
| any 4 of AKQJT of trumps | 100 | *regardless of* |
| all 5 of AKQJT of trumps | 150 | *doubling or* |
| all 4 Aces at no trump | 150 | *vulnerability* |

## Rubber scores

| | | |
|---|---|---|
| winning complete rubber | 700 | *if opponents won no game* |
| or. . . . . . .. | 500 | *if opponents won one game* |
| winning unfinished rubber | 300 | *if only one or two games completed* |
| and/or. . . . . . .. | 50 | *for being the only partnership with a part-score in an unfinished game* |

to that of previous undertricks. Thus, if the declaring side, vulnerable, bid five spades and was doubled, the possible range of scores according to the actual number of tricks taken is as follows:

*Declarers*:

13: 300 below, 200 above, 50 for insult
12: 300 below, 100 above, 50 for insult
11: 300 below, 50 above for insult

*Defenders (above)*:

10: 200   for 1st undertrick
 9: 500   = 200 + 300 for second
 8: 800   = 200+300+300
 7: 1200 = 200+300+300+400 . . .

and so on.

The score for honours is credited above the line to the side of whichever of the four players was dealt the four or five honours concerned. As it is lost if not claimed before the next deal, it is advisable for their holder (if not dummy) to announce 'honours' upon playing the last of them to a trick. The scores are minimal and are not affected by doubling or vulnerability.

A rubber can be won only by the declaring side and upon winning its second game. This carries a bonus of 700 if they won two games straight off, or 500 if three were played. If, for any reason, the rubber was not finished, but one game was completed, the side winning that game scores 300 for the rubber. If play ended before a game was completed, and if only one side has made a part-score (less than 100) in that game, then they score a bonus of 50. This is not of itself sufficient to carry an incomplete rubber bonus of 300, but may be made in addition to it if play ended during the second game.

## Notes on bidding and play

That Bridge is essentially a partnership game is nowhere more significant than in the auction. In the play of the cards, Declarer becomes the lone and star performer, and while there is scope for cooperation between the defenders, much of that is founded on information cooperatively exchanged during the auction, whether their own if they had a chance to bid, or, if not, by inference from that of the declaring side.

Bidding is a means of communication between partners. Its primary purpose is to ensure that they reach the best possible contract for the

26 cards held between them. To do this, they must convey as much information as possible to each other about their respective hands. The potential of bidding as a language derives from the fact that artificial bids may be used to convey specific information. Whereas a natural bid is one you would be quite happy for the partnership to engage in as a contract, an artificial bid is one made solely to request or convey information. It definitely does not represent a serious contract, which could well be disastrous if played.

The standard British bidding system, *Acol*, is widely used by both home and tournament players, and has considerable currency outside its country of origin. Its great merit is that it is based almost entirely on natural bids, but easily incorporates a number of artificial bids and bid sequences that have established their worth in other systems. It is important to note that the laws of the game permit neither partnership to use any system or individual convention which is unknown to the other side. Before play, therefore, both partnerships must state which system they are using (Acol, etc) and with what artificial bids and conventions.

*Strength and distribution.* The most basic information you want to communicate about your hand is its *strength*, in terms of high cards such as Aces and Kings, and its *shape*, or relative distribution of the four suits.

Strength is measured in high-card points, or 'hcp' for short. Count each Ace held as 4 hcp, each King 3, Queen 2, and Jack 1. As there are 10 hcp in each suit, and 40 in the whole pack, a hand counting 10 hcp is about average.

Shape, or distribution, denotes the relative numbers of cards you hold of each suit. If your 13 cards are divided 4–3–3–3 or 4–4–3–2, your hand is described as balanced, even, or 'flat', and suggests a no-trump bid. If it contains a long suit of five or more, your hand is unbalanced, and suggests a bid in the longest suit.

Borderline cases are 4–4–4–1 and 5–3–3–2. The first is not balanced but contains no obvious long suit. Whether it better suits a trump or no-trump contract depends on its hcp and how it fits in with your partner's hand. The pattern 5–3–3–2 contains a long suit, but if this is a minor suit you may consider it as potential no-trump material. This is because, at lower bidding levels, you score more for a no-trump contract than for a minor suit contract requiring a greater number of tricks.

Distribution can be usefully related to strength measurement to the extent that points may be added for distribution in certain well-defined circumstances. For example, in an opening bid of one in a suit, a point may be added for each card held in excess of four in the suit bid. Or, when partners have agreed on a trump suit between them, points may be added for shortages (two or fewer cards) in non-trump suits. Distributional points must be considered with caution, however, as they do not become a fixed quantity until a suit is agreed. Once added, you may subsequently have to remember to subtract them again.

*Bidding*. The aim of the auction is for the side with the best potential contract to discover and bid it. What you and your partner are looking for is a fit, which means either the suit in which you hold between you the greatest number of cards, or a complementary distributional pattern between both hands more suited to a no-trump contract. The minimum comfortable trump requirement for a one-in-suit contract is eight cards of that suit between you. Seven is feasible and even fewer may be playable, though with fewer than seven you will certainly be in the wrong contract. For no trumps, a fit means having all four suits stopped between you, i.e. headed by not less than an Ace or a guarded honour (Kx, Qxx, or, at worst, Jxxx).

In bidding towards a contract, you will be considering whether to aim for a part-score, a game, or a slam. A part-score is one that is not enough to win you the current game. 'Game' denotes a contract that brings your score to 100 or more below the line – i.e. from a score of zero, 3NT (100), four of a major suit (120), or five of a minor (100). If five in a minor looks probable, you will prefer to test the possibility of reaching 3NT instead, as this requires you to win only nine tricks for game, as opposed to eleven in a minor suit.

It helps to know that a game at NT or in a major suit requires 26 or more points between you, and in a minor suit at least 28. Standing at zero, your first concern will be to go for game if possible. If you already have a part-score, you will be looking for another part-score sufficient to complete the 100 points, and need not bid any higher than absolutely necessary to achieve this object and overcall your opponents' bids.

The table of points actually scored by all possible contracts (opposite), including slam bonuses but disregarding the effects of doubling and vulnerability, is worth examining for the light it throws on their relative values.

This makes it very clear that at lower levels, where the bidding mostly takes place, minor-suit contracts are hardly worth pressing if there is any chance of a major-suit or no-trump fit, even at a lower level, except for the purpose of overcalling the other side's bids. It is only at slam levels that this discrepancy is wiped out and minor suits come into their own.

**Table 4**  *Point score by contract*

|   | ♣ | ◇ | ♡ | ♠ | NT |
|---|------|------|------|------|------|
| 1 | 20   | 20   | 30   | 30   | 40   |
| 2 | 40   | 40   | 60   | 60   | 70   |
| 3 | 60   | 60   | 90   | 90   | 100  |
| 4 | 80   | 80   | 120  | 120  | 130  |
| 5 | 100  | 100  | 150  | 150  | 160  |
| 6 | 620  | 620  | 680  | 680  | 690  |
| 7 | 1140 | 1140 | 1210 | 1210 | 1220 |

The time to be more ambitious is when you gather from the early auction that a slam may be in the offing. A slam brings huge rewards if successful but does not lose any more than usual if unsuccessful – unless you are vulnerable, when you must bid more cautiously. A small slam normally requires about 31–33 points in a suit or 33–34 at no trump, and a grand slam 37 points.

This leaves a dead zone of rather unrewarding contracts between the levels of game and a small slam, i.e. four or five no trumps and five of a major suit. As we shall see later, this dead zone offers a patch of bidding space in which to exchange useful information about the possibility of attempting a slam.

We must, however, start at the beginning, which means with mundane low-level bids designed to convey preliminary information to one another about the nature of your hands. Here it is necessary to distinguish four types of bid as follows:

- An *opening bid* is the first one of the auction. Dealer has the first opportunity to make the opening bid, but, if he passes, the right to do so passes round the table until someone exercises it. Beginners sometimes fail to grasp the fact that the opening bid is by definition the first one of the whole auction, regardless of who makes it.
- A *responding* bid, or response, denotes, for our present purposes, the first bid made by the partner of the player who opens the bidding.
- A *rebid*, apart from its obvious general meaning, specifically denotes the second bid made by the opener in the light of his partner's response.
- An *intervening bid*, or overcall, is one made by either opponent of the opening bidder. Most significantly, it denotes the first bid made

by an opponent of the opening bidder. It may intervene between the opening bid and the response, or between the response and the opener's rebid.

For ease of discussion below, we will ignore intervening bids to start with and assume that the opening bidder and his partner make all the running. This does happen often enough to be realistic – perhaps not half the time, but not far off.

*Opening one in a suit.* The commonest opening bid of one in a suit is made on a hand containing 13 to 21 points and a reasonable re-bid in case partner responds by bidding in your weakest suit. The minimum 13 can be shaded to 12, or even (with experience) 11, but the potential rebid remains vital because of the 'unlimited' nature of this opening – for whether you have 13 or 20 points, or something in between, makes a big difference to how your partner assesses his hand. The very fact of opening invites partner, if strong enough, to respond in his best suit, and your sensible rebid will be necessary in case his best suit is your worst.

Suppose you hold:

♠ x x
♡ Q J x x
♢ A Q J x x
♣ K J

You can open one diamond without question, since you have a sensible rebid of two diamonds over any response except one heart, which you can raise to two. Given the minimum requirement, open with your longest suit. With two 5- or 6-card suits start with the suit higher in bidding value. This enables you to rebid the lower suit at the 2-level without losing the option of bidding 2 of the higher suit if appropriate.

Which to open of two four-card suits depends on whether or not they are 'touching', i.e. adjacent in bidding value, such as hearts and diamonds. Text-book procedure is to open the higher suit first. This enables you to name the lower suit if your partner responds, leaving either of you the possibility of going back to the first suit without having to raise to the level of three. Naming the lower first, then the higher at the next level, is a 'reverse' bid suggesting a high point-count (16+) and demanding a response. More recent practice, however, is to bid the lower suit first. Either way, the important thing is that you and your partner should agree a system and stick to it.

Of non-touching suits, bid clubs first if the other is spades. Otherwise, the choice is less easy. You may want to bid spades before diamonds in hope of finding a major suit fit first, or clubs before hearts in order to keep your exploratory opening bids at a safe level. If in doubt, the mechanical answer is to bid the four-card suit ranking immediately beneath the shortest suit held. A more creative guideline is to consider all the probable responses to either bid and make the one that will not give you a rebid problem.

If you want a rule for two four-card suits that is both easy to remember and likely to be safe whether the suits are touching or not, I suggest the following: bid hearts first if this is one of them, otherwise diamonds, otherwise clubs.

With three 4-card suits, bid the one below the singleton, or hearts if the singleton is clubs.

*Responses to 1 in a suit.* Now swap positions and suppose you are responding to an opening bid of one in a suit.

With fewer than 6 points, pass. Your partner could have a minimum 13, and will not thank you for your support if you turn out to have 18 or fewer between you. If he has substantially more, he can always bid again.

With four or more cards of the suit bid, raise it to two on 6–9 points, three on 10–12, four on 13–15.

Without a fit, but with a biddable suit of your own and up to 15 points, bid it at the lowest possible level. If the lowest level is one, 6 points will do; if two, at least 8 are needed. With 16 or more points, jump to one level higher than necessary. This is forcing to game: it shows you have enough strength between you for a contract worth at least 100 and possibly a slam, and tells your partner not to pass before reaching game level at least. You may also jump with slightly fewer points if your suit is six or more cards long.

With neither a fit nor a distinctive suit of your own, but with a balanced hand suitable for no trump, offer one no trump on 6–9 points, two on 10–12, three on 13–15.

*Opening two clubs.* The 2-club opening is a 'convention' which has nothing to do with your actual holding in clubs but denotes any hand counting at least 23 points and 5 quick tricks. Quick tricks are ones you can expect to make in the first two or three rounds of each suit. A suit headed by A K = 2 qt, A Q = 1½ qt, A = 1 qt, K Q = 1 qt, Kx = ½qt. It forces partner to keep bidding to game (unless you yourself stop it at 2NT).

The following hand counts 23 points and a total of 5 qt, and demands a two club opening:

♠ K Q x
♡ A K J x x
♢ A Q x
♣ K J

Partner is required to respond positively to this opening if he has at least 1½ quick tricks or a good 8–9 points, and can offer a major suit or no trumps at the two level, or three of a minor suit. As it is a forcing bid, however, which prevents him from passing, he must have access to a conventional negative response in case he has nothing to declare. In this case the negative reply is (logically enough) the lowest he can possibly make, i.e. two diamonds. If then you see no prospect of game, as here, you can sign off by bidding a perfectly acceptable 2NT.

If partner does respond, however, you can start developing the auction in other directions. For example, a response of two hearts would offer prospects of a slam in hearts, which you would explore by methods of slam bidding (see below). Two spades would be worth raising to four for an immediate game, and two of a minor suit would give you a safe rebid of three no trump. Either of these might then prompt your partner to start looking for a slam.

*Opening two in a suit other than clubs.* The so-called 'strong two' opening also has a special meaning, but, unlike two clubs, it is natural rather than conventional, in that you name a genuine prospective trump. It doesn't promise any particular number of points, but indicates strength in one of the following respects:

- Eight or more playing tricks and a long major suit headed by at least A–Q, such as:

  ♠ A Q J x x x x
  ♡ x
  ♢ A J
  ♣ A x x

- Two long suits, worth exploring for a possible fit, such as:

  ♠ –
  ♡ A Q J x x x
  ♢ x
  ♣ A K Q x x x

- A point-count almost high enough to open 2♣ but not meeting the requirement of five quick tricks, such as:

♠ K Q J
♡ K Q x x x x
♢ Q
♣ A K x

You must be prepared to bid again, as a strong two opening is forcing for one round. The negative response, in case partner has nothing to offer, is 2NT, which you can leave as the final contract.

What happens if you feel your only natural suit bid is two clubs, which you can't make because it doesn't qualify for the two-club convention? Well, you only have two choices. If the suit is long enough, open three clubs as described below. If not, open one club, and hope the auction stays open so you can repeat the suit at a higher level next time round.

*Opening three in a suit.* Open three on a weak hand containing one long suit, which, so far as you can see, is useless for anything but a bid in that suit, such as:

♠ x
♡ K Q J 9 8 6 5 3
♢ J x x
♣ x

A three-bid is described as pre-emptive, as its main value lies in preventing the other side from opening communications. The fact that you have such a long suit suggests an all-round uneven distribution with a possible game for the other side, but they may well be unable to risk entering the auction at such a high level. If they do, you have had it anyway. If not, and your partner has rubbish, you will go down by a trick or two. The main requirement for a pre-emptive bid of three in a suit is that you should reckon on being able to take six tricks in your own hand, or seven if vulnerable. It is best made from third position after two passes, in order to counter the probability that fourth-to-speak has a hand strong enough to open at the two-level. It is, of course, pointless to make it from fourth position, as you have no-one to pre-empt. Here, a bid of 'one' is all you need.

It is not usual to open more than three in a suit, since strength is indicated by opening at the two level, and a three-bid specifically implies weakness in all but one quarter. An opening bid of four may be regarded as the same as three, but stronger by one trick.

*1 NT opening and response.* No-trump openings are made on balanced hands (4–3–3–3 or 4–4–3–2), with stops (defensive tricks) in at least three suits, and falling, unlike one-in-suit openings, into a very narrow band of strength points. The main reason for this is that if your partner has an unbalanced hand, with a good prospective trump, he needs to know early on how much support he can expect from you in side suits in order to judge how far to go with his own suit in case a slam is on. Alternatively, he may also have a balanced hand, in which case, since no-trump contracts earn more points for fewer tricks, it is particularly desirable to bid to the most accurate level. For these reasons it is essential that you open in no trumps only within the agreed range of points for the level bid, never so much as one point below that range or, even more importantly (since the temptation is greater), above it.

One no trump may be opened 'weak' on 12–14 or 'strong' on 16–18 points. Which it is must be agreed between you and your partner beforehand. Some partners agree to play a 'variable' no trump, opening strong when vulnerable and weak when not. Some prefer a strong no-trump regardless of vulnerability, but the modern tendency is to prefer 'weak' throughout. A weak no trump has the advantage – except after three passes – of a pre-empt, in that it prevents the other side from opening communications below the level of two. At the same time, its limited nature enables your partner to assess more accurately how safe it is to respond at that level himself.

The following hands may be opened at 1NT (weak):

| | | |
|---|---|---|
| ♠ A K x | K x x x | x x x |
| ♡ x x | A Q x | K J x x |
| ♢ Q x x x | K x x x | A K x |
| ♣ Q J x x | J x | Q J x |

The following should not:

| | | |
|---|---|---|
| ♠ K x x x | K J | A x x |
| ♡ A K J x | A J x x | K x x |
| ♢ J x x | x x | K Q J x |
| ♣ Q x | K x x x x | Q x x |

The first should be opened one heart, as two suits are unstopped and you have good chances of a major suit fit instead. The second should be opened one club, being wrong in shape: 5–4–2–2 is acceptable for no trump, but not when one of the doubletons is unstopped and the other ill-headed against a bad break (of A–Q). The third counts 15, which is too many. Open one diamond and hope to bid at no trump later.

In responding to a NT opening, your options are to pass, to raise the NT bid, or to try a suit take-out.

Given a balanced hand, raise 1NT (weak) to 2NT on 11–12 points, 3NT on 13–17, 4NT on 18–19, 6NT on more. The 4NT response invites opener to go for the small slam (6NT) if he bid on not less than the maximum 14 points. However, points are not everything, especially at low levels, and hands counting less than 13 should be passed if containing an obvious weakness. Raise 1NT (strong) to 2NT on 8–9 points, 3NT on 10–14, 4NT on 15–16, 6NT on 17–19.

Given an unbalanced hand with a biddable major suit and at least 7 points, or 10 if vulnerable, bid two of that suit for a weak take-out. Partner is thereby obliged to pass and leave you in the suit contract. Take out into a minor suit if it is long enough – at least seven cards – to justify a three-bid. As two of a minor suit scores no more than 1 NT, be reluctant to take out into diamonds unless you are sure the suit contract is safer than one in no trumps. As for two clubs, this has a special meaning as described below.

With a good four-card major, you may employ the conventional 'Stayman' bid, provided this has been agreed beforehand. (And remembered. Stayman situations arise so rarely that occasional players sometimes forget to employ it or fail to notice it when used.) In response to 1NT, the Stayman bid of two clubs means. 'I have a good major suit: if you have one, bid it and see if they match'. If opener has no major strength, he replies two diamonds, otherwise two of his major suit. If the suit fits, they can explore further. If not, or in response to the negative two diamonds, the Stayman bidder can escape to an acceptable 2NT, or two of a major or three of a minor if convinced it is the best contract.

*2NT opening and responses.* Open two no trumps on a balanced hand containing 20–22 points. Partner should pass with 0–3 points, but with a balanced hand should reply 3NT on 4–10, 4NT on 11–12, 6NT on 13–14, leaving you to raise any of these if your count was maximum. Alternatively, he may take you out into three of a suit in which he holds at least five cards.

There is no point in opening a balanced hand at more than 2NT. If the hand is worth 3NT, indicate your strength by a opening a conventional two clubs. This is forcing to game level anyway, while allowing you plenty of bidding space in which to explore the possibility of a slam.

*Intervening bids.* We have so far taken it for granted that only one side is doing the bidding, their adversaries meanwhile respectfully murmuring 'no bid' and touching their forelocks from time to time. What often happens, however, is that one side starts the auction, the other side immediately intervenes, and a period of interaction at the one and two levels (or even higher, given freakish distributions) eventually results in one of the partnerships dropping out of the auction. An intervening bid is what you may make if the bidding has been opened by the player on your right, or on your left followed by two passes.

An intervening suit bid at the one level requires length rather than strength. A 10 point-count suffices with a five-card suit, and you can deduct a point for each card in excess. Thus

♠ x
♡ K Q x x x x
♢ x x x
♣ A x x

while not qualifying for an opening bid in first position, would rate a bid of one heart over a minor-suit opening from your right. With 13–15 points you can overcall at the two level. For example, change a minor-suit 'x' to a King on the above hand and you could overcall an opening one spade. With no long suit but 16 or more points you could overcall with 1NT.

*Informatory or 'take-out' double.* An intervening bid may take the form of a purely conventional double. This is typically made when the player on your right deals and opens one in a suit. A double in such a position cannot possibly arise from a genuine expectation that the auction will stop there and the contract be beaten. It therefore has a special use, indicating (in effect) 'My hand is strong enough to open but weak in the suit bid. Show me a suit and I will support it or make some other constructive response'. Partner should then respond as he would do if you had opened the bidding.

*Slam bidding.* When you obviously hold between you a lot of points and have agreed a suit with a good fit, the player who took the initiative will want to find out whether his partner has enough of the outstanding Aces and Kings for a playable slam. He will usually do this by means of the Blackwood convention, whereby bids of 4 and 5NT ask about Ace and King holdings respectively.

Suppose you deal and find yourself with this:

♠ K Q
♡ A Q J x x
♢ A K x
♣ K J x

With 23 points, you open two clubs. Your partner replies two hearts. Good! He has at least 1½ tricks and you have a fit in hearts. Translating his tricks into at least 6 or 7 points, you have at least 29–30 between you and will be thinking of a slam. The quick way of doing this is to bid a 4NT immediately. Since 3NT would be sufficient for game, 4NT should be interpreted as agreeing the heart suit and asking for information by means of the Blackwood convention.

Blackwood is a convention which asks partner to state how many Aces he holds by responding to 4NT as follows:

5♣ shows no Aces held (or all four)
5♢ shows 1 Ace
5♡ shows 2 Aces
5♠ shows 3 Aces

Suppose partner replies five hearts, showing two Aces. With four between you, a small slam is likely. Whether or not you can bid a grand slam depends on the position of the heart King. You therefore launch into phase 2 of Blackwood by bidding 5NT, asking for Kings on the same scale (except that four Kings is indicated not by 6 but by 7 clubs). If partner replies six diamonds, he has the King, and you can finally call seven hearts – not 7NT, as you could lose a trick in a minor suit.

If he replied six clubs, you would know the trump King to be off-side and would therefore sign off at six hearts. Similarly, if in response to your 4NT partner had shown only one Ace, you would have left it at five hearts. To have asked for Kings with 5NT, and got a negative response, would have left you in the impossible situation of having to bid the small slam lacking both an Ace and the trump King.

Blackwood need not be employed as precipitously as this. Given an agreed suit and the chance of a slam, bidding space can often be used to convey information to prevent the uncertainty described in the preceding paragraph. For example, let's suppose the hand described above were matched as follows:

| ♠ K Q | A x x |
| ♡ A Q J x x | K x x x |
| ♢ A K x | J x x x |
| ♣ K J x | A x |

The auction might more usefully proceed by showing 'controls' as follows. (First-round control is an Ace or a void, guaranteeing that its holder can win the first lead made in the stated suit. Second-round control is a King or a singleton.)

| West | East | | West | East |
|------|------|---|------|------|
| 2♣ (1) | 2♡ (2) | | 4NT (7) | 5♡ (8) |
| 3♡ (3) | 3♠ (4) | | 5NT (9) | 6♢ (10) |
| 3NT (5) | 4♣ (6) | | 7♡ | |

( 1) Showing 23+ points.
( 2) Showing long hearts and 1½ tricks.
( 3) Confirming hearts and keeping the auction open. A jump to four hearts would be taken as a recommendation to be content with game.
( 4) With hearts agreed, East shows first round control (Ace) in spades.
( 5) If West shows first round control in diamonds by bidding four, he prevents East from either showing club control with four clubs, or denying it with four hearts. As West is in the driving seat, it is more important to hear from East than to tell him things.
( 6) East shows first round control in clubs.
( 7) Blackwood, to confirm that East's first-round controls are Aces.
( 8) Replying 'two'.
( 9) Asking for Kings.
(10) Replying 'one'.
(11) Final bid of seven hearts. All you have to do now is make it. The problem card is the adverse diamond Queen.

It is important to note that 4NT call is only Blackwood if a suit has been agreed. If not, it is usually a natural bid. Especially is it natural when there can be no doubt that no trumps is intended, as in the opening sequence 1NT–4NT. Where no trumps has been agreed early on in the auction, recourse may be had to the Gerber convention, whereby Aces and Kings are asked for by bids of four and five clubs respectively.

For example:

| West | East |
|------|------|
| ♠ J x | K Q x x |
| ♡ A K x x x | Q x |
| ◇ K Q x | A x x x |
| ♣ A K x | J x x |

The bidding might start: 1♡–2NT, 3NT . . . West's no-trump confirmation suggests a hand worth at least 16 points (actually 20) with not more than one two-card suit, if any. East can therefore see a no-trump fit, with probable strength in his own weakest suit, and at least 28 points including his own 12. He therefore goes into Gerber, bidding 4♣ to ask West for Aces. The responses are four diamonds for none, clubs for one, hearts for two, spades for three, no trumps for four. West duly replies 4♡, showing two Aces. West calls 5♣, asking for

Kings, and the responding 5NT tells him that West holds the other three. East confirms the small slam by bidding 6NT.

*Declarer's play.* The unique challenge of Bridge lies in planning, and then putting into operation, the line of play which will yield all the tricks you need from the two hands you can see. Even when it is obvious that there are enough trick-winners between them, it is not always obvious without careful examination exactly how these cards should be played and in what order. One permanent occupational hazard of Declarer is that of taking a trick in the wrong hand so as to make it impossible to get back into the other hand to win subsequent tricks. The other is that of not having enough obvious tricks, and having to work out ways of developing the one or two extra you may need to make the contract.

Take, for example, the 6NT hand bid by East in the previous example of slam bidding. As Declarer, you can only afford to lose one trick, a spade to the Ace. The only other danger is the outstanding club Queen. To avoid being forced to play a losing club after leading Ace and King, your strategy must involve ridding yourself of a low club from each hand before entering that suit. You can only do this by discarding it to a trick won by your other hand in a long suit to which you cannot follow. One of your own low clubs must therefore be thrown to a heart trick in dummy, and dummy's low club to your last diamond or possibly spade trick in hand.

If South leads the spade Ace, your course is clear. You play an 'x' from each hand and wait. Given a second spade, you win with the Jack and play your winning diamonds in order King, Queen, Ace. This should oust all adverse diamonds, enabling you to lead the last from your own hand and discard a losing club. To these six tricks you add your two spades, then three in hearts by leading Queen, King, Ace, and finish with your two top clubs for twelve.

It's as easy as threading your way through a maze – which is to say easy in retrospect or from the air, but tricky at planning stage and on the ground. Incidentally, the success of this contract depends neither upon South's Ace lead nor on his pursuit of spades at trick two. Every alternative inaugurates a slightly different path through the maze, but all should get there in the end, except against the ridiculously freakish distribution which no-one can ever be expected to guard against.

In a trump contract it is usually right to attack and draw trumps as soon as possible, especially if you haven't as many of them as you would like and therefore need to establish winners in your long side suits without danger of their being ruffed. As to side suits, it is often important to avoid cashing your immediate winners, but to keep them as defensive strongholds while you attack the suit or suits in which you have top card weakness. In other words, hang on to the suits headed A–K until you have driven out the adverse high cards from your suits headed K–Q, Q–J–10 etc. Always calculate how many tricks you can afford to lose, and lose them earlier rather than later as part of a constructive strategy to establish future winners, trusting that those you were dealt originally will not have walked away in the meantime.

The process of weaving through a maze applies equally to trump contracts. Let's go back to the grand slam in hearts described above:

| | |
|---|---|
| ♠ K Q | A x x |
| ♡ A Q J x x | K x x x |
| ◇ A K x | J x x x |
| ♣ K J x | A x |

First, count your tricks. In spades, three, provided that you are careful to keep back the Ace until the King and Queen have made. In diamonds, two, and you must find a way of losing the 'x' in dummy to a trick won in hand, perhaps by ♠A. In clubs, two. In trumps, assuming the worst case that they fall two to a trick, five. Total twelve. One missing. Where is the thirteenth coming from? The only safe answer is to ensure that one of the trumps from the shorter holding, i.e. that in your own hand, can be used to ruff a lead from dummy. At some stage in the proceedings, you will want to lead ♣A from hand, followed by ♣x to the King, followed by dummy's third club for you to ruff.

How, then, will the hand go? It is quite probable that a club will be led. In keeping with your plan, you will take with the Ace, return a club to the King, lead your last club, and ruff it in hand, leaving you three tricks up with ten to go and clubs safe. Next, draw some trumps: lead an 'x' to the Jack, followed by the Queen to an 'x'. At this point, being in dummy, win tricks six and seven with the spade King and Queen. Now get back into hand with dummy's last low trump to the King, and play off the spade Ace, to which you can discard dummy's useless diamond. You now have only diamonds in hand, leaving dummy to take the remaining four tricks with the two top diamonds and two outstanding trumps.

Sometimes, when your initial survey reveals a trick short, you may find the only chance of developing another trick is to risk a finesse, which may be defined as an attempt to win a trick with a lower card when a higher one is held (or accessible). Suppose, in the above contract, dummy's diamond holding were A–Q–J and yours T–8–6–3. You might decide that the only way of getting home is to go for a second trick in the suit against the King. A finesse always depends upon the critical card lying in one rather than another of the adverse hands. For it to work here, the King must be in South's hand and you approach it by leading the Ten. If South has the King, you will win two tricks in the suit if he lets your Ten run, or three if he plays it and loses it to the Ace, which will leave dummy's Queen and Jack high. If North has the King, the finesse will fail. Situations do occur in which you can theoretically finesse against either defender, but you still have to choose which one to attack, as you cannot take on both at once. Whichever way you look at it, a finesse is always a 50/50 chance, and should be

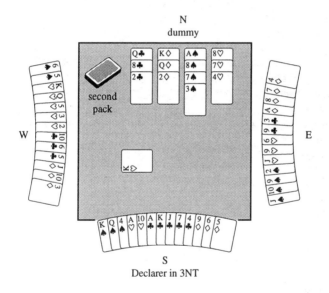

**Figure 13: Bridge** South deals at love all. (West will deal next, as indicated by the position of the second pack, which West will pass to the right for South to cut.) South, with 17 points and long clubs, opens 1 club. West intervenes with 1 heart. North, after some thought, rejects no trump and spade responses in favour of three clubs. East passes. South now counts at least 27 points between the two hands, which is borderline for a game in clubs, but safer at no trump. This is duly bid; North passes; West attacks hearts by leading the King; dummy goes down; and the situation is as illustrated. It is usual for trumps to be set out to the left of dummy, as seen by the Declarer, or clubs in a no-trump bid, as here. Declarer will probably make five clubs, one diamond, three spades and a heart, scoring 100 below the line and 30 above for the overtrick.

avoided if there is any safer way of winning the trick you need.

*Defenders' play.* Experience of Whist and any other intelligent card game will be of value to your play as a defender. The main problem is knowing what to lead first before the dummy has gone down. It will usually be desirable not to lead a suit mentioned by either opponent in the course of the auction, but rather to lead one mentioned by your partner, unless you have a long suit of your own headed by the Ace, which you will want to make before it can be ruffed.

If your partner has not mentioned a suit of his own, a standard opening lead is the fourth highest card (i.e. fourth from the top) of the longest non-trump suit in your hand. This gives your partner maximum information about the lie of the suit through application of the 'rule of eleven'. This is best explained from the receiving end. Suppose your partner leads his fourth highest and it is the Eight. Subtract the face value of the card led from eleven (= three), and you will know that his own hand lacks (in this case) three cards higher than the one led. The combination of this knowledge with what you can see in your own hand and in dummy will very often pinpoint exactly what Declarer holds in the suit, which can be very useful information indeed.

Another satisfactory lead is an honour heading a sequence of three or more, such as Jack from J–T–9– etc, or a low singleton so that you can trump that suit when returned by your partner.

# Four-deal Bridge

As noted in the introduction, this format of Bridge, also known as **Chicago**, is more suitable for home or club play involving several tables or a number of players greater than but not divisible by four. The equivalent of a rubber is always the playing of four contracts, which makes for a more economical use of the time available.

Choose partners and right of first deal in the usual way. The turn to deal passes to the left, but should any deal be passed out by all four players it does not pass but is made again by the same dealer. In all, then, everybody deals once.

A scoring characteristic of Four-deal Bridge is that vulnerability is not conferred by winning a game but instead is rotated in the following way: In the first deal neither side is vulnerable; in the second and third, the Dealer's side is vulnerable; and in the fourth deal both sides are vulnerable.

Scoring is the same as at Rubber Bridge except that there are no rubber scores, which are instead replaced by the following. Winning a game carries a bonus of 300 not vulnerable or 500 vulnerable. A new line is then drawn, as usual, and the next game starts from zero. On the fourth deal – and on this deal only – a side having the only part-score in the current game gets a bonus of 100.

Original Chicago scoring has now been widely superseded by a system derived from Duplicate Bridge. No distinction is made between above- and below-line scoring, and honours are ignored. Each deal yields a score for the declarers if the contract makes, or for the defenders if it goes down. For a failed contract, the defenders score as at Rubber Bridge, with vulnerability determined as described above. Otherwise the declarers score the full amount for all odd tricks actually won, plus 50 (for a 'part-score') if the contract was for less than game, or, if it was for game, 300 non-vulnerable or 500 vulnerable. The usual slam premiums also apply.

# 16

## —————— EUCHRE ——————

### *The Country and Western game*

Euchre is a fascinating partnership game nowadays mostly played in the West Country on a highly organised league and championship basis ranging from Bristol to Taunton to Exeter, where its popularity is equivalent to that of Cribbage in other parts of England. It will also be encountered in the Channel Islands and parts of Kent. Throughout the latter part of the 19th century it was one of the most popular home and social games of the United States, and it was only with the introduction of Bridge that it there suffered a decline from which it seems never to have recovered. It has fared better in Australia, however, especially in the advanced version called Five Hundred, a hybrid of Euchre and Bridge-Whist, which can nowadays be reckoned as Australia's national card game.

Like Ecarté, which could almost be called two-hand Euchre, it derives from the old French game of Triomphe. It first appeared under the spelling 'Jucker' in Alsace or thereabouts, and was evidently carried to the US by German immigrants. It is virtually Nap with the addition of a Joker and the promotion of two Jacks to the position of top trumps, or *bowers*. (Bower rhymes with power. It comes from the German *Bauer*, which literally means farmer but is also one of several words for a playing-card Jack.) Incidentally, Euchre was the game for which the Joker was invented. The Americans introduced it in the 1860s as an extra card or 'best bower' ranking higher than the right bower. The now customary design of a jester and the name 'Joker' did not appear until several years later. It is possible that the idea of a Joker was suggested by the word Euchre, which is pronounced *yewker*. The name 'Benny' is fairly recent and peculiarly English. Why the game now flourishes only in the West Country, and how it reached there in the first place, has yet to be discovered.

The following description is that of the modern game as governed by the British Euchre Association. It differs in slight respects from the 19th Century American game still recorded in most card-game books. The old version was played with 33 cards, including Sevens and Eights, which meant that virtually two fifths of the pack was out of play. The modern reduction to 25 cards has halved this chancy aspect and resulted in a more skill-rewarding game.

*Players.* Four, in fixed partnerships.

*Cards.* Twenty-five, consisting of A K Q J T 9 in each suit plus one Benny, which may be a Joker or the ♠2.

*Game.* In home play, a game is won by the first side to reach a previously agreed target score, traditionally 5 points. In tournament play, a match is the best of three legs, being won by the first side to win two. A leg is won by the first side to reach 21 points over as many deals as it takes.

*Shuffle and deal.* The cards are shuffled before each deal and cut by the player at Dealer's right. Deal five cards each in two rounds of three and two respectively. Place the undealt five face down to one side and turn the top card face up. The suit of this card is the proposed trump for the first round of bidding.

*Object.* Players bid for the right to go for game with the turned suit as trump, or, if all pass, with a trump of their own choice. Game is the winning of three or more tricks. Winning all five scores double, and a failed contract loses double. The bidding player has the further option of playing 'alone', without any contribution from his partner, for double.

*Rank of cards.* The Benny always belongs to the trump suit and is the highest of all. It is followed by the trump Jack (or 'right bower'), then the Jack of the other suit of the same colour as trumps ('left bower'), then Ace, King, Queen, Ten, Nine. Cards in all plain suits rank A K Q J T 9. Note that the suit of the same colour as trump will be one card short because its Jack belongs to the trump suit and not to its face suit.

*Bidding.* Each in turn, starting with the player at Dealer's left, must either pass or 'order it up', i.e. go for three or more tricks with the turned suit as trump. Ordering it up is so termed because, regardless of who makes the turned suit trump, Dealer is entitled to take the turned trump into his own hand in exchange for any unwanted card, which he discards face down. A player intending to play alone must announce 'Up, down' without a pause. Ordering up ends the auction.

If all pass, the faced card is turned down and there is another round of bidding. This time each in turn has the right to bid game by announcing a different trump suit, and Dealer does not have the privilege of taking the originally turned card. The first to make trumps ends the auction. If the maker intends to pay alone must announce this as part of his bid, e.g. 'Alone, spades', or 'Spades, down' without a pause.

If all pass again the cards are bunched and the deal passes to the next player in turn.

If the faced card is the Benny, Dealer announces what suit he wishes it to represent *before* looking at his own hand. The auction proceeds as normal, except that there is only one round. If all pass, the cards are bunched and the deal passes on.

*Going alone.* If the maker announced 'alone' or 'down', his partner lays his hand of cards face down before the first trick is led and takes no part in the play.

The maker's partner may turn his partner down and play alone himself, but Dealer cannot be turned down if he has taken the turned trump.

If the maker (or his partner) plays alone, either member of the opposing side may then also elect to turn his partner down and attack the contract alone. As before, Dealer cannot be opposed alone if he has taken the turned trump.

*Play.* The opening lead is made by the player to the left of the lone player, if any, otherwise to the Dealer's left. Normal rules of trick-play apply. Follow suit if possible (remembering that the Benny and left bower belong to the trump suit), otherwise play any card. A trick is taken by the highest card of the suit led, or by the highest trump if any are played, and the winner of each trick leads to the next.

*Score.* The maker's side, if successful, scores:

1 point for winning three or four tricks,
2 points for winning all five, or
4 for all five if played 'alone'.

The score of 4 does not apply if the originally turned card was the Benny. The maximum score is then 2 points.

If the maker's side wins fewer than three tricks it is 'euchred', and the opposing side scores 2 points if both played, or 4 points if one played alone.

*Revoke.* A revoke (and, in tournament play, a misdeal) incurs a penalty of 2 points.

## Notes on play

Euchre takes some getting used to if you approach it from Nap or Whist-like card games. The first point of difference is the status of Jacks as potential bowers. Suppose you deal yourself the following hand and turn up ♣9:

♠A Q ♣ – ♡A J ◇J

With spades as trump you can count your hand as worth two half-tricks. You might win a trick by trumping a club lead, but your trump Ace is otherwise worthless as it is only fourth highest in its suit, being covered by three bowers. You might win a trick with the red Ace, but, with only four outstanding hearts against you, it is more likely to be trumped. Your Jacks and Queen are of no account.

If the turn-up were ◇K, you would be rather better placed. Your red Jacks now put you in possession of the second and third best trumps, to which you can add the fifth best by taking the King in exchange for the black Queen. You are fairly sure to win two tricks, and would hope for a third from your own black Ace or, with a stroke of luck, your partner.

Best of all would be a heart turned, as you would then be playing with the second, third and fourth highest trump, the turned trump itself, and an outside Ace. Such a hand would be strong enough to play alone. Playing alone only nets a worth-while bonus if you win all five tricks, which is unlikely as the Benny is not in your hand. There is normally a 50–50 chance of its lying either in your partner's hand or in the undealt cards, but, as your partner will already have passed in order for the bidding to have reached you, you had better reckon without it. You might just play it as a loner on the off-chance that it lies among the four unknown cards.

With a club turned, your hand is hopeless. If all pass, however, and no-one bids before you on the second round, you are in a position to go for hearts yourself. With second, third and fourth best trumps you are assured of two tricks. Whether a third will be furnished by your partner or your black Ace remains to be seen. I wouldn't rate your chances higher than evens.

As may now be obvious, skill at Euchre lies almost entirely in the bidding: in deciding whether to order up the turned suit, whether to name one of your own, and whether to play alone. With so few cards in play, it is hardly possible to exercise much strategy in the actual play of tricks, as even the opening lead of a singleton Ace stands a good chance of being trumped. There is also little opportunity for communication between your own and your partner's hand. He may well hold an Ace which he is unable to make because you have none of that suit to lead him and he is unable to trump in.

Position is of particular importance in Euchre. In first or second position you should order it up if you have two good tricks and a possible third in your own hand, and have no especially strong suit that you would wish to call in the event that all should pass. In third position you need three good possibilities, as your partner has already shown weakness by passing. The same applies in fourth position, except that, as Dealer, you will reassess your hand more favourably by reference to the turn-up and the effect of your discard. In a second round of bidding, the opponents of the dealer should be more inclined to entrump the suit of the same colour as the turn-up ('make it next', in traditional terms), and Dealer's partner one of the opposite colour ('cross it'), for reasons which, if not obvious, will emerge from an examination of the following deal:

West deals and turns up ♣Q. (Jo denotes Joker):

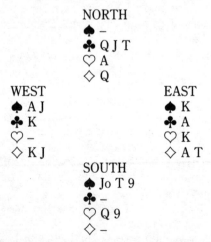

```
                    NORTH
                    ♠ –
                    ♣ Q J T
                    ♡ A
                    ◇ Q
      WEST                        EAST
      ♠ A J                       ♠ K
      ♣ K                         ♣ A
      ♡ –                         ♡ K
      ◇ K J                       ◇ A T
                    SOUTH
                    ♠ Jo T 9
                    ♣ –
                    ♡ Q 9
                    ◇ –
```

North passes, having nothing but the left bower (third highest). East passes, knowing that successful bids require trumps rather than the Aces and Kings which pass for strength in other games. South hesitates: he has three trumps, of which the Benny is unbeatable but the other two feeble. We will suppose he passes. West, also with three

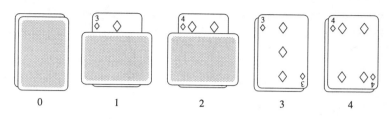

**Figure 14: Euchre** Euchre is played only with high cards, leaving low ones free for other purposes. Traditionally, each player or side has a spare Three and Four and arranges them on the table to indicate their current score, as shown here.

trumps after the exchange, orders it up and discards $\diamondsuit$J. North leads $\heartsuit$A, and, although this is trumped by West, North-South defeat the contract by three-two. Post mortem examination shows that South, though right to hesitate, could have bid and made the contract.

Let's change the turn-up to $\clubsuit$9. North now finds himself holding three trumps including second best, plus a bare outside Ace, and orders it up. West takes the turn-up in exchange for his red Jack, giving him three trumps including third best. By most lines of play, North-South win.

Change the turn-up, again, to $\heartsuit$J. North and East unhesitatingly pass. South holds three trumps, including the Benny, and order it up, though not without hesitation. West takes the red Jack turned up in exchange for his black Jack, and leads it to force out the Benny and weaken the contracting side in trumps. This deal could go either way. So far as I can make out, differing lines of play variously enable either side to win by one trick.

Finally, let's make the turn-up $\diamondsuit$9. The first three players again unhesitatingly pass. In West's position I would do the same. In the event, he would almost certainly win four-one by ordering it up, but he couldn't be expected to know about his partner's two helpful trumps. Suppose instead he also passes (by 'turning it down'). Is any player now in possession of a biddable hand? West's pass suggests weakness in red suits, so North and South will be looking to their red cards and East to his black. North and East will pass again. From previous inspection (above) we can see that South could successfully bid hearts. Whether he would do so in actual play remain an open question. I wouldn't. Would you?

# 17

## ——— QUINTO ———

### *Score for a bunch of fives*

This pleasant little game of tricks was invented around the turn of the century by Professor Hoffman, nom-de-plume of a cards expert with several 'Hoyles' to his credit. Easy to learn and not too demanding, it introduces two quite novel features into the field of Whist-like games from which it is derived. One is the 'hierarchic' order of suits for trumping purposes, which simply means that a card of any higher suit beats one of any lower suit, regardless of rank. (Interestingly, from a historical viewpoint, the order of suits is that of the old form of Bridge. The transference of spades from lowest to highest position produced the modern Bridge order, which is also to be seen in Contract Whist.)

The other novel feature is the invention of 'quints', which gives the game its name. A quint is simply a Five, or two cards of the same suit adding up to five, and it is from the making – and avoiding – of quints that the fun of the game is largely derived.

### The game

*Cards.* 53; a standard 52-card pack plus one Joker.

*Game.* A rubber is won by the first side to win two games. Game is 250 up, typically reached after two or three deals. Scores may be conveniently recorded on a Cribbage board (each peg counting five) or Bezique markers.

*Deal*. Twelve cards each, singly; place the last five face downwards to one side of the table to form the 'cachette'. The cachette may not be seen until the end of the round, when it is taken by the side winning the twelfth trick, and counts as a thirteenth.

*Object*. Points are scored for tricks in themselves, and also for certain combinations of cards – called quints – falling to a trick. Tricks are not counted until the end of the round, but quints are scored as they are taken. If a side makes game (250 points) as the result of winning a trick containing a quint, the rest of the hand is not played out.

*Trumps*. For trick-taking purposes, suits rank, in ascending order, spades, clubs, diamonds, hearts. A player void of the suit led can therefore trump by playing a card from any higher suit, spades being trumped by any other, clubs by any red suit, diamonds only by hearts, hearts not at all. Thus all 52 cards rank from ♠2 (lowest) up to ♡A, which cannot be beaten.

*Quints*. The Joker, each Five, and any two cards of the same suit totalling five in face value, are all quints. Thus a trick containing Ace and Four, or Three and Two, of the same suit scores a quint in that suit to its winner. A trick can contain more than one quint – for example, if Ace and Four of a suit fall to the same trick as any Five and the Joker, it contains three quints.

The value of quints is as follows:

| | |
|---|---|
| Joker (Quint Royal) | 25 |
| Any quint in♡ | 20 |
| Any quint in♢ | 15 |
| Any quint in♣ | 10 |
| Any quint in♠ | 5 |

*Doubling and redoubling*. After the cachette has been laid aside, but before any card is led, each in turn has one opportunity either to double, or to re-double an opponent's double. Doubling affects only the value of tricks, not of quints. Tricks are normally worth 5 each, but if doubled they count 10 each, and if re-doubled, 20 each.

*Tricks*. Player left of dealer leads to the first trick. Players must follow suit to the card led, except that the holder of the Joker may play it whenever he deems fit (*see below*). If unable to follow suit, a player may discard from a lower suit, or trump by playing any card of any higher suit. The trick is won by the person playing the highest card to it, bearing in mind that all cards have relative values from ♠2 to ♡A.

**Figure 15: Quinto** A trick full of quints. North leads an Ace; East can follow suit only with the Four, making a spade quint for 5. South, thinking partner's Ace is sure to win, throws the Joker for 25. But West, out of spades, trumps with the one-card diamond quint worth 20 – thus winning a trick worth 45 in quints, plus the basic trick value of 5 (or 10 or 20 if doubled or redoubled).

The winner of a trick scores the value of any quint it may contain, and leads to the next.

*Joker.* The holder of the Joker may play it at any time. It has no trick-taking value, but in its capacity as Quint Royal, worth 25, it counts to the credit of the side winning it in a trick. Its holder will therefore seek to play it to a trick being won by his partner.

(There is no official rule about leading the Joker, but the circumstance can arise in which the holder has no choice but to lead it. For this purpose I recommend that if a player leads the Joker, the player on his left determines the suit to follow.)

*Last trick.* Whoever takes the last (twelfth) trick takes the cachette of five cards and scores for any quint or quints it may contain. It also counts as an extra trick and scores accordingly.

*Score.* At the end of the round, each side adds to its score for quints a score for tricks it won, at the rate of 5 undoubled, 10 doubled or 20 re-doubled. If quints are enough to make game (250), tricks are not counted. If both sides make game on tricks, the side with the higher total wins. The first side to make two games wins the rubber, and scores an extra 100 for it.

There is no official ruling about ties, but I recommend that if both sides make equal game on tricks there should be another deal, in which case the first to score a quint is bound to win.

## Notes on play

The play of Quinto is entirely shaped by the hierarchic trumping system and the value of the last trick.

The winners of the last trick win the cachette, which is worth playing for, partly for its intrinsic value as the 'odd trick' and partly for the slightly less than one-in-nine chance of its containing at least one quint. Though its average value may be small, the cachette can in certain circumstances be worth 90 to its takers – for if it contains Quint Royal (25) in a re-doubled game (20), that makes 45 to you instead of 45 to your opponents.

The surest way of winning the cachette is for the holder of the unbeatable ♡A to hold on to it until the last moment. Since you cannot be sure from the outset that your partner does not hold ♡A if you do not have it yourself, there is no point in trying to force it out early. It is, however, possible to devise some sort of signalling system whereby a player can, by his choice of lead, indicate to his partner (and his opponents) whether or not he holds the top card.

Since it is virtually impossible to establish a black suit – i.e. to force out the higher red suits in order to lead into a long run of clubs – normal procedure is to start in spades and gradually progress through the suits in ascending order, leaving hearts till last. It is sometimes possible to establish diamonds, however, if you hold the suit long and have also either length or strength in hearts for the purpose of clearing them out first.

Whoever holds the Joker will be concerned to play it to a trick won by his partner, which means that if you yourself don't hold it you must give your partner the earliest opportunity of dropping it. For this reason leader should start with ♠A if he has it, or ♣A. Only in default of black Aces or guarded Kings should ◇A be led for this purpose, and ♡A would in any case be too valuable.

The making of quints injects some interesting elements into the play. For example, when playing second to the lead of a top card you should avoid throwing anything lower than Six for fear of giving away a quint. The 2+3 quint usually happens by accident, being forced out (as in the fifth trick of the sample game given later) when its holder has no choice in the matter.

The A+4 quint can be cooperatively worked up to between the partners. You may, for example, win a trick with a King when also holding the Ace, so that with an early return in the same suit your partner may throw, or even lead, the Four if he has it. There are two common ways of making the Five quint – one, which can easily be overlooked if you are not on the ball, is to trump or overtrump with a Five when unable to follow suit. Suppose, for example, your left-hand opponent leads ♣A and your partner drops the matching Four; then your right-hand opponent, being void in clubs, might profitably trump with ♢5. If you are also void you may simply be tempted to play a higher diamond and capture both quints. But of course what you should look for is ♡5, which gives you the trick and a third quint to boot! The other way of making the Five quint is simply to drop it to a trick you know your partner can win, or is already winning.

It is obvious that a two-card quint cannot be scored if you hold both cards yourself; you can therefore safely lead one of them out, and you should be on the alert for similar play from your partner. Even more significantly, if you hold Ace and Four, circumstances may arise in which you can lead or discard the Four in order to let your partner know you have the Ace as well.

Remember that five cards are out of play, lying in the cachette, so that with an even distribution of cards there may be two or three clean tricks to be made in each suit. With a fairly even distribution, you can expect in the lower suits to make with a guarded King, but possibly not with a guarded Queen. Do not bother to lead from a lower suit when play has reached a higher one. For example, by the seventh trick the play will probably be into diamonds, so it is not worth leading a black card. Reserve the residuals of lower suits to use as discards as necessary at a later stage. This is especially important if, as the result of long black suit holdings, you have kept hold of ♣5 or ♠5. Reserve them in the hope of dropping them, when void, to tricks won by your partner. Leading them out will force everyone to trump or overtrump, and may embarrass your partner considerably.

The lower the suit, the more valuable the void. If you have no spades to start with, you are in a strong position anyway and never more so than when playing second to the trick, as your partner then has a chance to drop his Joker, or the Five quint, or the Four to an Ace lead as the case may be. Since play normally starts in spades there is no point in going out of your way to void them. With two clubs or only one, however, it is often worth clearing them out as soon as possible, even by leading them before spades. A void in diamonds is only worth having if you have plenty of hearts with which to trump them. Needless to say, a void in hearts is useless!

You should certainly double or re-double if you feel you are in a position to do so. Since the cachette counts as the odd trick, one side is bound to take more for tricks than the other, so doubling or re-doubling increases the margin between the two sides. In the sample deal which follows, for example, the side that doubled finished up only 105 points off game and a good 55 in advance of their opponents. Had they not doubled, they would have lain only 30 in advance and a good 150 points off game. The effect is even greater in subsequent deals, where the difference between doubling and not doubling may mean the difference between making game on this round and losing it on the next.

To double or re-double you must be confident that your side will take seven tricks at least, or six and the last. Reckoning your own hand as four may not be enough if your partner can only make two, but if you can make five (or four and last) the opportunity should be seized. Your decision will be influenced, of course, by whether others have called or passed. Note, by the way, that you may only re-double an opponent's double, not your own partner's.

**Sample deal**

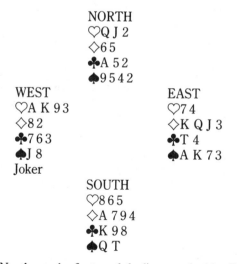

NORTH
♡Q J 2
◇6 5
♣A 5 2
♠9 5 4 2

WEST
♡A K 9 3
◇8 2
♣7 6 3
♠J 8
Joker

EAST
♡7 4
◇K Q J 3
♣T 4
♠A K 7 3

SOUTH
♡8 6 5
◇A 7 9 4
♣K 9 8
♠Q T

West dealt. North speaks first, and declines to double. East passes, not liking the look of his hearts, though he can probably count on two spade tricks, a trumped club, and a diamond in its own right. South is also unhappy with the trump situation, and passes. West doubles: he can surely trump a spade and a diamond, will make the two top hearts for four, and save one of them for the last trick, five. North leads.

| N | E | S | W | |
|---|---|---|---|---|
| ♣A | ♣T | ♣8 | ♣6 | Possibly North's only opportunity of testing South for the Joker . . . which he has not got. |
| ♠9 | ♠K | ♠T | Jo | East correctly divines from the previous trick that West has it. 25 to E-W. |
| ♠2 | ♠A | ♠Q | ♠8 | |
| ♣5 | ♣4 | ♣K | ♣7 | East has no further use for spades, except as discards, and now proceeds to void clubs. North duly plays the quint to his partner's win, scoring 10. |
| ♣2 | ◇3 | ♣9 | ♣3 | East happily trumps a two-card quint for 10. He might reasonably have taken high instead, on the off-chance of a later two-card quint in diamonds. |
| ♠5 | ♠7 | ◇4 | ♠J | East throws a cat to the pigeons, having a weak heart and preferring not to lead diamonds. South, by playing the Four, indicates to his partner that he also has the matching red Ace. |
| ◇6 | ◇J | ◇9 | ◇2 | |
| ♠4 | ♠3 | ◇7 | ◇8 | An amusing lead, but South refuses to relinquish his Ace. |
| ♡J | ♡7 | ♡5 | ♡9 | South gives his partner a quint worth 20. |
| ◇5 | ◇Q | ◇A | ♡3! | A good lead of a quint into a partner's known Ace, but unhappily trumped at the last minute. |
| ♡2 | ♡4 | ♡6 | ♡A | Just by chance, another lovely quint. |
| ♡Q | ◇K | ♡8 | ♡K | And the last trick. |

The cachette contains nothing of value (♡T ◇T ♣Q ♣J ♠6), but gives East-West their ninth trick, well justifying West's double. Thus the scores are:

| N-S | E-W | |
|---|---|---|
| 40 | 90 | for tricks (doubled, 10 each) |
| 50 | 55 | for quints |
| 90 | 145 | total |

# 18

## ———— BARBU ————

### *The bearded wonder*

This peculiar game for three or four players is an offshoot of the Hearts/
Black Maria family and apparently originated in the 1960s. *Le Barbu*
means 'the bearded man' and refers to the King of hearts, who plays
a prominent role in the game. A primitive version of it was first
described in a Belgian book (*Le Guide Marabout de tous les jeux de
cartes, 1966*) under the name *Le jeu du roi*, together with the assertion
that it derived from an English game called 'King' – of which, however,
I can find no source or trace in Britain or any English-language book
of card games. I am, however, informed by a reliable authority that
something substantially similar was being played in the 1960s at
St Petersburg under the English title 'King', though spelt, of course,
in Cyrillic (Russian) script. To add to the confusion, yet another French
book (*Cent jeux de cartes classiques*, 1975) describes a Parisian version
played with 32 cards and called *le Bambu*, as distinct from *Barbu*. At
time of writing, I know of at least one London card school that plays a
highly elaborated version of Barbu as a distinctly cut-throat gambling
game, though this need not be regarded as an essential part of the
proceedings if you enjoy (as I do) exploring games for their own sake.

As is so often the case with newish games, no two schools seem to
play it exactly alike. It will therefore be best to describe a very basic
version to which you can add your own rules and elaborations as the
fancy takes you.

## The game

*Players.* Four, but three possible.

*Cards.* Four use the full 52-card pack ranking A K Q J T 9 8 7 6 5 4 3 2. Three may use a 36-card pack made by omitting all numerals below Six.

*Game structure.* The turn to deal and play passes to the left, but each player deals seven times in succession before the next player takes over. Each set of seven deals is known as a quarter. When three play, a game consists of only three quarters, or 21 instead of 28 deals. Rule a scoresheet up into three or four columns, one for each player, and either 21 or 28 horizontal scoring spaces, one for each deal.

*Deal and game selection.* Deal, one at a time, 13 cards to each player, or 12 each if three play. When all have examined their cards, the dealer announces which of seven possible games will be played. This must be a different game on each of his seven deals, so that each game is played exactly once in his quarter. This means, of course, that his options grow progressively fewer, leaving him with only one possible game on his last deal.

The seven games are as follows. Note that five of them involve playing tricks at no trump and attract penalty scores or minus points, while the sixth and seventh attract plus scores whose combined total exactly matches that of the total number of penalties. This produces a zero-sum game, i.e. one in which the players' wins and losses cancel out to zero for ease of monetary settlement.

- *No tricks.* Play tricks at no trump and aim to win as few as possible. Each player scores 2 penalty points per trick won.
- *No hearts.* Play tricks at no trump and aim to avoid winning cards of the hearts suit. Each player scores 2 penalties per heart taken, or 6 for the heart Ace. (If three play, score 3 penalties per heart, including the Ace.)
- *No Queens.* Play tricks at no trump and aim to avoid winning any Queen in a trick. Each player scores 6 penalties per Queen taken.
- *No King* ('Barbu'). Play tricks at no trump. Whoever wins the trick containing ♡K scores 20 penalties.
- *No last.* Play tricks at no trump. The winner of the penultimate trick scores 10 penalties and of the last trick 20 penalties.
- *Trump.* Play tricks with a trump suit announced by Dealer, and aim to win as many as possible. Each player scores 5 plus points per trick won.
- *Domino.* The aim is to be the first to run out of cards in a game of

Domino, as described below. The winner scores 40 plus points. Second out scores 20 plus points, or 25 if three play. If four play, third out scores 5 plus points. The last player scores nothing.

Domino is played as follows: The player at Dealer's left plays any card face up to the table. The next must play, if possible, the next higher card of the same suit to its left, or the next lower card of the same suit to its right, or any other card of the same rank above or below it. This continues, with each in turn either passing or playing one card. Each card played must go side by side with a previous card, in such a way as to build up a rectangle of four suits of thirteen cards each, running in sequence from Two to Ace.

*Trick play.* In the six trick games, the opening lead is made by the player at Dealer's left. Suit must be followed if possible, otherwise any card may be played. The trick is taken by the highest card of the suit led, or (in the trump deal) by the highest trump if any are played, and the winner of each trick leads to the next.

*Variations.* In most of the accounts I have received, the game announcement is made by the player at Dealer's left, who also leads the first card. I favour the version described above. Those who play it

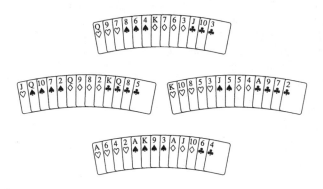

**Figure 16: Barbu** Consider each hand in turn as being that of the dealer at the start of play, when all options are open.

North has a horrible hand, and can do little more than take a chance on not taking the last trick ('no last').

East, by contrast, has several good possibilities, including either a trump game in hearts or its opposite, no hearts. But the hand is well placed for the tricky task of discarding the ♡K, and best calls for a bid of 'Barbu'.

South also might try a positive trump in either hearts or spades, and West has a very promising bid of 'no Queens'.

also incorporate an elaborate system of doubling, which nullifies the zero-sum effect but reportedly spices things up when played for money. They also play Domino differently, as follows.

Dealer announces which rank is to be played first, e.g. 'Five', 'Jack', etc, and the lead is made by the first player from the left able to comply with this specification. Cards are played to four overlapping columns (like the dummy at Bridge.) The first card played must be of the specified rank. Thereafter, anyone may start a new column by playing a card of the start rank, until all four columns are in progress. Cards are played upwards and downwards in suit from the start card in each column, and there is no relation between the suits. For example, if 'Five' is specified and the first three play Five, Six, Seven, the fourth may not play a Six or a Seven of a different suit. He may only continue the same suit by adding the Four or the Eight, or start a new one with another Five.

## Notes on play

Experience of Hearts or Black Maria will be of value in the play of Barbu, as the same underlying principles apply to the aim of losing unwanted tricks. What makes Barbu more exacting is the need to recognize which hands are most suited to which contracts. Bearing in mind that one's scope for choice becomes increasingly limited, it is probably best to leave till last the relatively straightforward contracts such as no tricks, no last, and trump. No Queens, no hearts, and Barbu (no King), being more specialized, should be dealt with as soon as the opportunity arises.

# 19

## —— HAVE A HEART ——

### *Black Maria and other games*

Black Maria is the British version of a family of Western card games derived from one called Hearts. In these games your aim is not to win tricks but to lose them – or, more precisely, to avoid winning tricks containing penalty cards, which are usually all those of the hearts suit. In one branch of the family, known as Black Widow or Black Lady Hearts, there is an additional penalty for taking the Queen of spades in a trick. Black Maria is a further extension of Black Widow, with penalties also for taking other high spades. It is a good game for three, and therefore described here primarily in that form. At the end of the chapter you will find brief descriptions of other members of the Hearts family and versions for other numbers of players. All are easy to learn and fun to play, making them good for children and those as yet unused to trick-taking games.

# Black Maria

*Cards.* Fifty-one – a standard pack from which ♣2 has been removed. Cards rank normally for trick-taking purposes, Ace high, Two low.

*Order.* Establish first dealer by any agreed means. The turn to deal the deal, and all play proceed clockwise around the table.

*Game.* For convenience, game may be set at 100 points – it finishes when one player reaches or exceeds that total, bearing in mind that the player with the highest score is the loser.

*Deal.* Seventeen cards to each player, dealt singly and face down.

*Object.* After an exchange of three cards, as described below, seventeen tricks are played out at no trump. The object is to avoid taking in penalty cards, which score against players capturing them as follows:

| | |
|---|---|
| Each heart | 1 |
| ♠A | 7 |
| ♠K | 10 |
| ♣Q (Black Maria) | 13 |

*The exchange.* Each player selects from his hand three cards which he does not want and passes them face down to the player on his *right* (anti-clockwise). Having passed them on, he takes up into hand the three cards similarly passed to him from the player on his left. The tricks are then played out.

*Tricks.* The player left of dealer leads any card to the first trick. Usual rules of trick-taking apply. You must follow suit to the card led if possible; if not possible you may discard from any suit. There are no trumps, and the trick is taken by the player of the highest card of the suit led. The winner of a trick leads to the next.

*Score.* Each player totals the values of all penalty cards he took in tricks and this number is entered against him on the score sheet. The three figures in each round should total 43. Scores are kept cumulatively.

## Notes on play

*The ideal hand.* The exchanging of cards gives players opportunity for the exercise of skill in shaping the final hands from which they play. The judgement called for in determining which cards to oust is compounded by the need to have regard to the cards one is likely to receive from the left. For example, rejecting three hearts is disastrous if three higher hearts are received subsequently. Thus, in deciding which cards to pass on it is desirable to have some idea of what constitutes strength and weakness in the final playing hand.

In hearts, the ideal holding is a number of low cards including Two or Three, and Four or Five as well. Low cards are 'guards' on higher ones: they ensure that if that suit is led you will be able to duck out of taking the trick. If you are safe in this respect it doesn't really matter if you have a long heart holding and/or a number of high cards, even including the Ace, since you can expect to lose these on tricks led in other suits when you have established voids in the hand. A bad heart holding is four or more with nothing lower than Five.

Spades lower than Queen are a good suit to hold, in moderation, and must be kept rather than thrown. Penalty spades (A, K, Q) are bad only if you have no low cards with which to avoid winning tricks with them when that suit is led. Counting as guards anything lower than Queen, you typically need three guards if you hold one or more penalty spades, four if the holding is Ace only or Ace and King.

In side suits – clubs and diamonds – the ideal is high winners and low losers. High winners you lead early in the game, when won tricks are unlikely to contain penalties; low losers you need for safely escaping from the lead when you have taken your fair share of inevitable (clean) tricks. If you have only middling cards the suit is probably safe if you hold four or fewer. A very long side suit can be dangerous if it does not make an early appearance, as you may be left later in the game with the lead of a suit in which the others are now void, but if it contains a safe loser, i.e. Two or Three (but remember Three is the lowest in clubs), it is probably safer than not.

A void is good defensively, in that it enables you to drop your clangers when led; but if you have too many high cards in other suits and are in danger of too frequently taking the lead, the void becomes a liability. (How often have I wished it possible to lead from a void suit!)

*Passing on.* Having a clear idea of the general framework of a good hand makes it that much easier to select your rejects. Look first at spades, since that suit accounts for 30 of the 43 penalty points. If you hold one or more penalty spades, make sure you have enough guards to keep them safe. If so, keep the penalties, as you will be well placed to control their destination; if not, pass on high spades from Ace downwards. Black Maria herself, if adequately guarded, is always better in the hand than out.

Hearts next, though here there is not so much you can do. There is no need to pass on high Hearts if you are safe in low, or to create a void except as a luxury (and irritant to your victim) if you are safe in other suits.

As to side suits, we have seen that the ideal is voids or long suits containing adequate low cards. A suit with three or fewer may as well be voided, though if it contains losing leaders (Two, Three) it may be more profitable to keep them yourself than donate them to an adversary. If you have a long suit with no low cards, get rid of as many of the highest as possible.

The passing on of cards gives their recipient some inkling of the nature of his left-hand opponent's cards, assuming that all tend to discard with the same principles in mind as outlined above. For example, if your neighbour gives you three of a suit including a low one, you can be fairly sure that he has created a void (though it might, of course, be nullified by the third player discarding from the same suit).

*The play*. Side suits are usually led first. Theoretically it is safe to lead high cards from side suits in order to take probably inevitable tricks while they are still 'clean'. In practice the procedure comes unstuck as soon as it leads into someone else's void. Since a player can only have voided if he held three or fewer, chances are that the lead of a high card from your side suit will be safe if the suit is short, risky if you have too many.

When following suit and losing the trick it is natural to play the highest card beneath the highest one already showing. Thus if you lead $\diamondsuit$J and the next plays $\diamondsuit$7 you might reasonably assume that he has something lower, making it safe for you to lead Diamonds again. But if third then plays $\diamondsuit$3 or thereabouts, you must be prepared to find him void next time that suit comes round. Drawing such inferences from the appearance of particular cards at particular times is an essential ingredient in the skill of the game.

If you are safe in spades, and especially lack the penalties in it, they often make a splendid lead. Ideally, play the Jack. If someone else takes the trick it can only be with a penalty, which achieves your object. If not, and the worst you can do is pick up a single Heart, you have the lead and can do the same again – this time with the Ten, if possible.

Heart leads (low, of course, by preference) are not worth making unless you have no other way of losing the lead, and premature heart leads are the sign of the beginner at the game. But if you have a longish run of hearts and seem destined to take a trick or two, it is best to do so early and get them over with. If left too late, you may find another player void and pick up a nasty spade, or you may be left with a lead you cannot escape from. Often, you will lead a dubious heart (say the Ten from a holding of T 6 4 2) and find it overtaken twice because the others are following the same principle of taking necessary evils early on.

By and large, you should make the tricks you have to make early on, then bow out and stay out for the rest of the round. About the worst thing that can happen to you is to be dealt four or five safe cards in a suit, which you retain, then find your holding increased by the pass-on from your left-hand neighbour, and eventually take the lead at trick ten, with all seven of a suit in which the others are both void.

## Sample game

*First deal.* Charlie deals; the cards fall as follows:

| Abel | ♠4 2 ♡Q T 8 4 2 ♣Q 6 ◇A K Q T 7 5 4 2 |
|---|---|
| Baker | ♠K Q 7 5 3 ♡9 6 5 3 ♣A K 9 8 5 3 ◇6 3 |
| Charlie | ♠A J T 9 8 6 ♡A K J 7 ♣J T 7 4 ◇J 9 8 |

Abel's hand looks not too bad: he is good in spades and has his high hearts not unreasonably guarded. Going for a void, he ousts ♡Q ♣Q, 6. But what he gets from Baker ruins his spade holding.

Baker has safe hearts and good all-round low cards everywhere. He decides to void his diamonds and pass on ♠K (much to Abel's chagrin), in the hope of losing his Black Maria to the latter. This device is counterbalanced by the cards he now picks up, though the high hearts need not worry him as he has them well guarded in the original deal.

Charlie has cause for complaint, having a general shortage of cards with which to lose the lead and a particularly bad hearts holding. He rejects ♠A ♡A, K. The ♡Q picked up from Abel is a nail in the coffin, though the two clubs are nothing to argue about.

After the exchange, the playing hands are:

| Abel | ♠K 4 2 ♡T 8 4 2 ♣ – ◇A K Q T 7 6 5 4 3 2 |
|---|---|
| Baker | ♠A Q 7 5 3 ♡A K 9 6 5 3 ♣A K 9 8 5 3 ◇ – |
| Charlie | ♠J T 9 8 6 ♡Q J 7 ♣Q J T 7 6 4 ◇J 9 8 |

Abel can guess that Baker is void in diamonds, Charlie that Abel is void in clubs. Abel leads. Winning cards are in **bold** type:

| A | B | C | |
|---|---|---|---|
| ◇7 | ♠A | ◇J | Baker could equally well have thrown ♡A. Bad start for Charlie. |
| ♠4 | ♠7 | ♠J | Charlie hesitated between ♠J and ♣Q lead; decides to throw cat among the pigeons. |
| ♠2 | ♠5 | ♠T | Looks like the last of Abel's low Spades . . . |
| ♠K | ♠Q | ♠9 | And so it proves. Now Abel forces Charlie to take a penalty . . . |
| ◇6 | ♡A | ◇8 | |
| ♡T | ♣9 | ♣Q | Not such a lucky lead. Charlie thinks he can escape through Clubs, but it would be as well to void Diamonds first in the hope that Abel will later have to lead them. |
| ◇5 | ♡K | ◇9 | |
| ♡8 | ♣5 | ♣7 | Baker is undertaking battle with Charlie in Clubs. |
| ♡4 | ♣A | ♣6 | |
| ♡2 | ♠3 | ♠8 | |
| ◇A | ♣K | ♣J | A clean trick! |
| ◇K | ♣8 | ♣4 | |
| | ♣3 | | . . . and Charlie takes the remaining tricks. |
| 23 | 1 | 19 | Score (against) at end of first round |

## Widow Hearts

This is the most basic form of Hearts for any number of players. 'Widow' is a technical term denoting a small number of undealt cards, which in this case will be the ones left over after the pack has been dealt round as far as it will go so that every player has the same number of cards. The widow is left face down on the table and is awarded to the player winning the last trick – together with any penalty points it may contain. (As a variation, it may be dealt face up to enable players to calculate their hands better.)

The player at dealer's left leads to the first trick, after which the winner of each trick leads to the next. Suit must be followed if possible, otherwise any card may be played. There are no trumps, and the trick is always won by the highest card of the suit led. The cards of the widow are added to those captured by the winner of the last trick.

Each player scores one penalty point for each heart captured in his tricks, and the game ends when one player has reached a predetermined losing target. (E.g. 31 in this version, but raise it according to the total value of penalties in each variation. A good way of agreeing a target is to divide the total number of penalties by the number of players, multiply by ten and round it off, so that an average game lasts ten deals.)

In most Hearts games, a player who captures *all* the penalty cards scores their total value in his favour. This turns a really bad hand into a good one, and may be recommended.

There are several variations in the scoring of penalty points.

## Other Hearts games

*PINK LADY* is Black Maria with a further penalty score of 13 for taking ♡Q in a trick.

In *SPOT HEARTS*, each heart counts as its face value in penalties, the lowest being Two, worth 2, and with Jack 11, Queen 12, King 13 and Ace 14 against. Total penalties: 104.

In *GREEK HEARTS*, numeral hearts count 1 each, court hearts 10 each, ♡A 15 and ♠Q 50 – total 104.

In *OMNIBUS HEARTS*, ♢T (or some say ♢J) counts 10 points in favour of the player winning it in tricks, thus reducing the total number of penalties by ten.

In *TRUMP HEARTS*, hearts are not only penalties but also trumps, and a rule may be introduced making it obligatory to trump if unable to follow suit.

In *HEARTS AND FLOWERS*, hearts count against and clubs count the same amount in favour of their winners, so the total number of penalties is zero (in which case, find some other way of determining the target score!)

In *HEARTS, FLOWERS AND TRUMPS*, which I have just invented, hearts count against, clubs count in favour, and spades are trumps (but it is not obligatory to trump when void). Since diamonds have no part to play in this scheme of things, one might suggest *HEARTS, FLOWERS, TRUMPS AND DIAMONDS*, which is the same, except that spades can only trump tricks which do not contain diamonds – the appearance of a diamond in a trick leaves it won by the highest card of the suit led.

# 20

# – MORE WHIST GAMES –

## *Ideal for three – or more*

The following simple trick-taking games all have the merit of being suitable for three players, and most have the bonus of being equally playable by any number up to six, or seven at a pinch.

All may be classed as varieties of Whist to the extent that the following rules apply unless otherwise stated:

- Cards rank A K Q J T 9 8 7 6 5 4 3 2 in all suits, though in some games the pack may be reduced by the removal of lower numerals;
- The turn to deal and play (and bid, if relevant) passes to the left and the opening lead is made by the player at Dealer's left;
- Any card may be led. Follow suit if possible, otherwise play any card. The trick is taken by the highest card of the suit led, or by the highest trump if any are played, and the winner of each trick leads to the next.

## ——————————— Bismarck ———————————

A game for three.
Bismarck is a 'compendium' game, in that the object and conditions of play vary from deal to deal in accordance with a pre-determined menu.

A game consists of 12 deals. Each in turn deals, four times in succession, 16 cards to each player and the last four cards to himself. He then discards any four and play begins. The conditions of each of his four deals are as follows:

*First deal.* The aim is to win tricks, playing at no trump. Dealer scores 1 point for each trick he wins above eight, each opponent scores 1 point for each trick he takes above four.

*Second deal.* The aim is to win tricks, with a trump suit selected at random (such as by turning the last card, or cutting another pack). Score as above.

*Third deal.* The aim is to win tricks, with a trump suit declared by the dealer after examining his hand but before the first card is led. Score as above.

*Fourth deal.* The aim is to lose tricks, playing at no trump. Dealer scores 4 points less the number of tricks he took, and each opponent 6 points less the number taken by himself.

It is very easy to create more interesting variations on this simple game.

# Knockout

For 3–7 players.

A children's or gambling game, however you prefer to regard it, Knockout is widely played in schools and pubs, and appears to be of surprisingly recent origin. The name is actually short for Knockout Whist, and by younger players who have never heard of the real game of Whist it is often known simply as 'Whist', which can make life very confusing for card-game researchers.

There are many variations, but the underlying theme goes like this:

Everybody places a single stake in the pot. On the first deal each player receives seven cards, on the second six, the third five, and so on, reducing by one card on each occasion. Dealer turns the next card for trump and leads to the first trick.

Anyone who fails to win a trick is knocked out and takes no further part in the game. Those who remain contribute another stake to the pot. Whoever won most tricks (or, if equal, the tied player who cuts the higher card from the pack) gathers the cards up and deals to the next round.

This continues until one player wins the pot by winning every trick played – usually on the last deal of one card, though it can happen earlier.

# Nap

For 3–7 players.

Nap, or **Napoleon,** is a cross between Euchre and Bid-Whist that became popular throughout Europe in the latter part of the 19th century and is recorded in a wide variety of guises and formats. Jerome K Jerome, in one of the earliest English references to it, portrays it being played in *Three Men in a Boat,* and it subsequently became a staple amusement of British family life before television took over the world, since when it seems to have lost a lot of ground. Although full of Napoleonic associations, it was certainly invented too late to have been played by the original emperor, but may perhaps have been named with some sort of reference to Napoleon III, a well-known card-player of Victorian England.

Nap is more of a gambling than an intellectual game, but you can (if you like) increase the 'think' factor by stripping the pack according to the number of players. Three or four play with a 28-card pack containing nothing lower than the Eights, five with 36 or 40 cards, i.e. respectively Sixes and Fives low.

The cards are shuffled before the first deal, and are cut before each subsequent deal, but are not shuffled again until a player has won a bid of Nap or higher.

Deal five cards each, either one at a time or in batches of three and two, and stack the rest face down.

Each in turn either passes or makes a higher bid than any gone before. A bid is an offer to win at least the number of tricks stated, using a trump suit of the bidder's choice, which is not yet stated. From lowest to highest, the bids are:

Two
Three
Miz (no trump; lose every trick)
Four
Nap (five)
Wellington (five, for doubled score or stakes)
Blücher (five, for redoubled score or stakes).

Wellington may only be called over a previous bid of Nap, and Blücher only over a previous bid of Wellington.

The highest bidder leads to the first trick, and whatever suit he plays is trump, except when playing miz.

The bidder, if successful, wins from each player two, three or four units for the relevant bids, three for miz, 10 for Nap, 20 for Wellington, 40 for Blücher. If unsuccessful, he pays to each opponent the amount he would have won, though penalties are usually halved for lost bids of five.

If a Joker is added, it counts as the highest trump. In miz, it is the only trump: it may only be played when its holder cannot follow suit, and, if led, belongs to whatever suit its holder declares, which must be one in which he is otherwise void.

## ─────────── Oh Hell! ───────────

For 3–7 players

This game bears a faint resemblance to Knockout at first sight, but in practice will be found to require more thought. It first appeared in the 1930s under the name Oh Hell! and has since been recorded under dozens different names – such as Blackout, Jungle Bridge, Botheration, and various bowdlerisations of its original title. At time of writing, it is most often referred to as **Nomination Whist**, which is a pity, as this title more properly denotes an interesting version of Solo. Its principal feature is that of bidding to take an exact number of tricks rather than a minimum number, a concept more thoroughly explored in the game of Ninety-Nine.

Start by appointing a scorekeeper, who will rule up a scoresheet into as many columns as there are players. As in Knockout, a game consists of a number of deals with one card fewer dealt each time, so as to finish on a one-card deal.

Whoever cuts the lowest card starts by dealing all the cards round until everyone has the same number and a smaller number is left over. For example, if seven play, each receives seven cards and three remain. The top card of the undealt batch is faced for trump. If none remain, play at no trump.

The players look at their cards and each in turn, starting with the player at Dealer's left, announces how many tricks he proposes to win. If seven are dealt on the first round, for example, each player bids any number from none to seven. The scorekeeper notes each player's bid in his column on the scoresheet.

In some circles the Dealer, who bids last, is prohibited from bidding a number which would bring the total of bids to the number of tricks played. The purpose of this is to ensure that at least one player will fail. Decide in advance whether or not to follow this rule.

Tricks are played as in Whist.

Scoring varies from school to school. It has become much simplified with the passage of time, but the original schedule is as follows. Each player wins 1 point per trick taken, whether bid or not, and adds a bonus of 10 for fulfilling his bid. In any deal of five or more cards, a bonus of 50 is awarded for bidding and winning every trick played (grand slam) or 25 for bidding and winning all but one trick (small slam).

The winner is the player with the highest score at the end of the last deal, or the first to reach 100 points if this happens sooner.

In some schools the first deal is one card and each subsequent deal is one card more. In others, the number starts low and rises to the maximum, then goes back down to one again – or it starts high and goes down, then goes back up again. Either version is called Up the River, Down the River.

# 21

## —— NINETY-NINE ——

### *The game of the century (almost)*

I invented Ninety-Nine some years ago in response to the need for a three-player trick-taking game which would combine simple rules with strategic depth. British card play has been so long dominated by Whist and Bridge, which are essentially partnership games not satisfactorily adaptable for three, that games for this number have never had a chance to blossom. It is not that strategic three-handers are lacking from the treasury of card games: many major national games of Europe are designed for three, notably Skat in Germany, Preference in Russia, Tarock in Austria, Vira in Sweden, Tyzicha in Ukraine, and Ulti in Hungary; but all are based on card-playing principles foreign to Anglo-American players, and over the centuries have developed so many refinements and complications as to render them indigestible to Westerners brought up on the relatively plain fare of traditional Whist, Bridge and Solo.

Ninety-Nine was first published in *Games & Puzzles* magazine in 1974 and has since found its way into other books of card games, in various languages, suggesting that it did indeed fill a widely perceived gap. The fact that it has been well received by Bridge players, who are notoriously resistant to any other games, is particularly gratifying.

The basic idea of Ninety-Nine is that all three players bid to take a precise number of tricks, neither more nor less. It has the advantage over other bidding games that most hands can be bid in several different ways, and that all three can bid and even win their contracts in every deal, so you do not have to hang around waiting for a good hand to come up before you can bid. In this respect, at least, it beats even Bridge.

Versions of Ninety-Nine for two, four and five players follow the main description.

# Ninety-Nine

*Cards.* Thirty-six plus Joker, ranking normally, i.e. from high to low: A K Q J T 9 8 7 6.

*Order.* Determine seats and right of first deal by any agreed means. All play is clockwise.

*Scoring.* Scores are noted at the end of each round. (A typical score sheet is illustrated.)

*Game.* A game consists of nine rounds and lasts about 45 minutes. Deal passes regularly to the left so that each player deals three times in each game.

*Deal.* Light shuffling is sufficient. Deal twelve each, one at a time, face down.

*Trump.* Deal the last (37th) card face up to one side of the table. The suit of the turn-up establishes trumps for that deal. If the turn-up is the Joker or a Nine, the round is played at no trump. Dealer should clearly announce the trump situation.

*Joker.* The Joker has no independent status, but for the purposes of all play assumes the identity and powers of the turned up card. (Example: if the turn-up is ♣9 then whoever holds the Joker in that round treats it exactly as if it were the ♣9, both for bidding and for playing purposes. He may even, if he wishes, exchange it for the turn-up, though this is disadvantageous as it gives information about one of his cards.)

*Object.* Each player discards three cards face down and plays out the other nine to tricks. His three discards are called 'bid-cards', and by means of a code explained below they are selected to represent any number from nought to nine. This number constitutes his bid. Each player's object is to take *exactly* the number of tricks he has represented by his bidcards – no more, no less.

## Play

*Bidding.* This is the strategic crux of the game. A player can bid anything from nought to nine tricks by discarding three bid cards in accordance with the following code:

Any ♣ discarded means 3 tricks
Any ♡ discarded means 2 tricks
Any ♠ discarded means 1 trick
Any ◇ discarded means 0 tricks

Thus, for example, a player proposing to win three tricks could throw out ♠ ♠ ♠ (1+1+1), or ♡ ♠ ◇ (2+1+0), or ♣ ◇ ◇ (3+0+0). There are three different ways of bidding 3, 4, 5, 6 or 7 tricks, two ways of bidding 2 or 8, and only one of bidding 0 (◇ ◇ ◇) or 9 (♣ ♣ ♣).

The ranks of the bid-cards have no bearing at all on the meaning of the bid; it is only the suit that counts. The Joker, of course, counts as the suit of the turn-up.

Each player, then, selects three bid-cards and places them face down on the table before him. They should be spread slightly to avoid being confused with tricks won during the game. Normally, bids remain secret and are not revealed until the end of the game. But each player has the option of making a premium bid for a higher score, which involves giving certain information about his cards, as follows.

*Premium bids.* There are two premium bids: a declaration and a revelation.

**Figure 17: Ninety-Nine (1)** For ease of remembrance, the number of tricks represented by each suit is related to its shape. Thus a club has three blobs, a heart two cheeks, and a spade one point, while a diamond may be be regarded as a zero with straight sides.

*Declaration.* When a player declares, he turns his bid cards face up before play so that the others know how many tricks he is proposing to win. It will then be more profitable to them to beat him than to succeed in their own bids.

*Revelation.* In a revelation, the bidder not only reveals his bid but also plays with his hand of cards face open on the table.

Each of these bids carries a bonus, which goes to the bidder if he succeeds or to each opponent if he fails.

Only one player may make a premium bid in any round, and priority for doing so starts with the player on dealer's left.

After the bid cards have been laid aside, but before any card is led, each in turn, starting at dealer's left, announces whether or not he will declare or reveal. The first to offer to declare is 'on' but he may be overcalled by a subsequent player offering to play open (revealed). In this case the earlier player had one opportunity to raise his declaration to a revelation and so claim priority.

When a declaration is established, declarer immediately turns his bid-cards face up on the table and leaves them in view throughout the play.

When a revelation is established, revealer immediately turns his bid-cards face up on the table as for a declaration and lays his hand of cards

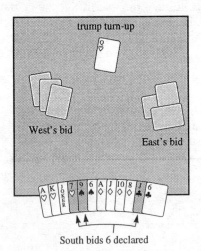

South bids 6 declared

**Figure 18: Ninety-Nine (2)** West dealt and turned the Queen of hearts for trump. South – whose Joker is the Queen of hearts by proxy – bids six ($\heartsuit$ + $\spadesuit$ + $\clubsuit$ = 2+1+3) and rather rashly declares it by laying his bid cards face up. This bid might have worked if South had had the lead and was correct in surmising that neither opponent was aiming to win a trick with a diamond honour.

face up on the table so that all are visible throughout play.

*Tricks.* The first lead is always made by the player left of dealer. Normal rules of trick-taking apply. Follow suit to the card led if possible; if not possible, either trump or discard from side suit. The trick is won by the highest card of the suit led or by the highest trump if any are played. The winner of a trick leads to the next.

*Claims.* When the last trick has gone, any player who has succeeded in his bid must turn his bid-cards face up to prove his entitlement to the full score. Any player who has failed is not obliged to reveal his bid (in fact, it is bad policy to do so).

## Scoring

Each player's score is made up of points for tricks taken, a bonus for succeeding in his bid, and a bonus for any premium bid that may have been made.

*For tricks.* Each player scores 1 point per trick actually taken, regardless of his bid. This may immediately be entered on the sheet, as bonuses are scored in tens and will not affect it. Trick points between the three players will obviously total nine.

*For succeeding.* Each player who succeeds in his bid gets a bonus for doing so, based on the number of players who succeeded in that round. Thus:

| | |
|---|---|
| If all three succeed | 10 each |
| If only two succeed | 20 each |
| If only one succeeds | 30 |

*For premium bids.* In addition to the success bonus, there is a bonus of 30 for a declared bid or 60 for a revealed bid. This bonus goes to the bidder if he succeeds; if he fails, it goes to each opponent, whether or not they also succeeded in their individual bids.

*Examples*

| | A | B | C | A | B | C |
|---|---|---|---|---|---|---|
| Tricks bid: | 4 | 3 | 1 dec. | 4 | 3 | 2 dec. |
| Tricks taken: | 5 | 3 | 1 | 5 | 3 | 1 |
| Success bonus: | – | 20 | 20 | – | 30 | – |
| Premium bonus: | – | – | 30 | 30 | 30 | – |
| Total score: | 5 | 23 | 51 | 35 | 61 | 1 |

*Settlement.* If the game is played for money, each pays to any with a higher score than himself an amount proportional to the difference. But scores are adjusted beforehand as follows: anyone failing to make 100 counts zero; a score in the two hundreds is doubled, in three hundreds trebled, and so on.

## Notes on play

*Approaching the bid.* The whole point of the game is that the cards you use to bid with, when removed, alter the hand you are left to play with. This makes for scope and variety. Almost any hand of cards at Ninety Nine is biddable, since there are ten different numbers of tricks to bid and no fewer than 220 different ways of discarding three cards from twelve. Not all the possibilities make sensible bids, of course, but more often than not you will find yourself confronted with a choice of two or three different bids to make and two or three different ways of expressing each bid. Deciding between them is where the basic strategy of the game comes in. You must be guided by various considerations, such as who has the lead, what suit is trumps (a factor which is more significant to the play of Ninety Nine than of any other card game, and to which we must return), what the other players are likely to bid (observing which cards are lacking from your hand helps here), and, above all, which of your cards are to be regarded as trick winners and which as trick losers.

This is the point at which you must begin to assess the hand. In Ninety Nine, you are required to win an exact number of tricks. This means that you are also required to lose a corresponding number of tricks. Thus a bid to win three tricks is the same as a bid to lose six. It follows that your first task is to classify your cards as probable winners (certain Aces, Kings and trumps), probable losers (Sixes and Sevens), and 'incalculables' – those of middle ranks, and especially Jack, Ten, Nine, any one of which is likely to win a trick when you want it to lose, or lose when you want it to win.

What you must aim to do, therefore, is as far as possible to retain extreme cards (winners and losers) and get rid of incalculables by using them to represent the bid. Choosing between several likely bids will often be controlled by the suits – that is, the bid values – of the cards you can most do without. You must enter the play with a clear idea of the intended destination of each card – which are to win tricks, which are to lose tricks, and which can be switched around from winner to loser or vice versa when something goes wrong.

*Imbalance of suits.* The ascription of values to suits for bidding purposes is unique to Ninety Nine, and it has a correspondingly unique effect on the relative strength in play of the four different suits. The point must be emphasised. In most card games there are a trump suit and three side suits. Apart from the fact that they have different symbols, there is no essential playing difference between one side suit and another. Similarly, one trump suit is as good as another. A game with spades as trumps may score higher than one with clubs (as in Bridge), but this has no effect on those suits' relative strength as trumps once the game is under way. The same does not apply in Ninety Nine. In Ninety Nine, clubs are nearly always a strong suit, and diamonds nearly always weak. Let us see why.

Not surprisingly, the commonest bid is that of three tricks. ('If in doubt, bid three' is a fundamental principle of Ninety Nine.) This can be represented in three different ways: ♠ ♠ ♠ or ♥ ♠ ◇ or ♣ ◇ ◇. From this bid alone it is apparent that spades and diamonds are *more likely* to be laid aside as bid cards than hearts or clubs. Studies from actual games confirm that – again, *on average* – the nine cards missing from the play of tricks comprise:

And there is a slightly greater tendency for diamonds to be out than spades, as zero is the second commonest bid.

It follows that, in play, clubs and hearts tend to be long suits (eight and seven respectively), spades and diamonds short (six and five). Players are more frequently void in diamonds than any other suit, but only rarely void in clubs. In side suits, therefore, given a normal distribution of cards, you can usually expect ♣A ♣K to be trick winners, and probably also ♡A, but ♠A is not certain and ◇A is positively risky, standing the most chance of being trumped.

Similarly, at the opposite extreme, if you have the lead and want to lose it, ♣7 is a much safer card than ◇7 – the latter can so easily be undercut by ◇6 and followed by a discard when the third player is void.

Thus in assessing your hand you are concerned not only with the suit of cards, in deciding which to keep and which to use as bidders, but also with their ranks. The ◇T is from all points of view the likeliest candidate for discarding, as it is the most incalculable rank of the most unreliable suit.

This imbalance of suits also has its effect on trumps. Thus if diamonds are trumps and a player is dealt ♦A K Q he will very often discard them for a certain bid of nought. In which case the player holding ♦J has the top trump and may well be forced to take an unwanted trick with it. Should he therefore count ♦J as a probable winner? Not at all – for an opponent dealt ♦A K Q might equally well keep them in hand and bid at least three.

But at the other extreme of suits, clubs are reliable as trumps. Thus if clubs are trumps and your highest trump is the Jack, you can be pretty certain that it's the fourth highest in play. The upper trumps are unlikely to be out in bids, because they imply bids of high numbers of tricks, for which purpose they would need to be retained!

It follows from the above that premium bids (declarations and revelations) tend to be safer in reliable suits (clubs, hearts) than in the others.

*The Play.* You will normally go into play with cards previously earmarked as winners and losers. Inevitably, you will have one or more of middle ranks or weak suits which are winners or losers – in other words, the incalculables. General procedure for all players is to get the lead as early as possible and lead out the incalculables. If they win you can work out in advance which probable winners you must now reclassify as losers. If they lose, you must perform the opposite calculation.

With incalculables out of the way, or if you have none to start with, begin by making your surest winners other than trumps and then lose the lead. Trumps normally play their role as leads at the end of the around, though of course circumstances occur in which they are better led early on.

Note carefully what cards others are playing. Frequently it is possible to work out what they have bid from what they play; even if not, a great deal of scope exists for playing thwarting tactics.

For example, if one leads ♦7 and the other follows ♦6 you can be sure that neither wants the trick. If void in diamonds it may be better to discard from a side suit than trump, even if you want a trick, solely to discomfit the first player, who probably counted it as a sure loser. On the whole, if you are not sure whether a particular lead means a player wants the trick or not, it generally proves best to let him have it. The fact is – and I offer no explanation for it – that in Ninety Nine players tend to underbid rather than overbid, and therefore more often find themselves trying to lose unwanted strong cards than win with weak ones.

If one player has declared or revealed, it will benefit you to spoil his game (working in collaboration with the other player) rather than make your own bid. If you can do both, of course, so much the better.

*Length of suit.* Long suits are weak; voids are strong. If you can discard so as to void yourself in a suit, you have splendid opportunities for either trumping or losing unwanted cards when that suit is led. Often the desirability of establishing a void is the chief determinant of a suitable bid.

A long suit is bad unless it contains safe low cards. Thus, suppose you hold ♣A Q 9 8 6 when some other suit is trumps. Normally you expect to be dealt three of each suit, given an even distribution. Here you have five. Chances are that an opponent received two or one and succeeded in voiding himself of clubs, thus bidding high and intending to trump. With this danger in mind, it is wise not to regard the Ace as a winner. A much safer procedure is to treat all five as sure *losers* and bid accordingly. This particular holding is quite safe: you can never be forced to take with a club. The situation would be different, however, if the five you held were ♣A Q T 9 8 for now you have neither a sure winner (the Ace may be trumped) nor a sure loser. Leading the Eight would be a sure signal of your intentions, and the others would, on principle, force you to take the trick.

*Premium bids.* For a declared bid you should have extreme cards in at least three suits and a void if possible. Remember that your bid-cards will be revealed, and that opponents can learn something from them. For example, if you bid three with three spades they may assume you have a void in that suit, and will probably refrain from leading it. This could be awkward if you were relying on the void as a means of making your trumps or losing some risky cards.

In order to reveal, you must be absolutely certain of the future destination of every card in your hand. Extreme cards or voids are necessary in every suit.

*Unbiddable hands.* Some hands look unbiddable at first sight. And they may so be, in the sense that you need the same cards for bidding as for making the tricks you bid. For example (with the trump suit quoted first):

$$\diamond A6 \quad \clubsuit J \, T \quad \heartsuit K \, J \, 9 \, 7 \, 6 \quad \spadesuit Q \, T \, 7$$

Here the only sensible bid, of one trick, can only be made by throwing out the very card ($\diamond$A) needed to make it with. Two can be bid, by throwing two spades and $\diamond$6, but the chance of taking a heart trick is slender indeed.

In this example, it is impossible to make a 'sensible' bid, i.e. one that you can be sure of fulfilling. What you do instead is adopt the Technique of the Meaningless Bid (TOMB for short), which involves throwing out bid cards solely for the surprise value of their absence from play. In this case the throw-outs are ◇A and both clubs. The chances of making six tricks are remote, but the likelihood of spoiling your opponent's bids is most promising. See the first player's surprise when you trump his ♣A with ◇6, and the second player's astonishment when he finds you out of trumps and is forced to take with ◇7!

Fortunately, few hands are completely unbiddable in this way, and it is better to avoid the meaingless bid. But laying aside a card for its surprise absence is always good tactics. Strong Aces and high trumps are ideal candidates for this practice.

## Sample Game

*First deal.* Charlie deals. The turn-up is ♠8. As Charlie is dealt the Joker we simply record it as ♠8, as it has no other power.

| Abel | ♠A J T ◇J 9 ♣Q T 8 6 ♡K Q 7 |
| Baker | ♠K 7 6 ◇K T 6 ♣A J 7 ♡A 9 8 |
| Charlie | ♠Q 9 8 ◇A Q 8 7 ♣K 9 ♡J T 6 |

A fairly even distribution. Abel has no difficulty in assessing hearts as one trick and clubs as none. Spades is an unreliable trump suit and there is a chance that both monarchs are out in bids, leaving his ♠J T high after the Ace. He bids three, discarding ♣Q, ◇J, ◇9 and thus voiding himself in his most awkward suit.

Baker's hand is tricky. There seem to be three winners (Aces and ♠K) and four losers (Sixes and Sevens), giving a sensible bidding range of three to five tricks. One possibility is to discard ♣J, getting rid of a problematical middling card, together with the two high diamonds for a bid of three. This leaves ♡9, ♡8 as nasty incalculables, for when the Ace is gone a low lead from another player could mean disaster. Another possibility is to discard ♡9, ♡8, ◇T for a bid of four. This relieves him of the problematical hearts and calls for a fourth trick from either the guarded ◇K or a low trump to a heart lead after the Ace has gone, In the event, Baker goes for a 'surprise' bid, throwing out his three spades for a bid of three and putting his trust in his three high cards.

Charlie's hand looks most unpromising at first sight, containing middling ranks, especially in the unreliable trump suit. The only sure loser is ♡6, and the nearest approach to a winner is ♣K. His most sensible bid is two, discarding ♡J, ◇A, ◇Q and intending to win with ♣K and ♠Q.

Abel leads. (winners in bold.)

| A | B | C | |
|---|---|---|---|
| ♡ K | ♡ **A** | ♡ T | Abel forces out the Ace and gets rid of an unwanted high card. |
| ♣ T | ♣**A** | ♣ 9 | |
| ♣ 6 | ◇**T** | ◇ 8 | |
| ♣ 8 | ◇ 6 | ◇**7** | Charlie wins with an unplanned card. He must now revise his tactics and count ♣K as a loser instead of a winner. |
| ♡**Q** | ♡ 9 | ♡ 6 | Abel makes with one of his planned winners. |
| ♡ 7 | ♡**8** | ♣ K | Baker takes an unwanted trick, but Charlie succeeds in losing his now unwanted King. |
| ♠J | ♣ 7 | ♠ 9 | |
| ♠ T | ♣ J | ♠**Q** | |
| ♠**A** | ◇ K | ♠ 8 | |
| 3 | 4 | 2 | Tricks |
| 20 | | 20 | Success bonus |
| 23 | 4 | 22 | |

Obviously, players will not all succeed if their bids do not total nine.
*Second deal.* Abel deals; hearts are trumps.

| Abel | ♡J T 9 ◇Q 8 7 ♣Q 7 6 ♠A Q 8 |
|---|---|
| Baker | ♡8 6 ♠A K J T ◇K 9 ♣K T 9 7 |
| Charlie | ♡A K Q 7 ♠9 6 ◇A J T 8 ♣J 6 |

Abel has awkward trumps and clubs. He would like to keep losers in weak suits, but cannot bid four. Instead, he voids spades for a bid of three.

Baker has two long suits – a decided weakness. He discards ♡6 and voids diamonds for a bid of two.

Charlie, however, has what appears to be an astonishingly good hand. Running down his hearts and diamonds will almost certainly give him eight tricks, though he can't bid it. In any case, he must retain ♣6 as a sure loser. Discarding ♡7, ♣J, ♠9 for a bid of six, Charlie declares and reveals his bid-cards. Baker leads.

| A | B | C | |
|---|---|---|---|
| ♡ 9 | ♠ K | ♠ 6 | Baker really wanted the trick – he only played King as a cover-up |
| ♣ A | ♣ T | ♣ 6 | Charlie now plans to lose the third trick and take the remainder. |
| ♣ Q | ♣ K | ◇ 8 | |
| ♣ 8 | ♠ A | ♡ Q | As Charlie planned. Now to run through his red suits. |
| ♡ T | ♡ 6 | ♡ A | |
| ♡ J | ♣ 7 | ♡ K | |
| ◇ 7 | ♣ 9 | ◇ A | |
| ◇ 6 | ♠ J | ◇ J | |
| ◇ Q! | ♠ T | ◇ T | Pipped at the post. |

| | | | |
|---|---|---|---|
| 3 | 1 | 5 | Tricks |
| 30 | | | Success bonus |
| 30 | 30 | | Premium bonus (C declared, failed) |
| 63 | 31 | 5 | Score |
| 23 | 4 | 22 | Previous total |
| 86 | 35 | 27 | Current total |

It was unfortunate for Charlie that Abel had a guarded Queen and wanted her to win. The declaration was sound in principle.

*Third deal.* Baker deals; diamonds are trump.

| Abel | ◇ 8 6 ♣ A K Q 8 6 ♡ K Q 7 ♠ J T |
|---|---|
| Baker | ◇ A T 9 7 ♣ J T ♡ A J T 9 ♠ A Q |
| Charlie | ◇ K Q J ♣ 9 7 ♡ 8 6 ♠ K 9 8 7 6 |

Abel correctly counts all his clubs as losers, but one trick must be taken as he cannot bid lower. He discards ♠ J, ♠ T, ◇ 8. The intention is to make one trick with a high heart and the other with either the second high heart or by trumping a spade.

Baker can guess from his card distribution that the others will be making low bids. He must therefore bid high, though that gap in diamonds could be awkward. He discards ♣ J, ♣ T, ♠ Q, for a bid of seven, intending to lose two hearts.

Charlie has an obvious bid: all diamonds out for a bid of nought. Despite (or perhaps because of) his defeated declaration in the previous round he decides to make a premium bid of it, and has little hesitation in offering to reveal.

| A | B | C | |
|---|---|---|---|
| ♡7 | ♡A | ♥ 8 | Charlie leads his safest suit. |
| ♡K | ♡9 | ♡ 6 | Baker, void in clubs, returns the lead to Abel, hoping that his temporary partner can lead the lowest club. |
| ♣6 | ♡T | ♣9 | He does, and Charlie goes down. Now Abel and Baker can concentrate on their own bids. |
| ♣A | ◇7 | ♣7 | |
| ◇6 | ◇A | ♠ 6 | |
| ♣8 | ◇T | ♠ 7 | |
| ♣Q | ◇9 | ♠ 8 | |
| ♡Q | ◇A | ♠ 9 | Abel and Baker both want the last trick. Baker must decide whether Abel's last card is more likely to be a club or a heart. |
| ♣K | ♡A | ♠ K | Wrong! Abel should have discarded the club and won the last trick with the Queen. |

| | | | |
|---|---|---|---|
| 1 | 7 | 1 | Tricks |
| 0 | 30 | 0 | Success bonus |
| 60 | 60 | 0 | Premium bonus |
| 61 | 97 | 1 | Score |
| 86 | 35 | 27 | Previous total |
| 147 | 132 | 28 | Current total |

### Ninety-Nine for two

There are two ways of adapting Ninety-Nine for two. The simpler is to strip the pack to 24 cards plus Joker by removing cards below Nine. The bonus for success is 20 if one player succeeds, or 10 if both. Only one player may declare, non-dealer having first choice, and the bonus for this is 20 to the declarer if successful or to his opponent if not. The game ends when a player fulfils his contract and thereby reaches a score of 100 or more. It is not sufficient to reach 100 on tricks alone or by beating a declaration.

The better version is **Dummy Ninety-Nine**. The dummy counts as a third player and can even, in theory, 'win' a bid, though this is incidental to the main point of the contest.

Use a 36-card pack plus Joker and deal three hands in the usual way, first to the live player, then to dummy, then to oneself, and so on. Dummy's last three cards are dealt face down to one side to represent its bid. These remain unseen until end of play.

Each live player bids in the usual way, and may declare but may not reveal.

Before play begins, Dealer turns up Dummy's cards, sorts them into suits and ranks and lays them face up on the table for ease of access by both players.

Non-dealer leads to the first trick, Dealer plays second, and non-dealer plays third from dummy. Whoever wins the trick places it in front of himself if he won it in hand or in front of the dummy if he won it in dummy. He then leads from whichever hand won the trick, waits for his opponent to play second, then plays third from the remaining hand. This continues until all nine tricks have been played and won.

Dummy's bid is then turned up and compared with the number of tricks it took, as though it were a third live player. Each live player, and dummy too, scores exactly as in the three-hand game: 1 point per trick won, 30 if the only player to succeed, 20 if one of two to succeed and 10 if one of three, plus 30 for a successful declaration or 30 for beating one.

## Ninety-Nine for four

Use a 52-card pack plus Joker and deal 13 cards each. Bids are made by means of three discards in the usual way. Since 10 tricks are to be played, 10 may be bid by discarding three diamonds. This also stands for a bid of none, but, of course, there cannot possibly be any confusion between the two. Indeed, a player who declares or reveals a bid of three diamonds need not specify which he intends, and will win if he fulfils either contract.

The bonus for fulfilling one's bid is 30 if the only player to do so, 20 if one of two, or 10 if one of three. No such bonus applies if all four either succeed or fail. Declarations and revelations carry their usual bonuses of 30 and 60 respectively.

## Ninety-Nine for five

This is best played with the 60-card Australian '500' pack – ignoring the red Thirteens – obtainable from any good card dealer. Deal 12 each and bid in the usual way. There is no bonus if all five succeed or fail, but a bonus of 10 applies to each of four who succeed, 20 to each of three, 30 to each of two, and 50 for a lone success. Declarations and revelations count 30 and 60 as usual.

If using a 52-card pack, deal 10 each and turn the last two face up. If these are of different suits, the trump is that of the higher-ranking card, or, if equal, of the higher-ranking suit (clubs high, diamonds low). If both are of the same suit, play at no trump.

Bid from 0 to 8 tricks by discarding two bid-cards. The combination ◇◇ represents nought or eight tricks, and ◇♠ one or seven.

# 22

## —— FIVE HUNDRED ——

### *The whizz game from Oz*

Five Hundred, devised around the turn of the 20th century as a cross between Euchre and Bid Whist, is a good game for three. It is also a good game for two, four, five and six. Though invented in the USA and originally copyrighted by the American Playing Card Company, it never withstood the competition of its contemporary, Auction Bridge, and soon died out almost everywhere except in Australia. Euchre had always been popular here, and this improvement of it has resulted in its becoming the Australians' national card game, and so remaining to this day.

Five Hundred involves tricks and bidding. It was originally played as a three-hander with the 32-card Euchre pack plus Joker, each player receiving 10 cards and three being laid aside as a widow. As this basic format applies regardless of the number of players, it follows that four play with 43 cards, five with 53, and six with 63. For the latter purpose, the Australian '500' pack contains 10 extra cards in the form of Elevens and Twelves in each suit, and Thirteens in hearts and diamonds, plus one Joker in the form of a kookaburra. It is possible to obtain genuine '500' packs in this country through specialist dealers such as Somerville of Edinburgh, and they are well worth having if you like tinkering about with card games for peculiar numbers of players such as five and six.

However, they are not absolutely essential to your enjoyment of Five Hundred, as I am told by the natives that very few people bother to play the game six up – that it is, indeed, most often encountered as a four-player partnership game. For the purpose of description, I will start with the original three-hander, and append notes on versions for other numbers of players.

As noted in the chapter on Euchre, 'bower' rhymes with 'power' and derives from a German word for Jack.

## Five Hundred for three

*Cards*. Thirty-three, consisting of one Joker plus A K Q J T 9 8 7 in each suit.

*Game*. Scores are accumulated at the end of each deal. They may be plus or minus and it is possible for a score to sink below zero. The game ends when one or more players reach 500 points, either plus or (more rarely) minus, and the winner is the player with the highest score.

*Deal*. The turn to deal and play pass to the left. Deal in batches as follows: three to each player, three face down to the table, four to each player, then three again all around so that each player has 10 cards. The undealt cards form the 'kitty'.

*Object*. The highest bidder takes the kitty, discards three in its place, and aims to win at least as many tricks as he bid after declaring a trump suit or no trump. A player may also bid misère, i.e. to lose every trick playing at no trump. Opponents also score for any tricks they take individually.

*Rank of cards*. When there is a trump suit, cards rank from high to low as follows:

Joker (best bower)
Jack of trumps (right bower)
Other Jack of same colour as trumps (left bower)
A K Q (J) T 9 8 7 in each suit (except where Jack promoted).

Note that the left bower is the third highest card of the trump suit and does not belong to the suit marked on its face. The trump suit is therefore one card longer (nine) than plain suits of the opposite colour (eight each), while the suit of the same colour as trumps is one card short (seven).

In a so-called no-trump game, all Jacks revert to their normal position between Ten and Queen, and the Joker is the only trump.

*Auction*. Starting with the player at Dealer's left, each in turn must pass or make a higher bid than any gone before. Passing does not prevent a player from bidding again later (it did originally, but modern players have dropped this restriction), except when two players pass in succession, when the last-named bid becomes the contract and its bidder the declarer. If all pass without bidding the game is played at no trump and each player aims to win as many tricks as possible.

The lowest bid is 'six spades', i.e. an offer to win at least six tricks with spades as trump. This can be overcalled by bidding six in a higher suit, for which purpose they rank spades, clubs, diamonds, hearts, no trumps (or 'no-ies'), or by increasing the number of tricks. Alternatively, bids may be made by announcing their scoring values as shown in the table. Thus a bid of 'six spades' may be announced simply as '40'.

| Bid = | 6 | 7 | 8 | 9 | 10 |
|---|---|---|---|---|---|
| ♠ spades | 40 | 140 | 240 | 340 | 440 |
| ♣ clubs | 60 | 160 | 260 | 360 | 460 |
| ◇ diamonds | 80 | 180 | 280 | 380 | 480 |
| ♡ hearts | 100 | 200 | 300 | 400 | 500 |
| No trump | 120 | 220 | 320 | 420 | 520 |
| Misère | 250, | | 520 | exposed | |

Misère is a bid to lose every trick, playing at no trump. Although it counts 250, it is overcalled by any bid of eight or more tricks, including eight spades for 240. Open misère, played with Declarer's cards face up on the table, overcalls everything, including the equally valued ten no trump.

*Kitty.* Unless everybody passed without bidding, in which case the kitty is left out of play face down and untouched, the highest bidder takes the kitty and adds it to his hand without showing it. He then throws out any three cards face down in its place.

*Play.* The opening lead is made by Declarer, or, if all passed without bidding, by the player at Dealer's left. If playing open misère, Declarer lays cards face up on the table before leading.

Suit must be followed if possible, otherwise any card may be played. A trick is taken by the highest card of the suit led or by the highest trump if any are played. The winner of each trick leads to the next. Each player stores his won tricks separately from everyone else's.

In any no-trump contract, including misère, the Joker is a trump and belongs to no suit of its own. Its holder may not play it if able to follow suit to the card led. If he leads it, he names a suit which others are required to follow if possible. This must not be one in which he has already shown himself void.

*Score.* Declarer, if successful, scores the value of his contract. For winning all 10 tricks he scores this or 250, whichever is the greater. If unsuccessful, he deducts the value of his contract from his current total. Each opponent scores 10 for each trick he took individually, or, in a failed misère, 10 for each trick taken by Declarer. (Misères must therefore be played through to the bitter end.) If all passed without bidding, each player scores 10 per trick won.

The winner is the player with the highest score when someone reaches 500 points plus or minus. If two or more players reach 500 simultaneously, and one of them is the Declarer, Declarer wins the game.

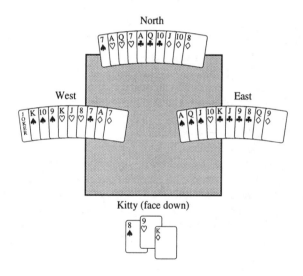

North

West          East

Kitty (face down)

**Figure 19: Five Hundred** West dealt. North has one bower (◇J) but nothing to bid. East has the black bowers and bids six clubs. West has the best and heart bowers, and overcalls six hearts. He takes the kitty and discards his Sevens and the lowest spade, leaving himself with five trumps, two solid diamonds, and a void in clubs. He makes his 100 points despite the adverse 4–1 break in trumps (North's are headed by the left bower and Ace), by leading his two bowers, cashing his two diamonds, and playing a third round of trumps. He trumps the club return for a fifth trick, and then leads low in spades. His sixth will come from trumping another club lead or forcing North's excess trump out with a spade.

## Notes on play

*General.* The first thing to be aware of in Five Hundred, if you are already used to other trick-taking games with bidding, is that of the thirty cards in play no fewer than ten are trumps – that is, one-third of the pack as opposed to only one-quarter in other games. Usually, five or six of the ten tricks are won by a trump (whether to a trump or a plain suit lead).

*Assessing the hand.* We may first dismiss No Trump hands as somewhat exceptional. A solidly reliable no trumper does not often appear, and can hardly be missed when it does. Certainly you should not attempt it without the Joker, as that is the one and only way of getting back into a suit in which you have a high gap. You will need strength in all four suits besides, since once you allow someone else to establish their suit your good cards will simply be whisked out of your hand before you get back in.

There being ten trumps and only two 'sides' to the game – you versus them – it follows that your minimum requirement is five trumps, together with strength in at least one other suit, in order to establish your 'book' of five tricks (i.e. the basis on which your actual bid must be built). A bid may be considered if you have only four trumps, provided that at least two are in the top three. And don't forget that the top three are the Joker and the bowers: Ace of trumps is only the fourth highest card.

Strength in side suits means at least an Ace or a high-guarded King. The high guard (Queen, or either Jack or Ten depending on the bower situation) is necessary for you to be able to make the King by leading from below and forcing out the Ace. A side suit headed by a guarded Queen is almost certain not to make a trick; in any case, the three cards involved in a guarded Queen are more strongly employed by being discarded to form a void. Which brings us to the second indicator of strength in a side suit, namely, a void or the possibility of creating one by means of the discard. Finally, a long side suit, one with four or more cards, is a particularly desirable feature.

*The kitty.* The primary purpose of exchanging through the kitty is to improve the balance (or imbalance) of your suits by creating a void and/or a long suit – it is not, as the beginner might assume, to furnish the Declarer with one or more winning cards. This is not to say that it will contribute nothing useful to the hand – you can often rely upon it to produce an extra trick if you are already sure of seven, and perhaps two if you are sure of six. But the important thing is not to rely on it to provide a single specific card (such as the Joker) without which a risky bid may be lost as a foregone conclusion. Holding four of a suit, the chances of finding a fifth in the widow are 5 to 3 in favour; holding five, the chances of finding a sixth drop to 5 to 4.

*Bidding.* The bidding procedure of Five Hundred allows no room for manoeuvre. With most hands you will have only one potential trump suit; only occasionally will you have the luxury of switching to another suit in order to overcall on the same number of tricks. Furthermore, once you have made your bid you must lie on it – you can't increase it for a higher score. If, therefore, you have a probable eight hearts don't bother to sneak up on it by starting at six. That being the highest suit, neither of the others may wish to raise you to seven, in which event they will pass and leave you to make a certain 100 instead of a probable 300. You must start by bidding the highest you dare, and know in advance whether or not you will allow yourself to be forced up.

Note carefully what the others bid, as this can give you a good idea not only of their strong suits but also of the distribution of the Joker and Bowers.

*Discarding* rarely presents problems. Retain all trumps, consecutive top cards, and a suit of four or more – in that order. Create a void if possible. (Don't let your discard physically get in the way of your won tricks – beginners have been known to miscount it as a trick and then fall short in the final reckoning! To be on the safe side, spread the discards to form a small fan, and put it out of reach.)

*The play.* The usual pattern is that Declarer leads into trumps in order to draw his opponents' teeth so that he can later succeed in establishing a long suit of four or more. If you have no long suit, you will gain greater control over potential trick-winners in other suits by letting the player on your left gain the lead rather than his partner. In other words, if not leading, your best position is playing third to a trick. At No Trump, lead from your longest rather than your strongest suit, and return to it whenever possible.

As an opponent of the Declarer, your primary objective is normally to defeat his contract rather than make tricks of your own. (Unusually, you might find yourself playing to the score. Thus, if Declarer is unable to make game – i.e. reach 500 pts. – on succeeding at his contract, but your temporary partner is not only well ahead of you but also only ten or twenty points off target, you will obviously prefer to prevent your partner from taking tricks wherever possible.)

When Declarer leads trumps, prefer to play low if your partner will win the trick, since Declarer's chief preoccupation is to leave himself with all the highest trumps in play. Indeed, you can nearly always afford to undercut his lead as second player if it is obvious that Declarer is trying to force out a higher trump which, since it isn't in your own hand, must be in your partner's. For example, suppose your partner made a bid in spades before Declarer established his contract of (say) seven Clubs. Declarer leads ♠K and you have ♠A but nothing higher. You might now, as second player, drop your next to useless ♠7 and leave the trick to be taken by your partner. The fact that Declarer led a middling trump means he is trying to force out something higher; the fact that your partner bid Spades implies that he must have at least one Joker and two black Bowers. And the fact that you let your partner have it means that Declarer will be playing second to the next trick and you third. All of which is very good – for the partners.

When leading, generally try to avoid opening up new suits, and stick by preference to your own longest or strongest. Once Declarer has shown a void, however, the partners should lead into it as hard as possible in order to force him to waste trumps.

## Sample game

[Jo = Joker]

| | | |
|---|---|---|
| Abel | ♠7 ♡A T 7 ♣K T 8 7 ◇J T | |
| Baker | ♠K J 9 8 ♡K 9 ♣J 9 ◇9 7 | |
| Charlie | Jo ♠Q T ♡Q 8 ♣A ◇A K 8 | |

Abel's clubs are long but hopeless – lacking Joker and either black Bower he has no bid here. Neither do his ♡A and potential Left Bower (◇J) justify the bid of hearts he actually is foolhardy enough to make.

Baker is strong in spades, with both Bowers, but has weak supporting cards in side suits. A niggardly kitty would ruin his game.

Charlie's good diamond suit (counting the Left Bower, ♡J) is better supported on the side by his clubs.

The bidding goes: Abel 6♡ (bluffing!), Baker 7♠, Charlie 7◇. Abel and Baker pass. Charlie draws from the kitty ♣Q ◇Q ♡A – a good draw, increasing his trumps and adding a side-suit Ace. He discards ♡Q, ♡8, ♠T to create a void in hearts. His hand is good, and probably worth eight tricks, instead of the seven he bid, should the four other trumps lie evenly. Charlie, as Declarer, leads. (Winning cards in **bold**.)

| A | B | C | |
|---|---|---|---|
| ◇T | ◇7 | **Jo** | |
| ◇J | ◇9 | ♡J | They did lie evenly, and the game is assured. |
| ♠7 | ♠8 | **♠A** | |

| | | | |
|---|---|---|---|
| ♣7 | ♠K | ♠Q | |
| ♡7 | ♡K | ◇8 | |
| ♣8 | ♣9 | ♣A | |
| ♡A | ♡9 | ◇A | |
| ♡T | ♠9 | ◇K | |
| ♣T | ♣J | ◇Q | |
| ♣K | ♠J | ♣Q | |
| 1 | 1 | 8 | Tricks |
| 10 | 10 | 180 | Score (contract only seven) |

Having assured himself of success at trick two, Charlie continued somewhat deviously, perhaps amusing himself by trying to make nine tricks. Such showing off can sometimes have disastrous consequences.

## Five Hundred for 2–6 players

The cards used for each number of players, in addition to the Joker, are as follows:

*Two players*: 24, namely A K Q J T 9 of each suit.

*Four players*: 42, consisting of A K Q J T 9 8 7 6 5 in each suit, plus the two red Fours.

*Five players*: The standard 52-card pack.

*Six players*: The full Australian '500' pack, with Elevens and Twelves in all four suits, and Thirteens in red suits only, these additional cards ranking immediately above the Tens.

Four and six players play in respectively two or three partnerships, the members of each partnership sitting opposite each other. For example, if six play, then, designating the three partnerships A, B, C, the rotation of players around the table is A-B-C-A-B-C.

In all partnership versions, it is only the declarer who takes the kitty and discards in its place. In serious four-hand partnership play it is common to omit the Joker and make only a two-card kitty.

Five play on an 'optional call' basis, that is, after taking the kitty and discarding, the declarer must either announce that he is playing alone against four, or else call for a partner by naming a card not in his own hand. Whoever holds that card becomes Declarer's partner and identifies himself immediately. The plus or minus score made by the partnership is ascribed equally to both members of it.

There is no reason why four should not also play on the optional call basis.

# 23

## —— PREFERENCE ——

### *The game of Russian intelligence*

Preference has been the national card game of the Russian educated classes for 200 years. Like many European national games, it is usually played by four at a table but involves only three active players at each deal, one of whom undertakes to win a minimum number of tricks by playing alone against the other two. Although its name is French (it should properly be written *Préférence*), I can find no historical evidence for the usual claim that it is of French origin. As the earliest description of it appears in a German book of 1802, and the game is still much played in Austria, its French connections more probably reflect the attachment to French language and culture of the Russian aristocracy of the time.

For many years the game has only been known to Western players in its Austrian form, of which a highly simplified account has long been perpetuated in American card game books. With the fall of the Iron Curtain, however, increasing cultural contacts between East and West have produced several descriptions of the game in English, notably by members of the International Playing-Card Society. The description which follows is based on an article in the Society's Journal of May 1992 by Dr Anthony Smith, to whom I am greatly indebted for his prompt and patient response to numerous requests for elucidation and revision.

If Preference looks more daunting than it really is to play, this is chiefly because of its extremely complicated scoring system, which shows all the signs of having undergone refinements and variations over a long period of time in a vast area where each centre of play is a law to itself. For this reason, and because I lack experience of the game, I cannot here offer more than a bare description of the rules of play. Space alone would preclude the addition of sample games and notes on strategy, even if I were competent to prepare them. It may be asked whether Preference should appear at all in a book not primarily aimed at experienced card-players. I hope I am right in thinking that it will be more useful for the general literature of card games to ensure that it appears in the more generally accessible format of a book as well as in the pages of a learned periodical of limited circulation. Perhaps it will encourage adventurous card-players to start exploring this fascinating and exotic game.

It must be emphasised that Preference is played in many local forms and varieties, of which the version described below is but one.

*Players*. There are three active players, but often four at a table, each in turn sitting out the hand to which he deals.

*Cards*. 32, ranking A–K–Q–J–T–9–8–7 in each suit.

*General idea*. In each deal, the highest bidder plays alone against the other two in a contract either to win from six to ten tricks with or without a trump suit of his own choosing, or to lose every trick at no trump. In low-level positive contracts, the opponents must win a quota of tricks to escape penalty, but may evade penalty by declining to play. If both decline, the declarer wins without play.

*Scoresheet*. Each player records wins and losses on a scoresheet illustrated in Figure 20, the purpose of which is to reproduce the effect of cash payments between individual players without burdening the table with myriads of coins or counters. It consists of two concentric squares diagonally sectioned into triangular quadrants. Within a circle drawn around the central point is written an agreed target number of points for the game, typically 10 or a multiple of 10. Player's names are written around the outer square in reflection of their relative positions at the table, one quadrant being ignored if only three play. Each player's quadrant consists of three parts as follows:

The inmost section, or *hole*, chiefly records penalty points exacted when the player, as declarer, fails a contract.

The middle section, or *pool*, records scoring points that accrue when the player, as declarer, fulfils a contract. The game ends when everyone has reached the target score (e.g. 10) recorded in this section of his quadrant.

The outer section, or *side*, records incidental credits due to him 'on

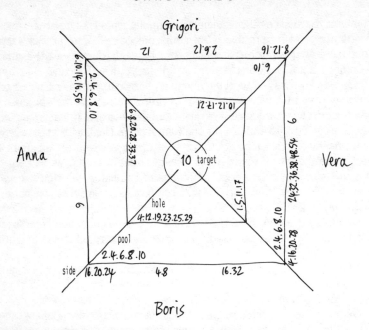

**Figure 20: Preference** A scoresheet from the viewpoint of Boris, one of four players. (Words in brackets are not actually written on the sheet.) In the centre is the target score, 10. The game ends when everyone has reached this target in their *pool* scoring area. Each row of numbers is a cumulative series, the one at the right being that player's current total. Thus Boris has reached 10 by making five scores of 2 each, some of which may have been 'donated' by opponents who have scored in excess of 10, in return for points recorded by them 'on the side' against Boris. Pool scores only record the progress of the game. They do not figure in the settlement, which is calculated from side scores and hole scores.

*Side scores* are reckoned first. These are scores made 'on the side' by each player against each opponent. Here, Boris has 24 against Anna, 8 against Grigori, and 32 against Vera, total 64; and against him Anna has 6, Grigori 12, and Vera 28, total 46. This leaves Boris 18 up (64−46). Similar computations leave Anna 28 down, Grigori 30 down, and Vera 40 up.

*Hole scores* (penalty points) are then taken into account. Boris has 29 against him, Anna 37, Grigori 21, Vera 17. The total is 104 and the average 26. Each player counts 10 times the difference between the average and his or her individual total. This puts Boris and Anna respectively 30 and 110 down, and Grigori and Vera respectively 50 and 90 up.

The final scores are therefore as follows:

|       | Boris | Anna | Grigori | Vera |
|-------|-------|------|---------|------|
| Side  | +18   | −28  | −30     | +40  |
| Hole  | −30   | −110 | +50     | +90  |
| Total | −12   | −138 | +20     | +130 |

the side' from each other player. Credits due from his left-hand opponent are recorded from the outer left corner, those from his right-hand opponent towards the outer right corner, and those from the other player (if four play) in the centre. In the final settlement, one hole point will be found equivalent to (the loss of) 10 points made on the side.

(Note: The respective Russian words are *gorka*, 'heap', *pool'ka*, 'pool', and *veest*, literally 'Whist', i.e. trick-play. The terms given above are not translations, but my suggestions for descriptive equivalents.)

*Deal.* Highest cut confers the first deal. The turn to deal passes to the left – except after a passed-out deal or a failed misère (a no-trump bid to lose every trick) – as does the turn to bid and play. The dealer, after shuffling and having the cards cut from the right, deals 10 cards, two at a time, to each active player, i.e. none to himself if four play. At any stage in the deal, the two excess cards are dealt face down to the table as a *talon*.

*Auction.* The possible bids are, from lowest to highest: six spades, six clubs, six diamonds, six hearts, then seven, eight and nine of these suits in the same order, then misère, and finally ten spades, clubs, diamonds, hearts. (The suits are usually designated respectively first, second, third and fourth preference. For example, the lowest bid is 'six of the first', the highest 'ten of the fourth'.) The highest bidder becomes the declarer, takes the talon, makes any two discards, and names his final contract, which may be higher than the one bid.

Forehand, the player at dealer's left, speaks first. He alone has the privilege of starting the auction with 'Six in the dark', which he may only do if he has not yet looked at his cards. Though risky, it is equivalent to the lowest possible bid of 'six spades' and has a pre-emptive value in that it may not be overcalled by anything less than *seven clubs*.

If he does not bid 'in the dark', he must either pass or make a normal bid. Each in turn must then either bid higher or pass. Jump-bidding is allowed. A player having passed may not come in again. When two pass in succession, the last to bid becomes the Declarer. If all three pass immediately, a special game called *raspasi* is played as follows.

*Raspasi.* There is no trump and the aim is to avoid winning tricks. Forehand turns the top card of the talon and leads a card of that suit to the first trick. Suit must be followed if possible. Whoever wins the trick adds the turned card to it, turns the second card of the talon, and leads a card of its suit to the second trick. Thereafter, the winner of each trick is free to lead any card to the next. After ten tricks, each player records in his 'hole' a penalty of 1 point for each trick he has won. If two *raspasi* are played in succession, the second is scored at

2 per trick; if three, the third at 3 per trick; and so on indefinitely. The deal immediately following any *raspasi* is always made by the same dealer – it does not pass to the next player, no matter how many *raspasi* are played in succession, and regardless of whether there are three or four players at the table.

*Announcements*. The declarer exposes the two cards of the talon for all to see, adds them to his hand, and makes any two discards face down in their place. In the light of his revised hand, he then either confirms his bid or announces any higher contract. He may, for example, offer the same number of tricks in a higher-ranking suit or at no trump, or a higher number of tricks in any suit or at no trump, or misère if he originally bid nine or less, or ten tricks if he originally bid misère. Note that final contracts are valid at no trump even though they may not be bid in the auction.

*Conditions of play*. Various conditions and procedures apply to particular contracts as follows.

*Declarer*. If Declarer contracts to win six or seven tricks, and can subsequently be shown (by post mortem) to have had a certain eight or nine, he will be penalised for undercontracting.

*Opponents*. In a contract of six, seven or eight, the opponents are obliged (unless they concede defeat without play) to win a collective quota of, respectively, four, two, or one trick between them in order to avoid penalty. If they fail in this, penalty will be exacted on either opponent who fails to meet an individual quota of two tricks in a six contract, or one trick in a contract of seven or eight. No such obligation attaches to higher contracts.

*Misère*. Declarer must tell his opponents what his 12 cards are, but need not say which two he discarded. The opponents are allowed to write this information down before the first trick is led. All ten tricks must be played, as the Declarer's penalty for failure depends on how many he takes.

After a failed misère, the deal does not pass round but remains with the same player.

*Slam (ten tricks)*. All three players lay their hands of cards face up on the table before the first trick is led. The defending partners may consult with each other about their play.

*Play or pass*. Each opponent, starting with the one at Declarer's left, now states whether he will 'play' or 'pass' (sit out) – unless the contract is six spades, when both must play. A particular incentive for passing a contract of six, seven or eight is the fear of incurring penalty for failing to fulfil one's required quota of tricks.

If both 'pass', the Declarer wins by default. If both 'play' – a situation

I will refer to as 'collaborating' – each stores his own won tricks separately.

If only one passes, he nevertheless actually plays, but can neither win nor lose points, all relevant scores or penalties being ascribed to the partner who said 'play'. The latter – whom I will refer to as the 'governor' – keeps and may score for all tricks won by both partners. In this situation, the partners have the option of playing 'in the open', i.e. with their hands of cards exposed on the table and with consultation permitted, the final decision resting with the governor. This option must be exercised before either of them plays a card; but, if Declarer has first lead, they may wait to see it before deciding.

*Play.* Forehand leads to the first trick. Players must follow suit if possible, otherwise must play a trump if possible. The trick is taken by the highest card of the suit led or by the highest trump if any are played, and the winner of each trick leads to the next.

*Score.* The score for *raspasi* (when all pass) has already been described. All other scores are based on the value of the contract as follows:

| Six | = | 2 | Nine | = | 8 |
|-----|---|---|------|---|---|
| Seven | = | 4 | Misère | = | 10 |
| Eight | = | 6 | Ten | = | 10 |

*Declarer, if successful*, scores in his pool the game value of his contract. This also applies if he won by default, his opponents having conceded without play. But it does not apply if, in a contract of six or seven, he can be shown by post mortem to have been able with complete safety to call eight or nine respectively. In this case he is penalised for underbidding to the tune of 10 penalty points 'in the hole'.

If the contract was for six, seven or eight, and the partners played but failed to win their collective quota of four, two or one trick respectively, Declarer scores 'on the side' against any opponent who failed to fulfil his individual quota of tricks, i.e. two in a six contract, otherwise one. The score so made is equivalent to the game value of the contract for each trick by which that partner fell short of his individual quota. If one partner passed, Declarer scores against the Governor alone the game value for each trick short of the required collective quota.

*Declarer, if unsuccessful*, records penalty points in his 'hole' equivalent to the game value for *each* undertrick. For example, winning only five tricks in a seven-trick contract incurs an 8-point penalty (two down times game value four). A failed misère incurs 10 penalty points for every trick he took.

In addition, whatever amount he records 'in the hole' is simultaneously scored 'on the side' by each opponent if both played, or by the Governor alone if one passed. This is called the 'consolation'.

*Successful collaboration.* If the partners collaborated and won their collective quota of tricks (four in a six contract, two in a seven, one in an eight, otherwise none), then each of them scores 'on the side' and against the Declarer the game value for each trick he won individually, regardless of how the quota was divided between them. This is additional to the 'consolation' scored should Declarer fail to make his contract.

*Unsuccessful collaboration.* If the partners collaborated but failed to win their collective quota of tricks, Declarer scores 'on the side' against whichever of them (both if applicable) failed to meet his individual quota of two in a six contract, or one in a contract of seven or eight. The amount so scored is equivalent to the game value for each trick short of the individual quota.

If the collective quota was missed but one partner nevertheless fulfilled his individual quota, he then scores 'on the side' against the Declarer the game value for each trick he took of his quota, but not for any overtricks. Declarer then scores against the other partner the game value amount of the collective shortfall (which in these circumstances will not exceed, and may be less than, his individual shortfall).

*If only one said 'play'*, and the partners fulfil their collective quota, the Governor scores 'on the side' against the Declarer the game value for each trick he and his non-playing partner took between them. If this quota is not fulfilled, Declarer scores 'on the side' against the Governor alone the game value for each trick by which they fell short of it.

*Game.* As stated, the rubber ends when every player has the target number of points – say 10 – recorded in his pool. When a player reaches this number, he no longer records points for won contracts in his pool. Any point won in excess of 10 is instead added to the 'pool' score of an opponent who has not yet reached that target, typically the one closest to it. In return for this apparent generosity (satirically known as 'American aid'), the donor records for each such game point 10 points 'on the side' against the beneficiary of his gift.

In this way everyone will eventually reach ten. Any points above 10 yielded by the final contract are ignored, as there is no-one to sell them to.

*Settlement.* Final scores or settlements are made by each player on two accounts: first, in respect of each opponent as individually recorded in scores made 'on the side', and secondly as modified by the number of penalty points recorded 'in the hole'. Pool points are irrelevant, of course, being equal.

Individual accounts are sorted out as between every combination of two players. For example, if Anna has 16 on the side against Boris, and Boris 9 against Anna, then Anna counts +7 in respect of Boris and Boris −7 in respect of Anna. In this way every player will count plus or minus in respect of every other player, and each player's three or four plus or minus scores will together yield an overall plus or minus total as the first component of his or her final score.

For the second component, each player multiplies the number of penalties recorded 'in the hole' by 10, and then reckons as final penalties the difference between his own tenfold score and that of the average of all three or four players. For example, if A, B and C recorded respectively 18, 23 and 32 penalties, the tenfold average will be 243 (i.e. 730÷3), and A will reckon 63 against (243−180), B 13 against (243−230), and C 77 in credit (243−320: a minus penalty, of course, yields a plus score).

The two components for each player are then put together to yield a final plus or minus score. The totality of all the players' scores will be zero, or within a fraction of it caused by the non-integral division of 'hole' points. It may be agreed that any such fraction or odd point be awarded to the player cutting the highest card.

# 24

## —— SKAT ——

### *Germany's national card game*

Skat was developed at Altenburg, near Leipzig, between 1810 and
1820, and by the end of the century had become the most popular card
game of all classes of German society. The German Skat Federation
was then formed to arrange national tournaments and to codify the
rules, for the game is extraordinarily rich in possibilities and even now
is still played in a variety of non-standard ways which are the bane of
all right-minded Skat officials.

There is no disguising the fact that Skat is hard to get into without
prior experience of card-point games – where the aim is not just to win
tricks but to capture counting-cards contained in them. It is, nevertheless, one of the deepest, most varied and most exciting games ever
invented, and well repays the effort of mastering its intricate scoring
system. The best possible way of approaching it is through the two-
handed game of Sixty-Six. Also helpful is some experience of the use
of Jacks as trumps, as, for example, through the play of Euchre and
Five Hundred.

*Players.* There are three active players, but usually four at a table,
each in turn dealing to the other three but not taking part in that hand.
The turn to deal and play passes to the left. The player at Dealer's
left, who will lead to the first trick, is called Forehand; the next one
round is Middlehand; and the last (Dealer himself if only three play) is
Rearhand.

*Cards.* Thirty-two, omitting numerals 2–6.

*Value of cards*. Cards won in tricks count as follows: each Ace 11, Ten 10, King 4, Queen 3, Jack 2, 9–8–7 zero. Tricks have no value in themselves apart from that of any counters they may contain. There are 30 card-points in each suit and hence 120 in all. In most deals one player contracts to take at least 61 card-points in tricks, and his opponents try to prevent this by taking at least 60 between them, playing as a partnership.

*Rank of cards*. The Jack of clubs is the highest trump, followed downwards by the Jacks of spades, hearts and diamonds.

- In a trump suit contract, the cards of that suit follow below the diamond Jack in order A–T–K–Q–9–8–7, giving eleven trumps and seven cards in each of three plain suits, thus:

| ♣J ♠J ♡J ♢J | A | T | K | Q | 9 | 8 | 7 | = | 11 trumps |
|---|---|---|---|---|---|---|---|---|---|
| | A | T | K | Q | 9 | 8 | 7 | = | 7 in each of 3 side suits |
| *2 2 2 2* | *11* | *10* | *4* | *3* | *0* | *0* | *0* | = | *card-points* |

- In a 'grand' contract, the Jacks form a four-card trump suit of their own, and there are seven cards in each of four plain suits:

| ♣J ♠J ♡J ♢J | = | 4-card trump suit |
|---|---|---|
| A T K Q 9 8 7 | = | 7 in each of 4 side suits |

- In a null (misère) contract, there are no trumps, and cards rank in Whist/Bridge order: A–K–Q–J–T–9–8–7.

*Object*. In each deal an auction determines who will play a solo contract against the other two. The basic contracts are: grand, a trump game in one of four suits, and null. At grand or in suit, the soloist's aim is normally to capture at least 61 card-points in tricks; at null, it is to lose every trick.

Each of these may be played either *with the skat* or *from the hand*.

- In a skat game, the soloist takes the skat, adds it to his hand, makes any two discards face down in its place, and then announces grand, suit or null before play begins. (This may improve the shape of his hand and enable him to bid a safer or higher contract than originally envisaged.)

- In a hand game, the soloist leaves the skat untouched and announces grand, suit or null immediately. (This carries a higher potential score.)

In either case, any card-points contained in the skat will count to the soloist at end of play as if he had won them in tricks (except at null, where they are irrelevant).

The soloist scores plus if successful and minus if not. The winner is the player with the highest cumulative score at the end of a previously agreed number of deals. This may be any number, so long as everyone deals the same number of times.

*Deal.* Deal 10 cards each in batches of 3–(2)–4–3, with two face down to the table after the first round of three. These two form the *skat*, which eventually goes to the highest bidder.

*Contracts and game values.* Bidding is done by game valuation – that is, the soloist is the player offering to undertake the highest-scoring contract. Players must therefore calculate the scoring value of their proposed game before entering the auction. This is complicated by the fact that most game values are not fixed but are affected by such factors as the number of trumps held.

Null contracts have fixed game values as follows: null with skat 23, from hand 35, ouvert with skat 46, ouvert from hand 59. 'Ouvert' means the soloist plays with his hand of cards face up on the table.

All other game values are found by multiplying the *base value* of your proposed trump by a number of *playing factors* as described below. The base values are: diamonds 9, hearts 10, spades 11, clubs 12, grand 24.

To calculate the number of playing factors by which the base value is to be multiplied, work through the following checklist:

- First, count your consecutive top trumps, or 'tops' (*Spitze*). If you hold ♣J, then you are playing 'with' as many tops as you hold. For example, with ♣J–♠J–♡J, but not ♢J, count yourself 'with three'. Holding ♣J but not ♠J, you are 'with one'. Holding all four Jacks and the Ace of your proposed trump, but lacking the Ten, you are 'with five'; and so on.

If you don't hold ♠J, then you are 'without' as many top consecutive trumps as you lack – i.e., as many as lie over the highest trump you *do* hold. Thus, if your highest trump is ♡J, you are 'without two' (lacking ♣J–♠J); if it is the Ten of your proposed trump, you are 'without five'; and so on.

Note that, at grand, the most one can be 'with' or 'without' is four, as only Jacks are trumps. Note also that, as the skat belongs to the soloist and counts as part of his hand, any Jacks it may contain may change the number of applicable tops and so increase or decrease the eventual game value.

- To the number of tops you are counting, add 1 factor for 'game'. This always applies as a matter of course.
- If you intend to play from the hand, add 1 factor for 'hand'.

- If you think you can capture 90 or more card-points (roughly equivalent to nine tricks), add 1 factor for *schneider*. If you think you can win all ten tricks, add a second factor for *schwarz*.

- If, and only if, playing from the hand, you may declare in advance that you are aiming to win *schneider*. This entitles you to add 1 factor for declaring it in addition to the 1 for (hopefully) making it.

- If, and only if, playing from the hand, you may declare in advance that you are aiming to win *schwarz*. This entitles you to add a fourth factor (to the 1 each for the included schneider and schneider declared and the 1 for winning all ten).

- If, and only if, playing from the hand and declaring schwarz – i.e. all ten – you may add 1 more factor for playing the hand *ouvert*, i.e. with your cards face up on the table. This, however, only applies to a suit game, because:

- If you can play grand, hand, with schwarz declared, and open on the table, then the 'grand' base value of 24 is replaced by a 'grand ouvert' base value of 36, and the extra multiplier for 'ouvert' is not applied. (A hand strong enough for 'ouvert' with a trump suit can almost invariably be played at 'grand ouvert' instead. Since this is worth more, suit ouverts are hardly ever played.)

**Table 5** *Game valuation*

| | | | | |
|---|---|---|---|---|
| ◇ | diamonds | 9 | | 1 per 'top' |
| ♡ | hearts | 10 | | +1 for game (always) |
| ♠ | spades | 11 | *times* | +1 for hand |
| ♣ | clubs | 12 | | +1 for *schneider* or 2 if declared[a] |
| | grand | 24 | | +1 for *schwarz* or 2 if declared[a,b] |
| | grand ouvert | 36 | | +1 for ouvert[c] (unless grand) |

[a] Schneider and schwarz may only be declared if played from hand
[b] Additional to points for schneider and schneider declared
[c] Ouvert may only be played if schwarz is declared

Fixed game values: Null 23, null hand 35, null ouvert 46, null ouvert hand 59

The lowest possible bid is 18: the lowest possible game value, diamonds, with or without 1, game 2, times 9 = 18. The highest possible suit game is 216: clubs, with or without 11, game 12, hand 13, schwarz declared 17, ouvert 18, times 12 = 216. The highest possible game is grand ouvert, with 4, game 5, hand 6, schwarz declared 10, times 36 = 360. All possible game values up to 100 are:

| 18 | 20 | 22 | 23 | 24 | 27 |
|----|----|----|----|----|----|
|    | 30 | 33 | 35 | 36 |    |
|    | 40 | 44 | 45 | 46 | 48 |
|    | 50 | 54 | 55 | 59 |    |
|    | 60 | 63 | 66 |    |    |
|    | 70 | 72 | 77 |    |    |
|    | 80 | 81 | 84 | 88 |    |
|    | 90 | 96 | 99 | 100 |   |

## Examples of game valuation

Consider a hand:

♣J ♠J ♣ A K ♠ K ♡ Q ◇ T K 8 7

The obvious contract is diamonds, and the skat is needed to get rid of the two useless singletons. Count, therefore: With 2, game 3, times diamonds 9 = 27. If the hand is played and takes in 90 or more card-points, it will gain an extra multiplier for schneider and so score 36. On these cards Forehand, having the lead, might bid up to 72 with a view to playing grand (3x24).

♡J ◇J ♣T Q 8 ♠ A T 9 ♡ – ◇ –

Here the obvious contract is clubs from the hand: Without 2, game 3, hand 4, times clubs 12 = 48.

♠J ♡J ◇J ♣ T ♠ A 7 ♡ A T 9 ◇ 7

Now the obvious contract is hearts – without 1, game 2, times hearts 10 = 20. If pushed, you might go to 30 in hope of taking the skat and either making schneider (without 1, game 2, schneider 3 x 10 = 30) or, with a good draw, playing grand (without 1, game 2 x 24 = 48). It doesn't look safe enough to permit hearts from the hand for 30.

◇J ♣ - ♠ A T Q 9 8 7 ♡ - ◇A K 7

This is certainly spades from the hand, and probably good for schneider. Count, therefore: Without 3, game 4, hand 5, schneider 6, declared 7, times spades 11 = 77.

♡J ♣ K T 8 7 ♠ 8 ♡ A 9 7 ◇ Q

A null contract worth 23. If pushed by the bidding, you would reject null from the hand for 35 because of the singleton Queen, but might risk taking the skat, burying the Queen and playing ouvert for 46.

*The auction.* The auction is conducted entirely by numbers, starting with '18' and continuing as shown above without any omissions.

Middlehand must either start the auction by bidding '18' against Forehand, or pass. If he passes, Rearhand must bid '18' or pass. If he also passes, Forehand wins the auction and becomes the soloist – unless he also passes, when the hands are thrown in and the deal passes round to the next dealer.

Assuming Middlehand does not pass, he bids by stating in succession '18, 20, 22, 23 . . .', and so on, as shown in the table. To each of these Forehand replies 'Yes' if he is willing to play a contract worth at least that amount, or 'Pass' if not. This continues until one of them passes – either Forehand because he cannot accept the value proposed by Middlehand, or Middlehand because his last bid was accepted by Forehand and he will not go higher. Rearhand may then continue the auction by bidding the next higher game value against the survivor, or may pass.

This continues as before, until one of them passes. The survivor becomes the soloist, and is obliged to play a contract worth not less than the amount of the last bid.

*Declaring the contract.* If playing from the hand, the soloist immediately announces the trump suit, or grand or null if applicable, adding 'hand', and any further declaration he may wish to make, such as 'schneider declared' or 'ouvert'. If playing ouvert, he simultaneously spreads his hand face up on the table.

If not, the soloist picks up the skat, adds it to his hand without showing it, makes any two discards in its place, and then announces the trump suit, or grand, null, or null ouvert as appropriate. No other announcement is required or permitted.

*Conceding.* The soloist may throw his hand in before playing to the first trick. This usually happens when he takes the skat and finds it useless. He must, however, name a contract, however unsuited to his hand, in order to determine what game value is to be deducted from his score.

*Play.* Forehand always leads to the first trick. Suit must be followed if possible, otherwise any card may be played. The trick is taken by the highest card of the suit led, or by the highest trump if any are played. The winner of each trick leads to the next. The two partners pile all their won cards together in a single heap: there is no need to separate them into tricks.

It is important to note that Jacks belong to the trump suit and not necessarily to the suits they display.

- At grand, the lead of a Jack calls for Jacks to be played if possible, and the highest Jack wins the trick. If a plain suit is led, a player unable to follow may trump by playing a Jack if able and willing.
- In a suit game, the lead of any trump calls for the play of any other trump, regardless of whether or not either is a Jack.
- At null, there are no trumps, and cards rank A–K–Q–J–T–9–8–7 in all suits.

All ten tricks must be played, unless the soloist concedes before playing to the first trick, or takes a trick in a null contract.

*Score.* At end of play, the skat is turned up (except at null) and counted as part of the soloist's won tricks.

To fulfil his contract, the soloist must have taken at least 61 card-points in tricks, or 90 if he declared schneider, or ten tricks if he declared schwarz, or no trick if he bid null. If so, the game value of his contract is recalculated in retrospect by the base value of the trump times the number of applicable game factors, including those for schneider and schwarz if made but not declared. If this game value is not less than the amount he bid, he scores it in full. If less, he is deemed to have lost.

If the soloist fails to make his contract, he loses the full game value as recalculated above. If he declared schneider and failed to make it, his (lost) game value is increased by one multiplier for the failed schneider as well as for the declaration. The same applies to schwarz declared. If he himself is schneidered (takes fewer than 31 card-points), his (lost) game value is increased by one multiplier.

If the game value of the contract played is less than his bid, it must be increased by as many more multipliers as are necessary to make it equal or exceed his bid. For example, if he bid up to 45 but found his spade game contract worth only 33, the latter must be increased to 55.

If he took the skat, the game value recalculated by the above rules is doubled before being deducted from his score. This applies to all skat contracts without exception, including null. The doubling is not taken into account as a way of bringing his game value up to the level of the amount bid.

If the soloist takes the skat and concedes without play, he must nevertheless declare a contract in order to calculate the amount of his penalty score, which is calculated in the normal way as if he had played it, and is doubled for taking the skat.

## Notes on bidding and play

Pick out any Jacks and put them together in high-low order. Sort the other cards by suit and place your likeliest trump suit next to the Jacks in the same high-low order.

If you haven't any Jacks, you are unlikely to have a game on unless you have one of the following three types of hand:

♣A K Q 9 8 7 ♡A K Q ◇A

With six or more trumps and safety in side suits you can try for a game 'without four', or even five, in the long suit. With a fair break, the opposition should not make more than about 40 on this example of 'without four, game five, hand six, times clubs 12 = 72'. But change the diamond Ace to a lower diamond or spade, and you will need a favourable skat to make the game safe.

♣A T 7 ♠A T 7 ♡A K 7 ◇A

This is a 'grand hand without four', worth 144, if you are prepared to chance a balanced distribution of Jacks and suits in the partners' hands. One or more Jacks could be in the skat.

♣A T 9 7 ♠T 8 7 ♡9 7 ◇8

Given the lead (the low diamond), this is virtually a cast-iron 'null ouvert hand' for 59. Even without the lead, the opponents would need a freak-ish distribution and clever play to beat it.

If you are holding one or more Jacks, consider whether your hand looks best for a suit bid, grand, null, or no bid. Most hands are either a suit bid or nothing; relatively few are right for grand or null. As a very rough guide.

- If about half your cards are Nines, Kings and Queens, pass.
- If about half your cards consist of Jacks and good suit, consider a game in that suit. With six or more trumps and a void suit, consider playing it from the hand. With both black Jacks and a long suit headed Ace-Ten, consider grand.
- If about half are Jacks and Aces, especially Ace-Tens, consider grand.
- If about half are Sevens, Eights and Nines, and you have no more than one Ace, King or Queen, consider null. Null bids have fixed game values. If you can lose every trick with the hand as dealt, you can bid up to 35, or 59 if you can play it ouvert. If you need to take the skat in order to get rid of a dangerous card, you can bid up to 23, or 46 if you can play it ouvert.

*Suit bids*. For a safe game in suit the normal requirement is at least five trumps including Ace or Ten, at least two side suits which are either void or headed by an Ace, and not more than five losing cards. If dealt such a hand, you can reckon on playing it from the hand – for example:

♣J ♡J ♣A K 9 ♠- ♡A T 8 ◇Q 9

This is a game at clubs, hand. The opposition will probably make up to 20 in clubs and 28 in diamonds, giving you a safety margin of 12 card-points to compensate for an Ace or Ten drop on the other's winning trump.

It is always best to look for a 'hand' game first because if you win you get a higher score, whereas if you lose you don't lose double. Furthermore, a void suit is a strong playing factor, and taking the skat is apt to ruin it by producing two middling cards of the suit you lack. Playing from hand also entitles you to declare schneider in advance. To do this, you must be sure of winning preferably nine tricks, possibly eight. It is the equivalent of a small slam at Bridge.

The time to think of a skat game is when you need the draw and discard in order to produce the sort of hand on which you would have bid 'hand' if originally dealt it. For example:

♣J ♡J ♠A K 9 ♠K ♡A T 8 ◇Q

In a hand game, the opposition could make 49 straight off in spades and diamonds, and finish you off with the trump Ten. Here, you need the skat to enable you to ditch the two dangerous singletons, or one of them if the skat offers support to the other.

Two points to watch in bidding suit games are Jacks and non-trump Tens.

The danger besetting a Ten is that of being caught by the Ace, giving the opposition, in a single trick, one third of the points needed to beat you. A Ten in hand is obviously safest when covered by the Ace, and most dangerous when held singleton. With a singleton Ten, therefore, you should only consider playing from hand if you can be sure of winning most of the other tricks. It is not unknown for the soloist, playing third to the first trick, to win it with a singleton Ten; but of course it would be unwise to count on it. A Ten once guarded (e.g. T–9) is a natural risk. On a low lead from your right, you may play the Ten and find it captured by the Ace on your left; or you throw the Nine, and then lose the Ten to the Ace on a subsequent trick. A Ten twice guarded (e.g. T–Q–7) is safer, except for the danger of its being trumped on the third round of the suit. If dealt one T–x combination and playing with the skat, it is usually acceptable to keep it; if dealt two, it is usually best to lay aside both Tens to ensure 20 towards your 61 card-points.

The point to watch about Jacks is the danger of bidding 'without' too many of them. Suppose you have only the diamond Jack and take the game at 36, bidding on the basis of 'without 3, game 4, times spades' = 44. You turn the skat and find it contains, say, the heart Jack. Now your game is devalued: you are 'without 2, game 3, times spades' = 33. Having bid 36, you are 'bust', and threatened with loss. The best thing to do is to play on, hoping to make schneider. This will give you the extra multiplier you need to justify your bid. If you turned a black Jack, you would be 'with (or without) 1, game 2, times spades' = 22 – worse still. In this case you must look for other ways of justifying your bid. Can you make clubs trump and win schneider? If so, you will score 'with 1, game 2, schneider 3, times clubs' = 36. If not, can you make a brave attempt at a grand (48), or a clever discard for null ouvert (46)? Generally, it is not wise to bid too high when playing 'without' Jacks, unless you can tell from the auction that the higher trumps are in one player's hand rather than lurking in the skat. Being double-crossed by Jacks in the skat tends to disconcert inexperienced players. Experts take this danger into account intuitively and are very rarely caught out by it.

*Grand bids.* American Skat expert Joe Wergin has shown that for a 'grand hand' you need at least five of nine power factors, they being the four Jacks, the four Aces, and the lead, and should not hold more than four sure losers. You therefore bid grand hand on:

    ♣J ♢J ♣T K Q ♠A T ♡A 9 8 and the lead
    ♣J ♠J ♣A T K 9 ♠7 ♡9 8 ♢A and the lead
    ♠J ♡J ♢J ♣- ♠T K Q 9 ♡A T K ♢- not leading

If just short of these values, you may consider playing grand with the skat. For example:

    ♣J ♡J ♣A K 9 ♠- ♡A T 8 ♢Q 9

This is the same as the hand which we saw earlier was good for a bid of clubs, hand. Given the lead, you have five of the requisite power factors, but five probable losers – one Jack, and two each in clubs and diamonds. If the auction forces you beyond 36 for your hand game in clubs, you may make the mental switch to grand and go up to 48.

*Null bids.* Starting at the top, for a bid of 'null ouvert hand', worth

59, it goes without saying that any void suit is an unbeatable advantage. Any other suit must be bottomed on a Seven, and no card higher than a Seven should be separated by more than one gaps from the one below it. Thus a holding of J-9-7 is unbeatable, and even A-J-9-7 would lose only if one opponent held the other four of that suit and was able to lead them from the bottom up. A singleton Eight is not bad, especially if you have the lead and get rid of it immediately. With only one dangerous card you can play hand, but not ouvert, for 35. For example:

♣K J 9 7 ♠Q 8 7 ♡8 ♢9 7

The Queen is the danger card, and you could be forced to take that spade trick if you played ouvert. An alternative approach would be to take the skat, dump the Queen, and then play ouvert for 46. But if the skat yielded, for example, two high hearts, you could be lost. A simple null for 23, in which you take the skat and do not play ouvert, is a very chancy business, and one you should only call as a substitute for drawing a bad skat on a lower bid. Many German players only allow bids of null from the hand.

*Play.* Skat is full of opportunities for clever and subtle play, but there is only space here for one or two particular points of interest.

In a suit game, the soloist should generally lead trumps at every opportunity. With five or six trumps, a good procedure is to lead high, then low, then high again, attempting to win the third trick in order to prevent the opponent who has no trump left from throwing a high counter to a trump trick won by his partner.

From a side suit headed T–K, it is often best – sometimes even vital – to play the Ten at the earliest opportunity. This forces the Ace out, leaving your King in command of the suit, at a time when the other opponent is still able to follow suit and hence unable to fatten the 21-point trick by discarding another Ace or Ten. If you play the King, and the Ace-holder ducks, you could lose 31 or more card-points ('half the rent', as they say) on the next round.

Always keep track of the number of card-points currently won by yourself and your opponents. This takes practice, but soon becomes second nature, and is well worth while. For example, when a suit is led which you cannot follow, don't automatically trump. It may be worth throwing useless Kings and Queens to dud tricks in order to void your side suits without giving too many away, and you can only do this with safety so long as you know the score.

At grand, don't hesitate to use a long suit to force Jacks out if your own Jacks are either vulnerable or needed for a later purpose.

For example:

♡J ◇J ♠A T K 8 7 ♡A T 7

Given the lead, this is a 'grand, hand, without 2'. Don't lead a Jack: it could lose you the contract. Instead, play spades from the top down. If the Ace is trumped, come back in with a top heart or a red Jack, and lead the spade Ten. If this also is trumped, you are left with the only Jack in play and certainly five, probably six remaining tricks. (You will try to get rid of the heart loser cheaply, rather than rely on clearing the suit with your Ace-Ten.)

The main thing for the partners to do is to take advantage of every opportunity for plumping tricks out by dropping high-scoring cards – especially vulnerable Tens – on those won by their partner. A typical suit-game opening sees the soloist leading a red Jack and the second dropping a black Jack in case his partner can plump it with the Ace or Ten of trumps, which might otherwise be lost. Alternatively, the second to play, having no black Jack, will himself drop the Ace or Ten, hoping his partner can play a high Jack. If not, they are both in the soloist's hand (or hand and skat, same thing), and the fat trump would probably have been lost anyway, so there was no harm in trying.

One of the most important rules of play for the partners is to keep the soloist in the middle, i.e. playing second to a trick, whenever possible. If, therefore, you are leading to a trick to which he will be playing third, and have no good card to lead, lead low in a suit which your partner either heads or can trump, in order to get him into the lead.

In bidding, it is sensible to stop at a value from which your partner will be able to infer something about the nature of your hand. For example, if you stop at 24 when you could have gone to 27, you will leave your prospective partner under the impression that your suit is clubs when in fact it is diamonds. Such misinformation could be fatal.

## Sample deal

|  | Forehand | Middlehand | Rearhand |
|---|---|---|---|
| Jacks | ♡ ◇ | ♣ ♠ | - |
| ♣ | T Q 8 | A K | 9 7 |
| ♠ | A T 9 | K | Q |
| ♡ | - | Q | A T K 9 8 7 |
| ◇ | A Q | T K 8 7 | 9      *Skat:* ♠8 ♠7 |

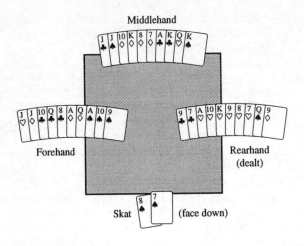

**Figure 21: Skat** The hands arranged for the sample deal described in the text.

Forehand has five of the nine factors required for a grand hand, but too many losers to justify the bid. He has, however, a certain 'hand' game in clubs, holding five trumps, an Ace-Ten, an Ace and a void. To go to the skat would not only fail to improve the hand, but could well ruin it by yielding two cards of his void suit. He also has the same number of spades, but clubs are better for two reasons: first, because they carry a higher score; second, because it is obviously better to hold the Ten of trumps and a side-suit Ace than the Ace of trumps and a Ten-headed side suit. He will bid up to 48, reckoning 'without 2, game 3, hand 4, clubs 48'.

Middlehand is 'with two', has a good potential trump in diamonds, and enjoys the support of a side-suit Ace (in clubs). His two useless singletons, however, threaten him with a loss of 49 card-points on two tricks alone, and it would be tempting providence to bid from the hand. The skat is needed, here, as a dump for the two singletons. His maximum is therefore 'with 2, game 3, diamonds 27', or perhaps 36 if he cares to risk playing from hand.

Rearhand has a theoretical 'hearts, without four', but too many losers to make this proposition worth while. His best chance is a null, for which he needs the skat to enable him to dump the Queen and Nine, unless it adds the Seven to the Nine. He will bid up to 23, unless prepared to risk taking the skat and playing open for 46.

Middlehand starts the bidding with '18'. Forehand replies 'Yes' to this, and to Middlehand's subsequent 20, 22, 23, 24, 27. At this point, Middlehand assumes that Forehand could be dangerous, decides against a hand game (for 36), and passes. Rearhand decides to go for his null ouvert – which, with a good skat, might conceivably turn into 'hearts, without four, game five, 50' – and continues bidding against Forehand: 30, 33, 35, 36, 40, 44, 45, 46. He must now stop, though we can see that the skat would have afforded him an unbeatable null ouvert.

Forehand, having won the auction, announces 'clubs, hand', which he can hardly fail to win for a score of 48. He will start by using his lower Jacks to force the high ones out, and a typical course of events might be as follows: (winning cards in **bold**):

| Forehand | Middlehand | Rearhand | | |
|---|---|---|---|---|
| ♦J | **♠J** | ♣7 | partners | 4 |
| ♦Q | ♡Q | ♡7 | partners | 6 |
| **♠A** | ♠K | ♠Q | soloist | 18 |
| ♣8 | **♣A** | ♣9 | partners | 11 |
| **♦A** | ♦7 | ♦9 | soloist | 11 |
| ♡J | **♣J** | ♡A | partners | 15 |
| **♣Q** | ♦8 | ♡8 | soloist | 3 |
| **♣T** | ♣K | ♡9 | soloist | 14 |
| **♠T** | ♦K | ♡K | soloist | 18 |
| **♠9** | ♦T | ♡T | soloist | 20 |

The soloist has 84 card-points to the partners' 36 – not far short of schneider.

Middlehand might have boxed clever by declining to cover the Jack led but instead playing the King, overtaking the next trump lead, and leading his top trumps to catch his partner's high-counting hearts. This would have brought them well into the 50s, but not enough to defeat the contract.

## Variants

Skat is played informally with many variations, despite the German Skat Federation's attempts to stamp out heresy. One of the most sensible variants is the base valuation of grand at 20 instead of 24. Grand occurs too often and succeeds too frequently to justify such a high score, and, to add insult to injury, is less interesting to play than a suit game. It was raised from 20 to 24 in the 1920s, and Federation purists uphold this decision on the grounds that it would be illogical to allow null ouvert, worth 46, to overcall a grand with or without one, which it would do if the latter scored only 40 instead of 48. If this argument is allowed, a better way of dealing with it is to follow the practice of those players who permit nulls only if played from the hand (35 or 59, not 23 or 46). Null could well be dropped completely. It was borrowed from Whist and is entirely out of keeping with the spirit of the game.

Another common variation is not to throw the hands in when all three players pass, but instead to play one round of a game called *Ramsch*. There are several ways of playing it, which have in common the fact that only Jacks are trumps, and each person plays for himself with the aim of taking the smallest number of card points. In the simplest version (point-Ramsch) the skat is left untouched. Forehand leads to the first trick, and tricks are played as at grand. Whoever wins the last trick adds the skat to his won tricks, together with any counting-cards it may contain. Tricks are then examined, and whoever has taken the greatest number of card-points deducts that number from his current score.

# 25

## ——— TWENTY-FIVE ———

### *An Irish five-finger exercise*

Ireland's national card game was formerly called **Spoil Five**, from the fact that five tricks are played and the aim is either to win a majority of them or else 'spoil' the play in such a way that no-one else can do so. Under this name it was scored in single points up to a target score of five. The habit later developed of scoring by fives instead of ones, with a consequent change of name from Spoil Five to Twenty-Five. It is nowadays often played in an extended form with a Joker, and under the name **Forty-Five**, reflecting its higher target score. All these titles emphasise the peculiar obsession it seems to exhibit for the number five: five is the best number of players; five tricks are played; the top trump is the trump Five, known as 'Five Fingers'; and even the Gaelic for 'trick', *cúig*, is the same as the word for 'five'.

Newcomers to the game may find it daunting at first sight because of the peculiar ranking of cards, which takes a little getting used to. But it is well worth the effort, as much for its intrinsic interest as for its cultural and historic significance – not to mention the fact that it is one of the very few games to work best for five players, though it can be played by any number from three to ten. Gaelic through and through, it first appears under the name Maw as the court game of James VI of Scotland (who later became James I of England), and was subsequently carried to the New World, where it remains popular in Canada, and especially in Novia Scotia ('New Scotland').

## The game

*Players.* Three to ten, five best.

*Cards.* Fifty-two. There is always a trump suit and three or four cards are always the highest trumps. From the top down, these are:

Five of trumps ('five fingers')
Jack of trumps
Ace of hearts
Ace of trumps (if not hearts)

The remaining cards rank from high to low according to the colour of their suit as follows:

in red     ($\heartsuit \diamondsuit$) K Q J T 9 8 7 6 5 4 3 2 A
in black   ($\spadesuit \clubsuit$) K Q J A 2 3 4 5 6 7 8 9 T

This may be remembered as 'high in red, low in black', or 'right up in red, back down in black'.

*Object.* If played for hard score, each player starts with 20 counters or chips and contributes one to a pool at the start of each deal. Five tricks are played, and the main object is to sweep the pool by winning three or more tricks. Failing this, the alternative aim is to 'spoil five (tricks)' by preventing anyone else from winning three, so that the pool is carried forward to the next deal and increased in value. If played with point-scoring, each trick counts five points and the target is twenty-five.

*Deal.* When everyone has added a chip to the pool, deal five cards to each player in batches of two and three. Stack the rest face down and turn the top card up for trumps.

*Robbing the pack.* If dealt the trump Ace, you *must*, just before playing to the first trick, declare that you hold it, and may 'rob the pack' by taking the turn-up and discarding an unwanted card face down. If you neither exchange nor declare, the Ace loses its high status and becomes the *lowest* trump when played to a trick.

If the turn-up is an Ace, the dealer may, just before playing to the first trick, rob the pack by taking the turned Ace in exchange for a face-down discard.

*Play.* The player at Dealer's left leads to the first trick.

To a plain-suit lead, you may either follow suit or trump, as preferred, but may only play anything else if forced.

To a trump lead, you must play a trump if possible, unless the only trump you hold is a top trump (trump-5, trump-J, $\heartsuit$A) and is higher than the one led. In this case you may 'renege' by discarding from another suit. Put another way, you cannot force someone to play out a top trump by leading a lower trump, only by leading a higher one.

*Jinking.* If you win the first three tricks straight off, you may claim the pool without further play. If instead you 'jink', i.e. lead to the fourth trick, this is taken as a bid to win all five, and you will lose if you fail to do so.

*Score.* Anyone winning three or more tricks wins the pool, plus an extra chip from each opponent for winning all five. If nobody wins three, or if a player who jinked won only four, the tricks are said to be 'spoiled'. The pool is then carried forward to the next deal and increased by one chip per player.

*Game.* The game ends when somebody runs out of chips.

# Forty-five

Play as above, but with these differences.

- Add a Joker to the pack. It counts as the fourth highest trump after trump Five, trump Jack and heart Ace. As with the higher trumps, its holder has the privilege of reneging.
- If the Joker is turned for trump, Dealer announces a suit of his own choice as trump, and whoever holds the trump Ace may rob the Joker.
- Each trick scores 5 points and the winner is the first to reach a target score of 45 points.
- There is no point in stopping after winning the first three tricks, as there is no penalty for falling short of five. Winning three scores 15 points and four 20 points. Winning all five ('jinking') brings a player to 45 points immediately and so wins the game outright.

### Sample game (Twenty-Five)

The turned card is ◇Q, making diamonds trump, and the hands are dealt as follows:

|     | Hand A | Hand B | Hand C | Hand D | Hand E |
|-----|--------|--------|--------|--------|--------|
| ◇   | –      | –      | 5♡A    | 9 4    | A      |
| ♡   | T 6 2  | –      | K      | –      | J 4    |
| ♠   | 3      | J 8    | 5      | Q 4 7  | –      |
| ♣   | 7      | 2 6 9  | A      | –      | Q T    |

Only C and E are strong enough to think about going for three tricks: C with two top trumps and a King, E with the trump Ace entitling him to take the turned trump Queen in exchange for his lowest card, the club Ten. With heart Ten led, the play goes:

| A | B | C | D | E |
|---|---|---|---|---|
| ♡T | ♣9 | ♡K | ◇4 | ◇Q |
| ♡6 | ♠8 | ♡A | ◇9 | ♡4 |
| ♡2 | ♣6 | ◇5 | ♠7 | ◇A |
| ♣7 | ♣2 | ♣A | ♠4 | ♣Q |
| ♠3 | ♠J | ♠5 | ♠Q | ♡J |

At trick 1, D is obliged to trump, E elects to do so and wins the trick. He leads a low heart in the expectation that, with a round of hearts already played, the others will mostly be forced to trump, thus enabling him to come in later with his Queen and make J his final, and hopefully winning, lead.

At 2, C's ♡A is a trump, since he cannot follow suit.

At 3, C now leads the unbeatable ◇5, which will force out any top trumps that anyone else might otherwise be saving, and hopefully, the trump Ace which C knows E to hold. E reluctantly complies.

At 4, however, C's ♣A is not good enough to win, and falls to E's Queen. E, having now re-entered by another route, leads the ♡J just as he had hoped, and wins the pool with three tricks.

If C had led ♣A to the third trick 3, E would still have won by leading ♡J to trick 4. C would have been obliged to trump, and E would then have held the last remaining trump.

*Notes.* As you will see from the sample game, most hands are run-of-the-mill, and the best thing to do with them is to try to ensure that tricks are evenly divided. One way of doing this is to refrain from playing a top trump to an early trick – by exercising the privilege of 'reneging' – so that you can employ it more profitably later against a player who has won a second trick, or is threatening to do so, with a view to a third.

To make three tricks worth the attempt you should have at least three trumps, one of them a top trump. A plain-suit King cannot be counted as a winner from the outset, but becomes more promising if you can retain it while trumps are being drawn in early tricks. Many a third trick is won by the lead at trick five of a card to which no-one can follow suit.

# 26

## —— GOING, ——
## GOING,
## GONE

### Simple going-out games for 3–7 players

There is a whole family of simple games, suitable for younger players or lighter moments, based on the idea of being the first to get rid of all your cards by discarding them one at a time to a wastepile. The catch is that you may only discard by matching the previous player's discard by rank or suit, and, if unable to do so, must draw more cards to increase your hand.

The earliest member of the family to be described in English was Rockaway, which appeared in the 1920s, followed by its close variant Eights, or Swedish Rummy. A variety called Mau-Mau became popular on the European mainland during the 1960s, and at about that time, or shortly after, British schoolchildren were playing a variety called Switch, or Two-Four-Jack. In the 1970s an elaboration of the basic idea was published as a proprietary card game under the name Uno, with great success.

## ———————— Rockaway ————————

*Preliminaries.* From a 52-card pack deal seven cards to each player and stack the rest face down. Turn the top card of the stock face up and lay it beside the stock to start a wastepile. If it is an Ace, bury it in the stock and turn the next. The aim is to be the first to play off all your cards to the wastepile.

*Play.* Each in turn, starting with the player at Dealer's left, may play one card face up to the top of the wastepile, provided that it matches the previous discard by rank or suit, or is an Ace. For example, if the first upcard is the Jack of spades, the first player must play a spade, a Jack, or an Ace.

A player unable to match the discard must draw cards from the top of the stock and add them to his hand until he can make a legal discard. If no cards remain in stock, anyone unable to pay must simply miss a turn.

*Ending and scoring.* The game ends when one player goes out by playing his last card, or when no-one can play. Each player scores a penalty according to the face value of all cards remaining in his hand, counting Aces 15 each, courts 10, and numerals at face value.

The overall winner is the player with the lowest penalty score after an agreed number of rounds or period of time, or when one one player reaches a total of 100 against.

*Variant.* **Swedish Rummy** is virtually identical, except that a player unable to match rank may play an Eight instead of an Ace, whence its alternative title '**Eights**'.

# Two-Four-Jack

Otherwise known as **Switch**.

*Preliminaries.* Two to four players use a single 52-card pack, from five to eight players use a doubled pack of 104 cards. Deal 12 cards each, or 10 each if four or eight play, and stack the rest face down. Turn the top card of the stock face up to start a wastepile. If it is an Ace, bury it in the stock and turn the next. The aim is to be the first to play off all your cards to the wastepile.

*Play.* The player at Dealer's left goes first, and play continues to the left until someone reverses direction by playing a Jack, as described below. Each in turn may play one card face up to the top of the wastepile, provided that it matches the previous discard by rank or suit, or is an Ace. For example, if the first upcard is the Jack of spades, the first player must play a spade, a Jack, or an Ace. A player who discards an Ace may specify what suit he means it to represent, which need not be that marked on its face. For example, if he discards the Ace of hearts and says nothing, the next player must discard an Ace or a heart, but if he says 'spades', then the next must discard an Ace or a spade.

A player unable to match the discard must draw cards from the top of the stock and add them to his hand until he can make a legal discard.

*Stock replacement.* When the last card has been drawn from stock, the Dealer gathers up all the cards of the wastepile except the one on top, shuffles them thoroughly, and lays them face down to start a new stock. If this happens while a player is still drawing from stock, he continues drawing as before until he can play.

*Twos and Fours.* Playing a Two forces the next player in turn either to play a Two himself or to draw from stock and miss a turn. If he misses a turn, the following player may continue by matching the Two by rank or suit. If he plays a Two, however, he forces the next to play a Two or draw four cards. If he also plays a Two, the next must do likewise or draw six cards; and so on, the number of cards to be drawn increasing by two for each consecutive Two played.

Fours have the same effect, except that the next player must play a Four or draw four, the next must draw eight if unable to match two Fours, then twelve and so on.

*Switching Jacks.* Playing a Jack reverses ('switches') the direction of play and forces the previous player to either play a Jack himself or miss a turn. The order of play changes from left to right or right to left throughout the game whenever a Jack is played.

*Ending and scoring.* A player who plays his last card but one, leaving only one in hand, must announce 'One left' as soon as he has played. If not, he must miss his next turn and draw a card instead.

The game ends when one player goes out by playing his last card, having previously announced that he is in a position to do so. Each player scores a penalty according to the face value of all cards remaining in his hand, counting Aces 20 each, Twos and Fours 15, courts 10, and others at face value.

The overall winner is the player with the lowest penalty score after an agreed number of rounds or period of time, or when one one player reaches an agreed total of penalty points.

# 27

# —— ADDING GAMES ——

## Three simple games for 3–7 players

Another family of simple games suitable for younger players or lighter moments (see also previous chapter) is based on the idea of adding up the face value of cards played as you go along, and trying to make or avoid certain totals. Games of this sort have only recently made their way to West from Eastern Europe. It is an odd fact that the only Western card game with anything like this feature is the peculiarly English game of Crib.

Here are a few such games, proceeding from the simplest to the more elaborate. You can easily make up others of your own.

## ————— One Hundred —————

Divide a 32-card pack evenly between from two to seven players. The cards have face values as follows:

| Card  | A  | K | Q | J | T  | 9 | 8 | 7 |
|-------|----|---|---|---|----|---|---|---|
| Value | 11 | 4 | 3 | 2 | 10 | 9 | 8 | 7 |

Any cards left undealt face up and Dealer announces their combined face value.

If a player brings the total to exactly 100, he wins the game. If not, whoever makes the total exceed 100 is the loser.

# —————— Obstacle Race ——————

Divide a 32-card pack evenly between from two to seven players. The cards have face values as follows:

| Card | A | K | Q | J | T | 9 | 8 | 7 |
|------|---|---|-----|---|----|---|---|---|
| *Value* | 1 | 4 | ±3 | 2 | 10 | 9 | 8 | 7 |

The player at Dealer's left starts by playing a card face up to the table and announcing its face value – or the total it makes with any cards left undealt. Each in turn then adds a card to the line and announces the new total. The cards so played should be spread out in an overlapping line so all remain visible. Note that the Queen either adds or subtracts 3 to or from the current total, as specified by its player.

The 'obstacles' in the eponymous race are 55, 66, 77, 88, 99 and 111. A player scores 1 point for bringing the total exactly to an obstacle number, but loses a point for causing the total to jump an obstacle number without making it exactly. Note that the subtraction facility of the Queen enables an obstacle to be hit or jumped either upwards or downwards, and more than once.

When the total reaches or exceeds 120 it is re-set to zero, and play continues as before. The winner is the player with the highest score after one or more deals, or the first to reach an agreed target.

# ——————— Ninety-Nine ———————

This one was reported to me as being a Romany game.

From two to seven players receive three each from a 52-card pack and the rest are stacked face down.

The order of play runs to the left around the table to start with, but may change (as in the game of Switch).

Each in turn, starting with the player at Dealer's left, plays a card face up to the table, announces the total face value of all cards so far played, and draws a replacement from stock.

Whoever brings the total over 99 ends the round and loses a life. Another deal follows, and the first player to loses three lives is the overall loser.

The cards have the following face values:

| | | | | | |
|---|---|---|---|---|---|
| Black Ace | *any* | Seven | 7 | | |
| Red Ace | 1 | Eight | 8 | | |
| Two | 2 | Nine *makes* | 99 | | |
| Three | 0 | Ten *minus* | 10 | | |
| Four | 0 | Jack | 10 | *and switches* | |
| Five | 5 | Queen | 10 | | |
| Six | 6 | King | 10 | | |

Playing a black Ace entitles you to make the total anything you like, from 0 to 99.

A Nine automatically brings the total to 99, and can therefore only be followed by a Three, Four, Ten, or black Ace.

Playing a Jack adds 10 and reverses the order of play. For example, when the first Jack is played, the next card is played by the person to the right of the one who played the Jack, and play continues to the right until another Jack is played.

# 28

# —— RUMMY ——

## *A collection of games for collectors*

Since its first appearance in the USA at the beginning of the 20th century, the game called Rum or Rummy has spread throughout the Western world and even reconquered the Orient, where it appears to have originated in the form of the tile game, Mah Jong. (Curiously enough, it has also been reconverted into a tile game in the West, under the proprietary name Rummikub.)

The basic idea – that of drawing and discarding with a view to collections sets or 'melds' of matched cards – is so simple that it has given rise to countless variants by way of elaboration. Among them are numbered Gin Rummy, for two players, and the game of Canasta, which for a brief while came to rival Bridge as a sociable partnership game, and itself spawned such offspring as Samba and Bolivia.

The simplest member of the family is basic Seven-Card Rummy, played with a single pack plus Joker(s), which reached its heyday in the Twenties and Thirties. Most Rummy-players nowadays play with a doubled pack and call the game Kaluki, or Kalookie. The precise rules of Kaluki vary from school to school. It is important to understand that in card games generally, and in Rummy games especially, both the rules and the names of popular games are constantly shifting, evolving, and changing places with one another.

Described below is the basic Seven-card Rummy, which forms a good introduction to the Rummy family for children and beginners. It is followed by the two-pack Kaluki. Both are suitable for three or more players. Gin Rummy for two and Canasta for four have chapters of their own.

Before we begin, here are some essential Rummy terms common to all varieties.

The general idea is to collect groups of three or more matched cards. Such a group is called a *meld*, and *to meld* is to lay it face up on the table.

A meld is either a *set* or a *sequence*. A set is three or more cards of the same rank, regardless of suit, such as A–A–A, 7–7–7–7, etc. A sequence is a series of three or more cards *of the same suit* and in numerical sequence, such as ♠2–3–4, ♡J–Q–K, etc. Whether Ace counts low (A–2–3) or high (Q–K–A) varies from game to game.

Jokers are *wild* – that is, you can use one to stand for any 'natural' card missing from a meld. For example, you can meld ♣3–4–Joker, counting the Joker as ♣5.

Exposed melds may be extended by the addition of extra cards one or more at a time. This is called *laying off*. For example, with ♠5–6–7 on the table you could lay off ♠8 to one end of it, or ♠4 to the other, or both. Some games only allow you to lay off cards to your own melds, not other players'.

As to the aim of the game, there are two sorts of Rummy. In the older sort, the winner is the first player to *go out* by playing off all his cards to melds, which are of no scoring value in themselves. Other players are then penalised according to the number and values of cards remaining in their hands (*deadwood*). In the newer sort, plus scores are made for melds, and the winner is the player melding the highest value of cards. This is usually combined with a smaller bonus for going out and penalties for other players' deadwood.

Finally, note that since all Rummy games by nature put the cards very much in order, it is essential to shuffle thoroughly between deals.

# Seven-card Rummy

*Players and cards.* Two to five players (three best) use a single 52-card pack without Jokers. Ace counts low in a sequence: A–2–3 is valid, Q–K–A is not.

*Deal.* Deal seven cards each in ones. Stack the rest face down. This is called the stockpile. Turn the top card of the stock and lay it face up to start the wastepile. Throughout play, the current top card of the wastepile is called the upcard.

*Object.* The aim is to be the first to go out by melding, laying off or discarding the last card from one's hand.

*Start.* The player at Dealer's left either passes or takes the upcard in exchange for any unwanted card from his hand. If he passes, the next in turn has the same option. This continues until someone starts the game by taking the upcard. If no-one takes it, the player at Dealer's left starts the game by drawing the top card of stock, adding it to his hand, melding if possible, and discarding one card face up to the wastepile.

*Play.* Thereafter, each in turn from the left of whoever started plays as follows:

- Draws either the upcard or the top card of the stockpile and adds it to his hand;
- (If able and willing:) Lays a meld face up on the table in front of himself, and-or (provided he has already made a meld of his own) lays a card off to anybody's meld already made;
- Ends his turn by discarding one card face up to the wastepile. If he drew from the wastepile, he may not discard the card he drew in the same turn.

*End of stock.* If a player draws the last card of the stockpile and does not go out in the same turn, then, after he has discarded, Dealer gathers up the wastepile, shuffles it thoroughly, lays it face down as a new stock, and turns the top card face up beside it to start a new wastepile.

*Going out.* Play ceases the moment one player goes out, whether by melding, laying off or discarding the last card from his hand. He scores, or is paid by each player, according to the total value of cards left in their hands, counting Ace to Ten at face value and courts 10 each. This amount is doubled if the winner went 'rummy', that is, disposed of all his cards in one turn without having previously made any meld.

# Kaluki

*Players.* Two to six, best for four.

*Cards.* 108, consisting of two 52-card packs and four Jokers. Ace counts low or high, that as, A–2–3 and Q–K–A are both valid. Jokers are wild.

For scoring purposes, Aces count 15 each, courts 10 each, numerals at face value. Jokers count 25 against if caught in hand at end of play.

*Deal.* Deal, one at a time, 15 cards to each player, or 13 if five play or 11 if six. Stack the rest face down as a stockpile. Turn the top card of the stock and lay it face up to start the wastepile. Throughout play, the current top card of the wastepile is called the upcard.

*Object.* The aim is to be the first to go out by melding, laying off or discarding the last card from one's hand.

*Start.* The player at Dealer's left either passes or takes the upcard in exchange for any unwanted card from his hand. If he passes, the next in turn has the same option. This continues until someone starts the game by taking the upcard. If no-one takes it, the player at Dealer's left starts the game by drawing the top card of stock, adding it to his hand, melding if possible, and discarding one card face up to the wastepile.

*Play.* Thereafter, each in turn from the left of whoever started plays as follows:

- Draws either the upcard or the top card of the stockpile and adds it to his hand;
- (If able and willing:) Lays a meld face up on the table in front of himself, in accordance with the rules of melding below, and-or (provided he has already made a meld of his own) lays a card off to anybody's meld already made;
- Ends his turn by discarding one card face up to the wastepile. If he drew from the wastepile, he may not discard the card he drew in the same turn.

*Melding.* You may not lay off cards to other players' melds before you have made a first meld of your own. Furthermore, the first time that you meld, you must dispose of cards with a total face value of not less than 51, for which purpose Jokers count as the cards they represent.

For example, ♡10–Joker–Q–K–A may be melded first, being worth 55. This value may be made up from one or more melds, or a meld and lay-offs to those of other players. For example, you could meld ♣6–7–8–9 for 30, ♣4–♡4 ♣4–♢4 for 16, making 46, and lay off ♢5 to another player's ♢A–2–3–4 to make up 51.

A meld may contain one or more Jokers, and it must be clearly stated what cards they represent. No meld may contain two identical cards, whether wild or natural. This means, in particular, that a set may contain not more than four cards of the same rank, and they must be of different suits.

*Taking Jokers.* If any meld contains a Joker, and you hold the natural card that Joker represents, you may, on your turn to play, take the Joker into hand in exchange for the natural card.

*End of stock.* If a player draws the last card of the stockpile and does not go out in the same turn, then, after he has discarded, Dealer gathers up the wastepile, shuffles it thoroughly, lays it face down as a new stock, and turns the top card face up beside it to start a new wastepile.

*Going out.* Play ceases the moment one player goes out, whether by melding, laying off or discarding the last card from his hand.

*Soft score.* Each player except the winner is penalised by the total value of cards left in hand, counting Jokers 25 each, Aces 15, courts 10, and numerals at face value. The game ends when a player's penalty total reaches 150, and the winner is the player with the lowest penalty score.

*Hard score.* The winner receives from each opponent two units for each Joker left in hand and one for every other card.

# 29

## CANASTA

### Game for basket-weavers

Canasta is an elaboration of Rummy developed in Uruguay some time around 1940. Originally a two-player game, it was in its four-hand partnership version that it swept its way across the United States before the end of that decade, becoming for a while the most preferred second-fiddle game of previously dedicated Bridge-players. Just as it reached craze proportions in 1950s Britain, the American version started developing even more complex varieties such as Samba and Bolivia. These have long since passed, and Canasta itself has now settled down into the relatively quiet life of a card game classic.

Its name is Spanish for 'basket'. According to the author of *Culbertson on Canasta* (London, 1950): 'The Spanish word for "weaving" is *tejiendo. Tejiendo las cartas*, that is, "weaving the cards", is a colourful Spanish way of saying that a meld of three of a kind, or more, is being "woven" together. And when the biggest meld of all, the canasta, is completed, you naturally have woven a "basket"'.

But enough of colourful Spanish phrases. (Have you ever met a black and white one?) It's time to get weaving.

### The game

*Cards.* 108, consisting of two standard 52-card packs with four Jokers. They need not all be of the same back design and colour, but must be of the same size.

*Game.* Partners sit opposite each other, North-South versus East-West. A game may consist of one or more deals and is won by the first side to reach or exceed 5000 points. If both sides reach it on the same deal the one with the higher total wins. Scores are recorded at the end of each deal.

*Deal.* Decide first dealer by any agreed means; thereafter the turn to deal passes to the left. Deal eleven cards each, in ones. Place the undealt cards face down and squared up in the middle of the table to form the *stock.* Turn up the top card of the stock and lay it face up beside the stock. This starts the discard pile – best referred to as the *pack* – which must also be kept squared up throughout the game. The card on top of the pack is known as the upcard. If the first upcard is a Joker, a Two or a red Three, it must immediately be covered by the next card of the stock, and so on until the upcard is of some other rank or a black Three.

With the stock and the first upcard settled, any player who has been dealt a red Three must place it face up on the table before him and is then dealt the top card of the stock to bring his hand back to eleven cards.

You are now ready to start play, but should first note the following basic facts about the game, which will give you an initial sense of direction.

*Object.* The object of the game is to collect and display on the table batches of three or more cards of the same rank, such batches being called melds. A meld of seven or more cards is a canasta, and no-one can end the game until his side has made at least one of them.

Jokers and Twos are 'wild' cards: they cannot be melded but can form part of melds based on 'natural' cards by themselves (i.e. ranks from Four up to Ace). Threes have special powers, as outlined below.

All meldable cards have a melding value, which at the end of the game counts to your credit if they are out in melds, but against you if still left in hand. The set values are:

| | |
|---|---|
| Jokers | 50 each |
| Aces and Twos | 20 each |
| High cards (K Q J T 9 8) | 10 each |
| Low cards (7 6 5 4 and black 3) | 5 each |

In addition to the melding value of individual cards, each completed canasta carries a bonus of 500 if it consists entirely of natural cards, 300 if it contains one or more wild cards. (These are known respectively as a 'natural' and a 'mixed' canasta.)

Black Threes may only be melded when you are 'going out', as explained later.

Red Threes are bonus cards. Every time you get one you must lay it face up on the table before you. They are worth 100 each (doubled if you get all four) and count in your favour if you have made any melds, but against you if you have not.

The game normally ends when one player 'goes out' by melding in one turn all the cards left in his hand.

Finally, you must be aware that Canasta is essentially a partnership game. Partners keep melds made by both of them together in one place on the table, not separately in front of each. And it is sometimes inadvisable to end the game by going out without first asking your partner's permission.

*Play*. Starting with the person at dealer's left, each player in turn does one or more of three things in the following order:

- Draw (top card of stock, or discard pile if permitted)
- Meld (if any possible, and subject to certain restrictions)
- Discard (unless gone out by melding all cards left in hand).

*Draw*. You may always take the top card of the stock and add it to your hand. If you draw a red Three, you place it face up before you and draw again.

Instead of drawing from stock, you may take the whole of the pack, provided that you can immediately meld the upcard – either by adding it to one of your existing melds on the table, or by using it to start a new meld in conjunction with two or more matching cards from your own hand (for which purpose a matching natural card plus one wild card is sufficient, though some insist that you must hold a natural pair to start a new meld with the upcard).

But you may not take the discard pile in this way if it is *frozen*, which it is in the following circumstances:

- It is frozen to you and your partner until your side has made its first meld.
- It is frozen to everybody whenever it contains a wild card (or a red Three as the result of the initial turn-up).

In these cases you may only take the pack if you can immediately use the upcard to start a new meld in conjunction with at least two matching *natural* cards from your own hand. (If you have none on the table already, this may count as your initial meld provided it meets the initial meld scoring requirement described below under 'melds'.)

Furthermore:

- The pack is 'stopped' to you personally if the upcard is a black Three. In this case you may not take it at all but can only draw from stock.

*Melds:* All melds made by one partnership are kept together in one place. Subject to rules governing composition and value of melds, you may in your turn start one or more new melds, and or add ('lay off') one or more natural or wild cards to any of your partnership's existing melds. Cards once melded cannot be retrieved for further play.

A meld must contain three or more cards, of which at least two must be natural cards, and not more than three may be wild. All natural cards in a meld must be of the same rank.

A canasta is a meld of seven (or more) cards, and may be melded outright or gradually built up by laying off additional cards to smaller melds. Once completed, the cards of a canasta are squared up in a pile, with a red card face up on top if it is a natural canasta (containing no wild cards), or a black card if it is 'mixed' (containing one or more wild).

A canasta must contain at least four natural cards, but there is no limit to the number of wild cards that may belong or be subsequently added to it. As soon as any wild card is laid off to a natural canasta, remember to replace the top red card by a black one.

Red Threes are not melded. Black Threes may only be melded if you go out on the same turn (*see below*).

*Initial meld:* The first melds or melds made by a partnership must total a certain minimum value (counting each Joker 50, Ace or Two 20, high card 10, low card 5). What that minimum value is depends on your partnership's cumulative score in the current game, as follows:

**Table 6**

| *Score so far* | *Required initial value* |
| --- | --- |
| A minus figure | any |
| Less than 1500 | 50 |
| 1500 but under 3000 | 90 |
| 3000 or more | 120 |

You may count the combined values of more than one meld towards this minimum requirement, but you may *not* count the 500 or 300 point canasta bonus towards it, nor any bonus deriving from red threes.

(Remember that the pack is frozen to your side until it has made an initial meld of the minimum required value. But the initial meld does not *have* to be made from the hand: provided it meets the requirement, it may be made by melding the upcard with at least two natural cards from your hand.)

*Discard:* Having drawn and either melded or not, you complete your turn by taking a card from your hand and placing it face up on the pack, unless in your turn you go out and have nothing left to discard.

You may not discard a red Three. If you discard a black Three, you thereby freeze the pack to your left-hand opponent for one turn only.

If you discard a wild card you thereby freeze the pack to everybody, and it remains frozen until taken.

To show that the pack is frozen, place the wild card not on the top but at the bottom of the pack, face up and sticking out sideways so that it is clearly visible. (It is, however, still the upcard for one turn and theoretically obscures the card visible on top. This means that your left-hand opponent may *not* immediately capture the pack by matching the visible card with a natural pair from his hand; but as soon as he has played, his discard becomes the upcard and thereafter the pack can be taken in accordance with the rule for capturing a frozen pack.)

*End by going out.* A player goes out and thereby ends the game when in one turn he gets rid of all the cards in his hand – either by melding them all, or by melding them all except one and discarding that last one.

You may not go out unless your side has made at least one canasta. But you can meet this requirement by melding or completing a canasta on the turn in which you go out. It is only when you are going out that you may meld black Threes – either three or four of them.

If after drawing from stock you are in a position to go out, you are permitted (not required) to ask your partner whether it suits him. If you do ask, you must do so before melding any card at all. The correct wording is 'May I go out, partner?', to which he must reply either Yes or No. You are then bound by his reply. (Indeed, if he says Yes and you find that you cannot go out after all, you are penalised 100 points.

You get a bonus of 100 for 'going out blind', that is, if you personally have not previously melded anything during the course of the current deal. But you only qualify for the bonus if all your cards are meldable in their own right – you don't get it if you lay off cards to your partner's melds.

*End by exhausting stock.* Somebody usually goes out before the stock is used up, but in case they don't, this is what happens: if the last card drawn from stock is a red Three, the player faces it, makes any melds he wishes, but does not discard. That ends the deal.

If not, he plays in the usual way and then discards. The next in turn must then take the pack (by melding the upcard) if he can legally do so; if not, the deal ends. If he can do so, he makes his play and then discards. From now on the 'pack' will only ever consist of the previous player's discard. If on your turn the previous discard matches one of your melds, you are forced to take it, lay it off, and then discard. If it does not match, but can still be melded with the aid of cards from your hand, you may either take no action, in which case the deal ends, or you may make your meld(s), in which case you must discard unless you go out.

This continues until any player in his turn either goes out or fails to take the previous player's discard because legally unable or unwilling to do so.

*Scores.* Each side reckons its score first for bonuses and then for cards; but note that if a side has melded nothing at all then any red Threes it has count against it instead of for it, their value being combined with the penalty for unmelded cards in hand.

*Bonuses*

| | |
|---|---|
| For going out | 100 |
| *or*, for going out blind | 200 |
| For each red Three | 100 |
| *or*, for having all four | 800 |
| For each natural canasta | 500 |
| For each mixed canasta | 300 |

To the score for bonuses is added the total meld value of melded cards, counting thus:

*Cards*

| | |
|---|---|
| Joker | 50 |
| Ace, Two | 20 |
| High card (K Q J T 9 8) | 10 |
| Low card (7 6 5 4 and black 3) | 5 |

From the combined total for bonuses and cards, each side now subtracts the total meld value of all cards remaining unmelded in the hand. (The side that went out, of course, will have cards left only in one hand; the other side will have two handfuls to count against them.)

If a player proves to have a red Three in hand, having failed to expose it on the table, it counts 500 against his side.

## Notes on play

Canasta is not one of those Rummy games in which the main object is to 'go out' for the sake of the bonus, regarding melds only as a means to that end. It is one of the other sort, in which the main object is to build up a large score by making as many melds as possible. The side that melds first gains an immediate advantage, having, as it were, hatched the goose that lays the golden eggs, and they should go on exploiting this advantage for all it is worth. As soon as the other side has caught up, the first side should be in or approaching the position at which it has the minimum canasta requirement for going out – not for the sake of using it quickly, but for its power as a threat to the opponents.

When going out has become a real possibility, it may eventually be effected for either of two good reasons: first, that despite your lead and initiative your opponents are now beginning to catch up or even threatening to overtake; or second, that your opponents are so far ahead that going out is your only way of defending against a huge loss. There is a third possible reason – that you have been dealt the sort of hand on which the surprise value of a 'quick out' will produce a small, quick profit for the minimum of intellectual investment – but this does not happen very often, and you need not go out of your way to look for it.

The strategy, then, is to be first to break into the scoring vein, get as much out of it as you can while the going is good, and pull out when your advance begins to lessen – or, if you find yourself on the wrong side, to prevent your opponents from succeeding in the same endeavour, even to the extent of pulling out prematurely if you consider the task hopeless. What about the tactics – the means by which this objective is to be achieved?

Inevitably, this aspect of the game revolves around the taking of the pack (i.e. the discard pile). Even if it contains no more than three or four cards the pack is always advantageous to the player who takes it, and most of your play will be directed towards this end. Usually the first side to take the pack is then able to seize the initiative and dictate the course of the game. If your opponents get it first, you must be prepared to play defensively until you can afford to meet them on their own ground.

*Initial meld.* At the start of the game your immediate objective is to make the initial meld that will entitle you to set out on your scoring spree. So strive for it – but not at the expense of all other considerations. In particular, try to meld as economically as possible. The fewer cards you keep in hand, the less chance you have of taking the pack, so to use up too many on the initial meld is largely self-defeating. For this reason it is unwise to make your initial meld entirely from the hand: wait until you can meld by taking the pack, and deplete your hand no more than necessary.

In subsequent rounds of play, when your initial meld requirement advances to 90 or 120, you may have to accept the sacrifice of more cards in order to compensate for the extra difficulty of meeting the minimum value. Even so, it is wise to expend to more than four cards for the 90, or six for the 120.

*Further melding.* Having started, make as many melds as you can, in order to keep up the pressure and increase your ability to take the pack. The more melds you can lay off to, the greater difficulty your opponents have in finding safe discards. Don't be frightened of sullying natural canastas by the addition of wild cards, and do not cripple yourself for the sake of working towards the bonus for going out concealed. If your hand happens to lend itself to that fortunate prospect, all well and good; if not, forget it.

There are circumstances in which restraint is worth exercising on the making of melds. The question of economy is one of them, as it was in the case of the initial meld: don't part with too many cards, and in particular don't part with any which may be of use in capturing the pack later. For the same reason it is also sensible to refrain from melding when the discard pile is large: the more cards you keep in hand the more chance you have of capturing it. Defer melding until the pack has been taken, even if not by yourself.

The importance of completing your first canasta is obvious, as it puts you in a position of constant threat (to go out). It is also important throughout the game not to fall behind in the completion of canastas, for which purpose mixed canastas, though less profitable than natural ones, are infinitely better than none at all.

*Freezing the pack.* It is a beginner's irritating habit to freeze the pack for no better reason than that he happens to be able to, and can think of nothing else to do. There are, of course, times when it is right to freeze the pack and times when it is wrong.

The most important time to freeze the pack is when your opponents have started melding and you have not, as it is your only effective defence against their ability to keep on recapturing it for continual rewards. Freezing is also a good defensive move when your opponents have too many cards in hand and melds on the table, as it enables you with relative safety to discard their players (cards which match their melds and would otherwise enable them to take the pack) and improve the overall meldability of your own hand.

When the pack is frozen it is good to have a hand containing many pairs, as they give you more opportunity to capture it. This does not mean, however, that a hand full of pairs is a good excuse for freezing the pack. It is obviously undesirable to freeze if there is a high probability that the other side will be able to take it. Finally, avoid freezing just because you are unable to find a safe discard. In such circumstances you are likely to do yourself more harm than good.

*Black Threes.* If you can find a better discard than a black Three, make it, and save the Three for the time when it is the only solution to an otherwise impossible position. Given a black Three early in the game, a good time to discard it is often when you have just made an initial meld. Since it freezes the pack to your left-hand opponent only, it prevents him from taking the pack before your partner has a chance to take advantage of the position.

Wild cards should be put to work, not hoarded. Each one added to a meld is a bird in the hand when it comes to the score. And do not lightly discard Aces. They, too, are better put to work.

*Discarding.* Discard low in early rounds, as such cards are not suitable for initial melds. Watch the discards made by your left-hand opponent and try to match them for as long as you feel he is genuinely throwing away unwanted cards. Since your right opponent will be watching you with the same objective in view, don't make things easy for him by sticking rigidly to the discard of singletons. At judicious times have no hesitation in discarding from three or more, so that when he subsequently discards the same rank you can capture the pack and meld. The only time to concern yourself seriously with your partner's discards is when there is a real danger of your opponents' going out. By matching your partner's discards in this situation you may save yourself a lot of penalties.

The time to throw out cards matching your opponents' melds is when the pack is frozen and they appear to have little chance of capturing it. Any cards that are of no use to you but possibly of use to them are best reserved for discarding until the pack is small.

*Going out.* We have already noted that going out is more of a defensive measure than anything else, either because you are too far behind and want to cut your losses, or because your opponents are beginning to catch up and you do not want to cut your profit margin. Watch the timing. A good time to go out is when your opponents have too many cards in hand.

## Sample game

All Rummy games are difficult to notate and inconvenient to play through in sample form, but Canasta, with 108 cards, is virtually impossible. Here instead is an illustration of the end position of a game, showing how the score is calculated.

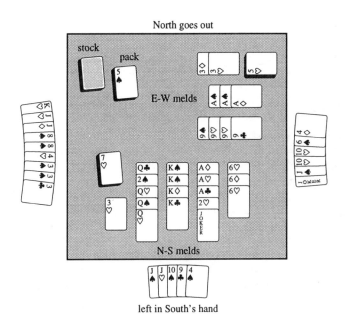

left in South's hand

**Figure 22: Canasta** You have just given your partner, North, leave to go out. Your side scores 100 for going out, 100 for the red Three, 300 for the mixed canasta (black Seven on top) and 90 for its component cards, 245 for melds on the table, total 835 less 45 in your own hand = 790. East-West score 200 for the red Threes, 500 for the natural canasta (red Five on top) and 35 for its component cards, 100 for melds on the table, total 835 less 160 for cards left in both hands = 675.

# 30

## CONCERTO

### A Poker-like game with partners

Concerto is a game of my invention and remains one of my favourites after 25 years of frequent play. My aim was to produce a partnership game involving coded communication between partners comparable to the sort of signalling that goes on in the auction at Bridge or in the conventional plays at Whist, but one that would not belong to the trick-taking family – partly because the vast majority of partnership games are already of this type, so there is no point in adding to them, and partly to offer something of comparable interest to regular card-players who are not so keen on trick-taking games. Instead, Concerto springs from the idea of making Poker hands. This does not mean it is a form of Poker, nor is it even a gambling game. Rather – well, see for yourself.

*Players.* Four, sitting crosswise in partnerships, which may be agreed in advance or decided by any agreed method.

*Cards.* Standard 52-card pack ranking A K Q J T 9 8 7 6 5 4 3 2, with Ace optionally low in certain instances.

*Deal.* Shuffle thoroughly and deal 13 cards to each player.

*General idea.* As each player has 13 cards, so each partnership has 26 between them. From these 26 you play cards out one by one to make up four Poker hands of five cards each. Each hand scores from 1 to 15 points according to how good a Poker hand it rates in the schedule below. After four hands there will be six cards left between you. Any

Poker hand contained in any five of these will count heavily against. Hence your overriding aim is to make the best Poker hands you can from the first 20 cards, and especially to ensure that you don't leave any hands unplayed.

*Poker hands and their values.* A Poker hand is any five cards. They may make one or more of the following combinations, here listed from lowest to highest ('x' means any unmatched card to make up five):

| | |
|---|---|
| One pair | Two cards of the same rank, e.g. A–A–x–x–x |
| Two pairs | Such as K–K–3–3–x |
| Three of a kind | Three of the same rank, e.g. Q–Q–Q–x–x |
| Straight | Five cards in numerical sequence, not all the same suit, Ace counting high or low, e.g. A–K–Q–J–T or A–2–3–4–5. |
| Flush | Five cards of the same suit, not all in sequence. |
| Full house | A triplet and a pair, e.g. J–J–J–8–8 |
| Four of a kind | Four cards of the same rank, e.g. 9–9–9–9–x |
| Straight flush | A straight with all five cards of the same suit. |

*Order of play.* The first dealer is designated West. North leads to the first hand, which is played between himself and South while East-West look on. Then East leads to the first East-West hand while North-South look on. The turn to lead passes regularly to the left. There is no interaction between one side and the other.

*Play.* The leader plays any card face up to the table. He may not pass. His partner may either play a second card or pass. This continues with both alternately playing or passing until five cards have been played. If these form a Poker combination the appropriate score is recorded on the score sheet as follows:

| | |
|---|---|
| One pair | 1 |
| Two pairs | 2 |
| Three of a kind | 3 |
| Straight | 5 |
| Flush | 6 |
| Full house | 8 |
| Four of a kind | 12 |
| Straight flush | 15 |

The hand is gathered up by its leader and left face up on the table in front of himself. All cards once played remain visible to both sides throughout the play, as Concerto is a game of deduction, not memory.

*Passing and playing.* The first card must be played by the official leader of the hand. Thereafter, each of the two players in turn may either play a card or pass. Passing is allowed to enable one player to make a complete Poker hand if he has one. However, not more than two passes may be made in succession. If the player in turn passes, and his partner also passes, then the player in turn must play. To keep track of the position, it helps for the first player to say 'Pass' and the second to say 'Pass back'.

A player who may legally say 'Pass' or 'Pass back' may instead say 'Play'. This forces his partner to complete the hand alone (or, if he hasn't enough cards left, to play out all he has), and so saves time.

*End of round.* The round ends when each player has led twice and has two Poker hands in front of himself. The scores are then totalled. If one side has a higher score than the other, they may score a bonus for 'left-overs'. This equals ten times the value of any one Poker combi-

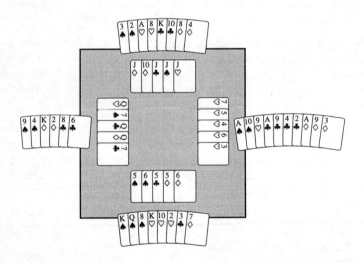

**Figure 23: Concerto** North opened Jack, Ten of diamonds and South's Jack made it four of a kind for 12. East led Seven, Five of hearts, showing the Six, and West completed the straight flush for 15. South played Five, Six of spades, suggesting the Eight or Nine, and North converted to a full house for 8. West's red Queen, black Seven showed three of one and two of the other, to which East replied 'Play', leaving a full house for 8. From the position shown here North led to a full house of Eights and Kings, East to four Nines, and South and West to two pairs (Threes and Twos, Aces and Twos respectively.) North-South therefore scored 30 to East-West's 37, increased to 47 for the pair of Tens left over.

nation they can make from the six cards left unplayed by the losing side. For example, if the left-overs are ♡J–8–7–4–2 ♠J they could score 10 for the pair – but, of course, they will prefer to score 60 for the flush. They can't score both, as only five cards may be used. (Exception: if the six cards form three pairs, the bonus is 30.) If no scorable hand can be made, there is no bonus.

If both sides tie for Poker hands made, the side who can make the higher bonus from the other side's left-overs gets the appropriate score. If both leave the same type of combination, it goes to the side with the that of lower face value. For example, if North-South leave K–K–7–7–5 and East-West J–J–T–T–2, East-West score 20 for two pairs, as Kings are higher than Jacks.

*Game.* A part-game ends after four deals, or at the end of an earlier deal if one side has reached 100 points. If both sides reach 100, or neither side reaches 100 after four deals, the side with the higher total scores one game point. If the winners reached 100 and the losers did not, they add a bonus of 100. Play up to any previously agreed target score, e.g. 500 or 1000.

## Sample game

Here is a sample game played by two experienced partnerships using a code of signals to indicate the nature of their hands by the order in which they play their cards. The signalling system is outlined later.

West deals as follows:

*North*
♠A K T
♡Q 2
♣J T 4 2
♢K J T 7

*West*
♠9 7 3 2
♡A 8 7 3
♣K 8 7
♢3 2

*East*
♠Q 6
♡K T 6 5 4
♣Q 3
♢Q 6 5 4

*South*
♠J 8 5 4
♡J 9
♣A 9 6 5
♢A 9 8

North-South play first, with North on lead. The following signs are used:

– for 'pass'
= for 'pass back'
× for 'play'

*North South hand 1*

| ◇J | – | |
|----|------|---|
| ◇T | ◇9 | North shows one lower card held, |
| ◇7 | ◇8 | and South has the other two |

| NS | 15 | for the straight flush |

*East West hand 1*

| ♡6 | – | |
|----|------|---|
| ♡4 | ♡7 | East shows three in sequence |
| ♡5 | ♡8 | and West can complete the straight flush |

| EW | 15 | for the straight flush |

*South North hand 2*

| ♣5 | – | |
|----|------|---|
| ♣6 | – | South asks for 7–8 or 7–9, which North can't provide. |
| = | ♣4 | South passes the initiative . . . |
| – | ♣2 | |
| ♣9 | | . . . and completes the flush |

| NS | 6 | for the flush, current total 21 |

*West East hand 2*

| ◇3 | – | |
|----|------|---|
| ♣7 | ♣ 3 | West show 3 Threes and 2 Sevens. |
| ♡3 | × | East says 'play' after contributing the other Three. |
| ♠3 | | |

| EW | 12 | for four Threes, current total 27 |

## *North South hand 3*

| | | |
|---|---|---|
| ♠A | – | |
| ♠K | ◇A | South knows they lack ♠Q and so aims for a full house, |
| – | ♣A | |
| – | × | North passed in case South had the fourth Ace. |
| ◇K | | |

| NS | 8 | for a full house, current total 29 |
|---|---|---|

## *East West hand 3*

| | | |
|---|---|---|
| ◇Q | – | |
| ♠6 | × | East shows a full house; West has no Queens or Sixes. |
| ♠Q | | |
| ♣Q | | |
| ◇6 | | |

| EW | 8 | for a full house, current total 35 |
|---|---|---|

## *South North hand 4*

| | | |
|---|---|---|
| ♠8 | – | |
| ♠J | ♠T | South shows four spades; North plays another |
| – | × | South was still hoping for a straight flush. |
| ♠5 | | |
| ♠4 | | |

| NS | 6 | for the flush, final total 35 |
|---|---|---|

## *West East hand 4*

| | | |
|---|---|---|
| ♠9 | – | |
| ♣8 | ♡T | West shows three to a straight. |
| ♠7 | × | East can contribute nothing useful. |
| ◇2 | | West cannot even make a pair! |

| EW | 0, | final total 35 |
|---|---|---|

As both sides have finished level, the remaining cards are shown to see which side scores for left-overs. North-South leave Q–J–J–T–9–2, East-West A–K–K–5–4–2. As both have one pair, it is decided on the basis of rank. Kings are higher than Jacks, so the bonus of 10 goes to North-South.

This sample deal well illustrates the fact that games are often decided on the last hand. North-South could have made a full house of Jacks and Tens on their fourth hand, and left nothing against them, if South had preferred to lead ♠J and pass, showing a pair. This would have brought them to 37. Similarly, though, East-West could have made two pairs from Kings and Twos, also bringing them to 37 and leaving no penalty.

## Concerto signals

The following signals, outlined as briefly as possible, are the ones I have found most useful over the years. You are welcome to simplify, elaborate, or discard them as you see fit.

When the leader plays a card he will normally have decided whether to go for a set of like cards (one pair, two pair, full house etc) or a straight-flush type of hand. In the first case he will want to play two cards of the same rank, in the second two of the same suit and in range (i.e. belonging to the same straight). His partner should therefore usually pass, and wait for leader to play a second card indicating which he has in mind. If the leader then passes in return, it will usually mean that he has no strong preference one way or the other, and leaves the decision up to his partner. Thus a 'signal' can be constituted by the relationship between the leader's first two cards, or by his first card if followed by a pass.

Because the best score is earned by a straight flush, leader should go for a straight flush first, provided that he has at least three cards belonging to one. If his partner then shows lack of support by passing, it will still be theoretically possible to convert the first two cards into the next highest combination, four of a kind, since it doesn't matter what the fifth card is.

*Straight flush signals.* A straight flush signal consists of two cards of the same suit and in the same range. These two cards may be consecutive (e.g. 3–4), or separated by one, two or three steps (e.g. 3–5, 3–6, 3–7), and they may be played either low-high (3–4) or high-low (4–3). This gives eight possible signals, to which the following meanings are attached:

In the following table, 'LH' means lower card played first, higher card second, and 'HL' high first, low second. The number of dashes between them shows how many ranks separate the two cards played.

| | | |
|---|---|---|
| **1** | L–––H | = 5 held: all in sequence |
| **2** | L––H | = 4 held: all in sequence |
| **3** | L–H | = 4 held: 3 in sequence, one higher or lower |
| **4** | LH | = 3 held: 2 in sequence, one higher |
| **5** | HL | = 3 held: 2 in sequence, one lower |
| **6** | H–L | = 3 held: all in sequence |
| **7** | H––L | = 4 held: 1 missing between |
| **8** | H–––L | = 3 or 4 held: 2 or 1 missing |

Examples:

**1** Holding 8 9 T J Q, play 8 then Q. Partner must then say 'Play'.

**2** Holding 8 9 T J, play 8 then J. Partner will play 7 or Q if held.

**3** Holding 2–4 5 6 or 4 5 6–8, play 4 then 6. Partner will play 3 or 7 if held, which may or may not be the required card.

**4** Holding 8 9–J or 8 9–Q, play 8 then 9. Partner will know Ten and one higher card are required and will play accordingly.

**5** Holding 6–8 9 or 5–8 9, play 9 then 8. Same argument as above, but in opposite direction.

**6** Holding 6 7 8 and no other card to the same straight flush, play 8 then 6.

**7** From 5 6–8 9 play either 9 then 6 or 8 then 5. May also be used as an alternative to signal 3 – e.g. from 2–4 5 6 play 5 then 2; from 4 5 6–8 play 8 then 6. Use whichever signal (or even signal 8, below) gives the better chance of converting to four of a kind or a full house if the straight flush falls through.

**8** From A–3–5 play 5 then A. If partner holds 2 and 4, he will complete the straight flush. This may also be used as an alternative to signal 7 for a four-card holding, e.g. from A 2–4 5 play 5 then 2, or 4 then A. If partner holds the intervening card he will know it is a false signal and accordingly play it.

*Matched rank signals.* Four of a kind is indicated by playing them out one at a time in any order. Meanings can be attached to the order in which suits or colours are played, but the opportunity to use them occurs too rarely to make these worth while. Other holdings are indicated by means of the first two cards played as follows:

Two or more sets of three: play one from each set, of different suits but alike in colour. For example, from ♠A–♣A–♢A ♡9–♣9–♢9 play black Ace then black Nine, or red Ace then red Nine, in either order. Partner will then add the fourth of either rank if held.

Full house: play two cards of opposite colour, from the trio first and the pair second. Partner will add the fourth if he can match the first card, or the third and fourth if he can match the second.

Two or more pairs, no triplet: Play a pair as the first two cards and then pass.

Three of a kind, no pair: Play a red card from the triplet, preferably a heart, then pass (but come back later if appropriate).

One pair: Play a black card from the pair, then pass. If both are red, play the diamond and pass.

*Weak signals*. These are almost invariably used on the fourth hand, often on the third, sometimes on the second, or, in general, whenever leading from a hand containing fewer than seven cards. The point is that an apparent straight flush signal may not mean what it would normally mean according to the table, partly because it is now necessary to make as much as possible from the fewer cards available, and partly because meanings can be checked by reference to the cards already played and remaining visible on the table.

Flush: holding a complete 5-card flush, play the lowest then the highest. For example, from 2–5–7–J–K play 2 then K. Holding only four to a flush, play low then high but in range. For example, from 2–7–J–K play 7 then J, or J then K. This allows possible conversion into a straight if the flush misses. From only three to a flush, play high then low, in range if possible.

Straight: holding a complete 5-card straight, play the lowest of them and then the highest (regardless of suit). From four to a straight, play low-high, as close together as possible and preferably in different suits. From only three to a straight, play high then low, in different suits if possible.

More elaborate signals than these have been devised, but 'if you want any more, you must sing it yourself'.

# 31

# —— THE BUM GAME ——

## *For the player who tends to come bottom*

This amusing but skill-rewarding game for two to five players (four is best) is based on a Chinese game called Zheng Shàngyóu, which was collected by John McLeod and first described by him in the Journal of the International Playing-Card Society. Other versions of it have been found in Japan and France, and it bears points of similarity to certain East European games such as the Russian Durak ('Fool') and Korol ('King').

Its Chinese title means 'Climbing Up', in the sense of climbing up to a higher position – social climbing perhaps. The Japanese version is called Dai Hin Min, meaning 'Very Poor Man', or possibly 'Drop-out'. The French name, Trouduc, is equivalent to the American 'ass-hole', meaning someone at the bottom of the social heap. The London Card Club refers to it as 'Pits', and in my own circle we play a modified version which we call the 'The Bum Game'.

All this should give you an idea of the general sociological flavour of the game, and may even put you off by its unsavouriness. But persevere! It is not only great fun to play, and unlike anything you've played before, but also, when you once get into it, turns out to call for unusual elements of skill.

The most novel feature of the game is that it is the only one in which players physically change positions from deal to deal. If you want to play it properly, you should even provide four different types of chair for them to sit on. The basic idea is that players race to play out all the cards from their hand. For the first deal it doesn't matter who sits where. The first to get rid of all his cards is designated 'the Boss', and takes his position on a dignified but comfortable chair at the head of the table. The second to go out becomes 'the Foreman', and moves to a more functional office chair placed to the left of the Boss. Third out becomes 'the Worker', and occupies a hard wooden chair to the left of the Foreman and opposite the Boss. The last player left with cards in hand is the Bum, or Dogsbody, referred to in the title. He sits on a broken stool or creaky packing-case at the fourth side of the table. Subsequent deals may produce different results, causing players to occupy higher or lower positions in the hierarchy. But, as you will see, the game is so designed as to favour the current Boss and Foreman at the expense of the Worker and Bum, so that it is not so easy to make your way up the ladder if you have the misfortune to find yourself at the bottom at the end of the first deal.

The following member of the social climbing family, as it has evolved in my group of players, is described for four players, with variations for two to five following the main description.

## The Game

*Cards and positions*. Use a 52-card pack plus two Jokers. Draw for initial positions, the lowest taking the Bum's place, the highest sitting at his left in the Boss's chair, and the others following the same principle.

*Deal*. The cards are always shuffled and dealt by the current Bum, or, in the first deal, by the player in the Bum's position. Deal all the cards out as far as they will go, so that two players receive 14 to the others' 13 each.

*Rank of cards*. The two Jokers are the highest cards. They are followed by the Deuces (Twos), Aces, Kings, Queens and so on down to the Threes, which are lowest of all. Suits are irrelevant. Jokers and Deuces are wild in certain circumstances, as explained below.

*Object*. The aim of the game is to get rid of all one's cards as soon as possible by playing them out to rounds of play which may be called 'tricks' for convenience.

*Play*. The opening lead is made by the player at dealer's left (the Boss), and the winner of each trick leads to the next. Won tricks are worthless in themselves and are thrown face down to a common pool. The advantage of winning a trick is the quite powerful one of being able to lead to the next.

The leader may lead:

- a single card, or
- two or more cards of the same rank, such as K–K, 4–4–4, etc, or
- a numerical sequence of three or more cards, such as 3–4–5 (the lowest possible), 9–T–J–Q–K, K–A–2–Joker, etc.

Each subsequent player must either pass or else play the same number and combination of cards as the previous player, but higher in rank.

Thus if a single card is led, each must play a higher card, and a Joker is unbeatable.

If a pair is led, each subsequent pair must be higher, and a pair of Jokers is unbeatable. If a triplet or quartet is led, such as 7–7–7(–7), each must play the same number of a higher rank, for which purpose 2–2–2(–2) is unbeatable. You cannot beat three of a kind by playing four of a kind, or a pair by playing three of a kind, as it is always necessary to play the same number of cards as the leader.

Similarly, the lead of a three-card sequence, such as 8–9–T, can only be beaten by a higher three-card sequence, such as 9–T–J: it cannot be beaten by, and indeed may not be followed by, a four-card sequence.

*Wild cards.* Jokers and Deuces may be used as wild cards in sets of matched cards. For example, 7–7–7–7 is beaten by 8–2–2–Joker, representing four Eights, and A–2–2 (three Aces) by 2–Joker–Joker (three Deuces). With the aid of wild cards it is possible, and permissible, to lead five or more of a kind. Jokers and Deuces may be used in sequences, but only in their normal positions (e.g. K–A–2–Joker), not as wild cards.

*Winning a trick.* Play continues with each in turn either passing or playing higher than the previous player. The turn may go round several times, and a player who has passed once is not debarred from playing again if able to do so. However, the same player may not play twice in succession. Three consecutive passes end the trick, and the person who played last must then turn it down and lead to the next. If he ran out of cards on his last play, the lead passes to his left.

*End of deal.* A player who runs out of cards ceases play. The first out of cards scores 3 points and becomes the next Boss, changing places if not already in that position. The second scores 2 and becomes the Foreman, the third 1 point and becomes the worker. The last player, or Bum, scores nothing, but bunches and shuffles the cards and deals to the next round, starting with the Boss and ending with the Foreman.

*Card exchange.* Before play, the Boss must remove the two lowest-ranking cards from his hand and pass them face down to the Bum, receiving in return the Bum's two highest-ranking cards. Similarly, the Foreman passes the Worker his lowest card – one only – in exchange for the Worker's highest. The purpose of this rule is to give the Boss and the Foreman an unfair advantage. The only consolation for the Bum and the Worker is that if either is dealt a Joker he is not obliged to give it away in the exchange, but may hang on to it.

When cards have been exchanged, the Boss leads to the first trick.

*End of game.* The game ends when one player wins by reaching a target score, say 20 for about three-quarters of an hour's play. One's final position in the hierarchy, whether Boss or Bum, is of no particular significance but may be used to break a tie.

*Variants.* Many variations are recorded in respect of scores and allowable combinations. As a matter of particular interest, the Chinese game also includes multiple sequences so that (for example) 6–6–7–7–8–8 is beaten by 7–7–8–8–9–9 or higher. In the Japanese game, if both Jokers are dealt to the Worker or the Bum, he may declare a revolution. The Boss then changes places with the Bum, and the Worker with the Foreman, with all the advantages of the exchange appertaining thereto.

The game may be played with varying numbers of Jokers. If they are differentiated from each other, for example by colour, it may be agreed that they beat one another in a particular order when played as singletons. In some versions of the game, Jokers may be used to represent Deuces but not to beat them in their own right.

It may be agreed that, in sequences, Jokers may be used as wild cards, and Deuces as natural low cards, so that 2–3–4 . . . etc is a valid sequence.

If, like my group of players, you are too lazy to keep changing places, you can instead prepare four place-cards labelled with the four titles, and simply shift them about at the end of each deal. In this case, however, you should ensure that when a player goes out, the next lead is made, not necessarily by the player on his left, but by the player occupying the highest hierarchical position from the previous deal.

## Other numbers of players

*Five players.* The third to run out of cards occupies a position between the Foreman and the Worker, and does not exchange any cards.

*Three players.* The positions are Boss, Middleman, Bum. The Boss passes his lowest card to the Bum and second lowest to the Middleman. The Bum passes his highest to the Boss and second highest to the Middleman. The Middleman passes to the Boss the highest card, and to the Bum the lowest card, from the hand originally dealt to him (before receipt of a card from each other player).

*Two players.* Deal 14 cards each and stack the rest face down. The first to run out of cards scores one point for each card remaining in the other's hand. The remaining cards are then dealt out and the Boss and Bum exchange their lowest and highest cards respectively. The Boss then leads from 13 cards and the Bum starts with 13 plus those remaining from the first deal. The same scoring applies at the end of the second deal.

## Notes on play

It is best not to arrange your cards in suits, which are irrelevant, but in ranking order, e.g.

Jo–2–A–K–J–9–9–9–7–6–5–5–3 (Jo = Joker)

The first thing you must do is to plan how to make the best of your combinations and how to get rid of your lowest-ranking cards, which are always the most most difficult. In the hand shown, for example, you must decide whether to play your Fives as a pair at the earliest opportunity, leaving you with two middling and one low singleton to dispose of (7–6–3), or to play 7–6–5 as a run, leaving you with two low stragglers (5–3). An advantage of the run 7–6–5 is that if the turn comes round again you can play your unbeatable Jo–2–A, or, with slight element of risk, your 2–A–K, enabling you to lead your Three upon winning the trick.

Having made a decision, it is usually best to stay with it. If the person on your right plays a pair of Threes or Fours, you should resist the temptation to play your Fives. If a single Five precedes you, the best response is the straggler Jack, which belongs to no set or sequence, rather than break into your three-card sequence or trio of Nines. Following a Three or Four, however, you would promptly throw a Five, as your decision to retain the sequence has turned it into a straggler.

You will aim to get rid of low cards as soon as possible and at every opportunity. For example, it is nearly always better to lead one Three than three Fives. If you lead four Threes early in the game you may well find opponents unable to follow to quadruplets, thus putting you well ahead; but if you get stuck with only Threes in hand, whether one or all four, and haven't got the lead, you'll certainly finish bottom. A minor exception is when you hold one very low rank and a lot of high ones, when you can sometimes bank on winning a round with a bunch of high cards and then going out by leading the low one – or pair, or however many you have of it.

If your highest card is, say, an Ace, you should, unless you can see a quick way of going out by playing it, hang on to it until you have counted out all the Deuces and Jokers, so that you can be sure of its winning a trick on a singleton lead. If you play it early and have it overtaken, you may never come in at all. If you have nothing higher than, say, Jacks, don't panic: just wait, and play carefully. You can hardly expect to win on such a hand, but it is by no means a foregone conclusion that you will come bottom. The all-important skill factor is a sense of timing.

## Sample game

After several rounds, Bum deals the following hands (Jo = Joker)

| | | | | | | | | | | | | | | | |
|------|----|---|---|---|---|---|---|---|---|---|---|---|---|---|---|
| Boss | Jo | 2 | A | Q | J | J | T | 9 | 8 | 8 | 7 | 4 | 3 | 3 | |
| Foreman | 2 | 2 | A | J | T | T | 9 | 9 | 8 | 7 | 7 | 5 | 5 | 3 | |
| Worker | A | K | K | K | Q | J | T | 6 | 6 | 6 | 5 | 4 | 4 | | |
| Bum | Jo | 2 | A | K | Q | Q | 9 | 8 | 7 | 6 | 5 | 4 | 3 | | |

After the exchange of high and low cards, these become:

| | | | | | | | | | | | | | | |
|------|----|---|---|---|---|---|---|---|---|---|---|---|---|---|
| Boss | Jo | 2 | 2 | A | A | Q | J | J | T | 9 | 8 | 8 | 7 | 4 |
| Foreman | 2 | 2 | A | A | J | T | T | 9 | 9 | 8 | 7 | 7 | 5 | 5 |
| Worker | K | K | K | Q | J | T | 6 | 6 | 6 | 5 | 4 | 4 | 3 | |
| Bum | Jo | K | Q | Q | 9 | 8 | 7 | 6 | 5 | 4 | 3 | 3 | 3 | |

The Boss kicks off with his long sequence of Seven to Queen, which no-one can follow, and leads his singleton Four to the next trick. Foreman plays an Ace, Worker passes, Bum wins with his Joker, and leads his long sequence from Three to Nine. After three tricks the hands are:

| | | | | | | | | | | | | | | |
|------|----|---|---|---|---|---|---|---|---|---|---|---|---|---|
| Boss | Jo | 2 | 2 | A | A | J | 8 | | | | | | | |
| Foreman | 2 | 2 | A | J | T | T | 9 | 9 | 8 | 7 | 7 | 5 | 5 | |
| Worker | K | K | K | Q | J | T | 6 | 6 | 6 | 5 | 4 | 4 | 3 | |
| Bum | K | Q | Q | 3 | 3 | | | | | | | | | |

Bum now leads his pair of Threes, followed by Eights (2–8 from the Boss), Tens, Kings, pass, Aces, and finally Deuces from the Foreman.

This leaves:

| Boss | Jo | 2 | J |   |   |   |   |   |   |   |   |
|------|----|----|----|----|----|----|----|----|----|----|----|
| Foreman | A | J | 9 | 9 | 8 | 7 | 7 | 5 | 5 |   |   |
| Worker | K | Q | J | T | 6 | 6 | 6 | 5 | 4 | 4 | 3 |
| Bum | K | Q | Q |   |   |   |   |   |   |   |   |

The Foreman, after much thought, leads his pair of Fives rather than 7–8–9, which would leave four straggly cards. These are followed by Sixes, Queens, and the Boss's unbeatable Deuce-Joker. The Boss now exits with his Jack, to which Foreman plays an unbeatable Ace to find himself on lead again from this position:

| Foreman | J | 9 | 9 | 8 | 7 | 7 |   |   |   |
|---------|---|---|---|---|---|---|---|---|---|
| Worker | K | Q | J | T | 6 | 5 | 4 | 4 | 3 |
| Bum | K | 3 | 3 |   |   |   |   |   |   |

This time he opts for the three-card sequence, 7–8–9. The Worker overtakes with T–J–Q, wins, leads 3–4–5–6, which no-one can follow. Neither can they follow his King, and he goes out second with the Four. Bum thereupon goes out with his King, leaving Foreman with J–9–7 and changing places with him in the hierarchy.

Had Foreman led his pair of Sevens from the above position, he would have held the trick, led Nines, held it again, and led the Eight, leaving himself with an odd Jack. He would then only have lost if Worker had been concentrating enough to realise that his King was now unbeatable and should be played. Otherwise he would have played the Ten (keeping J–Q–K intact), and Foreman would have dropped by only one position instead of two.

The more you play this extraordinary game, the more fascinating it becomes.

# 32

## —— NEWMARKET ——

### *An old favourite from start to finish*

This popular pastime of pubs and clubs has undergone a number of changes since it first appeared in the card-game textbooks. In various forms it goes right back to a game called Comet played at court in 17th century France. Other games of the same family bear such picturesque names as Yellow Dwarf, Pope Joan, Spinado and Pink Nines. Many are named after other racecourses, including Epsom and the American game of Michigan.

The following rules are typical of the modern game (South London, 1990s), but variations in detail may be encountered from place to place.

*Cards.* Standard 52-card pack. Cards run from low to high as follows:

A 2 3 4 5 6 7 8 9 T J Q K

*Players.* Three to eight; ideal for four.

*Deal.* Remove the four Kings and set them out face up on the table. Deal all the cards out one at a time, the last of each round going to a 'dead hand' which is left face down. It doesn't matter that some players have more cards than others.

*Staking.* Everybody stakes the same agreed amount to a pool or kitty, and another agreed amount on each of the four Kings.

*Object.* There are two aims. One is to be the first to play out all one's cards, thereby winning the kitty. If no-one goes out, the kitty is increased and carried forward to the next deal. The other is to win a King stake by playing the Queen of the same suit. The game ends when all four King stakes have been won. This takes several deals, and sometimes many more.

*Buying the dead hand.* If the dealer is unsatisfied with his hand, he may exchange it for the dead hand free of charge. If he declines, the option of buying it passes to the left until someone else has exercised it or everyone has passed. Anyone who takes the dead hand, except the dealer, must pay another stake to the kitty. The two hands may not then be changed back again.

*Play.* Each in turn plays a card face up to the table in front of himself. Whoever holds the lowest diamond starts by playing it. The holder of the next higher diamond plays next, then of the next up, and so on in numerical order one at a time. If this sequence gets as far as the Queen, the player of that card wins the stake on the diamond King, turns the King down, and starts a new sequence as described below.

More usually, the sequence will peter out because the next diamond in sequence is lying in the dead hand so no-one can play it. In this case the player of the last card starts a new sequence by playing the lowest card he holds of either black suit. If he has no black suit, the turn to start passes to the left until someone can go.

Play continues in the same way. Each sequence is continued by the player holding the next higher card of the same suit. Whoever plays a Queen wins the stake on the matching King (if it has not already been won in a previous deal), turns it down, and starts again. The starter of a sequence must play the lowest card he has of a suit *opposite in colour* from the one last played.

*End of hand.* There are two ways a hand can end.

- Whoever plays the last card from their hand ends the play and wins the kitty.
- If no-one can start a new sequence because they can't change colour, play ceases and the kitty is carried forward.

In either case, the cards are bunched, the deal passes to the left, and everyone adds another stake to the kitty.

*Burying the Jack.* When three King stakes have gone and only one remains, no-one may buy the dead hand, and a new rule comes into play. The player holding the Queen matching the last King announces 'Bury the Jack' – or, if he also holds the Jack, the next card below the lowest card he holds of the sequence headed by the Queen. (For example, holding 9–T–J–Q he would say 'Bury the Eight'.) The holder of the card called for burial must then exchange his hand for the dead one, free of charge.

If no-one holds the Queen, she being in the dead hand, play continues with the hands as dealt, and the King stake will be carried forward to the next deal.

*End of game.* The game ends when someone plays the Queen matching the last King. This wins both the King stake and the kitty.

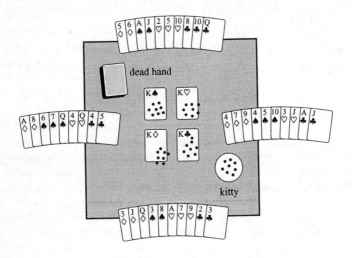

**Figure 24: Newmarket** West leads, holding the lowest diamond (Ace). No one has the Two, so West leads again, switching colour as required. The play continues:
West ♣4–5, ♡4
North ♡5 ♣8 ♡2
East ♡3 ♠4–5
West ♠6–7
South ♠8 ♡A ♣2–3 ◇3
East ◇4
North ◇5–6
East ◇7
West ◇8
East ◇9 ♣A ♡J
West ♡Q ♠Q, sweeping a King with each Queen and the kitty for going out.

This looks like the first deal played with a new pack. It is rare for the suits to be evenly distributed and for everyone who completes a sequence to be able to switch colour for a new lead. The nature of the game is such that in subsequent deals players are more likely to be dealt hands containing a void suit or dominated by cards of one colour.

# 33

## —— PONTOON ——

### A game by any other name...

This gambling game is played all over the world. Its most general and accurate title is **Twenty-One**, but different versions of it appear in different countries and in various social contexts under a variety of characteristic names. Pontoon, probably a corruption of its older French name, *vingt-un*, denotes the informal British game played at home, in school and (if permitted) in the pub. Its American equivalent is **Blackjack**, which differs in certain details from Pontoon, and is the form of the game played in British gaming establishments. As a casino game, it has the remarkable, if not unique, property of enabling an intelligent and assiduous player to consistently break even against the house, if not actually to stay ahead. This can be done by means of complex computer-aided analysis, but of course this makes the game less fun to play, especially as casino proprietors are quick to spot it and keen to stamp it out.

The following rules of the common or garden domestic British Pontoon are typical rather than definitive. As with all gambling games, details vary from school to school.

### The game

*Cards.* A standard 52-card pack.

*Preliminaries.* Pontoon is played for chips, counters or other manageable objects. Agree first on minimum and maximum permitted stakes (say, one to five), then each player should start with at least ten times the maximum stake (say fifty). Each deal is a separate event and is settled individually. The game ends when one player goes broke, or after an agreed time-limit. Choose first banker by drawing a card from the pack: Ace counts high, and highest banks first. The bankership subsequently passes to the first punter (player against the bank) to make a winning pontoon.

*Shuffling.* The cards are shuffled before the game starts, and by each player when he takes over the bank. After each deal the banker returns all played cards to the bottom of the pack and cuts, but does not shuffle, before dealing. (Players may agree beforehand to dispense with the cutting rule.)

*Value of cards.* Cards are only of interest for their numerical values, suit being completely irrelevant. Court cards count ten each, others their face value, and Ace either one or eleven at the discretion of the holder (and he may change his mind about it as often as he likes). Cards worth ten (T J Q K) are called tenths.

*Object of the game.* At each round of play each punter's object is to acquire a better hand of cards than the banker's. In the event of equality, the banker always wins. The value of a hand is the total value of the cards it comprises. The possible hands rank as follows:

| | |
|---|---|
| Bust (over 21) | – always loses, but banker wins equality. |
| A count of 16 to 21 | – the higher, the better. |
| Pontoon | – a count of 21 consisting of two cards, an Ace and a tenth. |
| Five-card trick | – five cards not exceeding 21 in sum. |
| Royal pontoon | – 21 made on three Sevens (only valid when held by a punter: in the banker's hand it is an ordinary '21'). |

*The deal and stake.* The banker deals one card face down to each player, in clockwise rotation ending with himself. Each punter (but not the banker) looks at his card and places a stake beside it, leaving the card face down on the table before him. The banker then deals everyone a second card face down.

*Pontoons?* The banker now looks at his cards, without revealing them, to see if he has a pontoon (an Ace and a tenth). If so he shows it, and each punter pays him twice his stake, unless he also has a pontoon, in which case he shows it and only loses his single stake. If the banker does not have a pontoon he leaves his cards face down and indicates his readiness to play further. In this event, any player holding a pontoon must face his Ace to show that he cannot lose and will be taking over the bankership.

*Pairs?* Any punter who has two cards of the same rank may split them, and play them as two separate hands. For this purpose they must be of the same rank: different tenths, such as a Queen and a Jack, will not do. The player indicates that he is splitting by separating the two cards, laying the whole of his stake against one of them and placing exactly the same amount as his stake against the other. The banker than deals him two more cards, one for each hand. Again, the punter looks at his second cards, and may split again if he has another pair. In all subsequent play, a punter who has split pairs must count himself as two (or more) separate people, and concern himself with each hand individually.

*Stick, buy, twist or bust.* The banker now addresses himself to each player in turn, dealing him as many more cards as requested, until the punter either sticks or announces himself bust. So long as the punter's count is less than 16 he must either buy or twist another card. At a count of 16 or more he may buy or twist, or else stick, thus indicating satisfaction with his hand and his intention to compete against the bank. At a count of 22 or more he must announce himself bust and hand his cards to the banket, who returns them to the bottom of the pack and appropriates the loser's stake.

If the punter says 'buy' the banker douls him a card face down; if he says 'twist', the card is dealt face up. In order to buy a card the punter must first increase his stake, but he must not pay less than he did for the previous card, nor more than the total already staked. As soon as he has twisted a card, he may only acquire more by twisting and may not revert to buying. If he gets a total of four cards with a combined count of 11 or less, so that he is bound to make a five-card trick, he may not buy but only twist a fifth. In any case, even when he (legally) buys a fifth card it is dealt face up instead of down. No player may have more than five cards in any one hand.

*The banker's play.* If everybody busts, the bank wins all stakes and there is no further play. If any punter is left in, however, the banker now reveals his two cards and continues to deal himself more cards, face up, until he either sticks or busts. (He may not split pairs.)

If the banker busts, each punter left in the game reveals his own cards and collects from the banker an amount equivalent to his stake if he has a count of 16 to 21, or twice his stake if he has a pontoon or a five-card trick, or three times his stake if he has a royal pontoon (three Sevens).

If the banker sticks at a count of 21 he wins the single stake of any punter with 21 or less, but is beaten by and pays out a single stake to a punter's pontoon, double stake to a five-card trick, treble stake to a royal pontoon. If his count is less than 21 he pays anyone with a higher count. (With a count of 17, for example, he says 'Pay 18', and anyone with 18 or more turns his cards face up to claim payment.)

If the banker has a five-card trick he beats anything except pontoon and royal pontoon. Banker's royal pontoon (three Sevens) counts only as an ordinary 21, and loses to pontoons and five-card tricks.

**Table 7** *Eventualities at Pontoon*

| Punter's hand | is beaten by banker's: | is paid if unbeaten: |
|---|---|---|
| bust (over 21) | anything | – |
| count of 16–21 | equal or higher count | single stake |
| pontoon (A + tenth) | pontoon only | double stake |
| five-card trick | five-card trick* | double stake |
| royal pontoon | (unbeatable) | treble stake |

\* Not pontoon, since if the banker had one nobody could have drawn five cards! In some circles, incidentally, a banker's five-card trick beats a pontoon. This marginally increases the excitement on some hands, but it contravenes the spirit of the game, and anything which further increases the banker's advantage (as this does) is to be deprecated.

### Notes on play

*Bank take-over*. The bank is taken over by any punter who wins a pontoon (not a royal pontoon or a five-card trick), but not if he does so on a split hand. If more than one has a pontoon, it goes to the first of them to the present banker's left.

Skill at gambling consists in playing systematically, though not necessarily to a 'system'; adjusting the amount of your stake to the probability of winning; and resisting the temptation to stake wildly when low on resources. My recommended one-to-five minimun/maximum stake enables you to (*a*) distinguish between a low, a middling and a high stake, in accordance with the probabilities, and (*b*) adjust this scale to your current resources. For example, when low on funds you should play cheese-paringly and fix your stakes at, say, 1, 2 or 3; when well off you may fix them at 2, 3, 4 or 3, 4, 5; or at any other time work to a 1, 3, 5 series of gradations.

Do not underestimate the bank's advantage. Most of the banker's income derives from punters who bust, for they still pay him whether or not the banker himself busts. Another large proportion comes from the fact that he wins from equals. And, in his own play, he has an advantage in knowing how many punters are standing against him. As a player, your safest course is to stick when you can – even at 16, since the mean value of a card is seven, and the chances of your not busting are 2–1 against. The banker may conceivably stick at 16 if there is only one punter against him, but with three against him (or up to six, counting split hands) the draw of another card is more likely to win than an agreement to 'pay seventeens'.

The probability that the banker has a pontoon, or that you will be dealt one from scratch, is about 0.024, equivalent to less than 2½ per cent, or one in every 41 hands. (Hence, in a four-player game expect to see a pontoon once in every ten deals.) The probability of being dealt a five-card trick from scratch, according to my calculations, is twice as high – amounting to about 0.045, or 4¼ per cent, or one in every 22–23 hands. If fewer actually appear than this figure suggests, it is clearly because many potential five-card tricks are not filled out, but abandoned at the fourth or even third card. The probability that the banker will bust after you have stuck is about 0.3, or three in ten. This figure assumes that he follows the policy of always sticking when he can; if not, your chances improve.

The fact that an Ace may count 1 or 11 introduces some fascinating complications. In Blackjack terminology a hand containing an Ace and not exceeding 21 is described as 'soft'; if it exceeds 21 by counting the Ace as 11 it is 'hard'. It is pretty obvious that you should always stick at, say, 18 – but what about a 'soft' 18, which alternatively counts 8? Here the answer depends in part on how many cards you have – with four, for example, a count of 8 guarantees you a five-card trick; with three, you must consider the possibility of drawing an Eight or Nine, which gives you a lower stickable number, an Ace, Two or Three, which gives you a 21 or a five-card trick, a tenth, which leaves you back where you started (with 18), or one of the other four ranks, which complicate matters further.

Whether or not to split pairs is not a difficult question provided that you follow a policy in deciding which counts are good and which bad. If the individual count of each card is better than the total count of both, split them; otherwise, don't. All you need then is a good policy.

In view of the possibility of a five-card trick, the number of cards on which you reach a given count is of considerable significance. The following suggestions for strategy are therefore subdivided into the numbers of cards held.

*First card.* Stake high on an Ace, for obvious reasons. The probability of being dealt a tenth next is about 0.38, giving two chances in five of making a pontoon. On a tenth, stake high, but with reservations. The probability of a pontoon is less than 0.08 (12–1 against). You have a three-in-ten chance of getting a second tenth, and must weigh that against the possibility that banker will make 20 or 21. In straitened circumstances, make it a middling stake. On anything else, prefer to stake low.

*Second card (no pair).* Stick on 16–20 (hard): your chances of *not* busting if you twist at 16 are barely two in five, and naturally worse on higher numbers. The banker will certainly beat your 16 if he sticks, but it is safer to bank on his busting than to try it yourself. On a soft 18–20, stick if you want to play it safe. Soft 16/17 is better counted as 6/7.

A hard count of 12–15 is the worst range of all, and the safest procedure is to twist. The fact that the mean value of a card is seven should not be taken to imply that 14 is the most promising count: 12 is clearly better, as it gives you the smallest chance of busting. A soft count of 12–15 should, of course, be regarded as 2–5.

A count of 10 or 11 is highly favourable – see *First card* for the probabilities. Buy, rather than twist.

On a count of less than 10, buy, for a modest amount. Do not start splashing out yet against the possibility of a five-card trick.

## Splitting pairs

Aces: you will do better to split than to regard them as the foundation of a five card trick.

Tenths: the question here is whether a count of 20 in the hand is better than two chances of a pontoon in the bush. It surely is. Don't split.

Nines: your choice is to stick at 18, or to try for two slightly-better-than-even chances of not doing worse. Don't split unless you can afford to indulge a delight in gambling for the sake of it.

Eights: your choice is to stick at 16, twist to a 5-in-13 chance of improving, or split on two 9-in-13 chances of improving a count of eight. Splitting is best; sticking worst.

Sevens, Sixes: neither rank allows you to stick, and both put you in the dreaded 12–15 range. Always split. (The odds against drawing a royal pontoon to a pair of Sevens are about 24–1.)

Don't split Fives, as 10 is a good count to buy to.

Split Fours: it's true that they are of a favourable average value for a five-card trick, but the chances are not good, and 8 is a bad count to buy to.

Don't split Threes or Twos: both 6 and 4 are acceptable counts to buy to, and you may be permitted the thought of a five-card trick.

*Third card.* Stick on hard 16–21. If you must gamble on soft 20, twist, don't buy: you have one chance of improving, four of equalising, eight of doing worse. Whether you count this as only a five-in-thirteen chance of not doing worse, or an eight-in-thirteen chance of not doing better, the odds are still not in your favour. Soft 18 or 19 is best left alone, but you may twist (or even buy, if you can afford it) to soft 16 or 17, either of which is at least in the running for a five-card trick.

With 12–15 (hard), twist, as for the same total on two cards. Count soft 14–15 as 4–5 and buy with a view to a five-card trick. If you have soft 13, you have been playing it all wrong, and soft 12 on three cards is only obtainable with a card counting zero, which Pontoon has not yet invented.

Buy gladly with 10 or 11, and with a view to a five-card trick on a count of 4–7. Buy cheaply or twist, on a count of 8–9.

*Fourth card.* If you have from 5 to 11, you are obliged to twist, as the five-card trick is beyond question. From 12 to 20, of course, your only concern is not to bust, and the probability of doing so gradually increases as follows:

*Count of*  12 : 0.31 *probability* (3 *in* 10 *chances of busting*)
             13 : 0.38
             14 : 0.46
             15 : 0.54
             16 : 0.62
             17 : 0.69
             18 : 0.77
             19 : 0.85
             20 : 0.92

In general, then, you may consider buying so long as your chances of not busting are better than even, i.e. up to a count of 14. You can't stick at 15, so whether you buy or twist is a question that must be answered by balancing the slightly-worse-than-even chance of improving against how much you can afford to gamble.

From 16 upwards the probability of making a five-card trick is exactly the same as that of improving a similar count on a smaller number of cards. However, the difference is that you now stand to win twice your stake if successful as against losing only your single stake if you bust. At 16, then, you have 62 chances in 100 of losing one stake (*total*: minus 62), but 38 chances of gaining two stakes (*total*: plus 76). This produces a balance of +8 in your favour, so at 16 it is worth buying if you can afford it, or twisting if not. At a count of 17, a similar calculation of the balance turns out to be almost the same amount against you, so it would be slightly better to stick. At 18 or more, you should stick.

*Banker's play.* The same suggestions as those made above for punters apply also when you are the banker, only more so, since you have a natural advantage. If you always stick when you can, you are bound to win in the long run. But, since you don't know how long a run you are going to get, you may be influenced in some of your decisions by the number of punters standing against you. For example, with three against you it is hardly worth sticking at 16; with only one against you, you will already have gained two stakes and can well afford to take another card to a count of 16.

## Sample round

The players are Abel, Baker, Charlie and Dealer (banker), who distributes cards as follows:

*First two cards*
A is dealt ♣3, stakes 3, dealt ♣2 for a count of 5.
B is dealt ♡K, stakes 4, dealt ♠2 for a count of 12.
C is dealt ♡8, stakes 2, dealt ♠8, splits, staking 2 on each count of 8.
C-right is dealt ◇6, counts 14.
C-left is dealt ♠3, counts 11.
D deals himself ♠A ◇2, counts 3 or 13.

*Further transactions*
A (staking 3 on 5) buys ♣T for 2, counts 15 (staking 5 on 15) twists ♡5, sticks at 20.
B (staking 4 on 12) twists ♣9, sticks at 21.
C-right (staking 2 on 14) twists ♠K, busts.
C-left (staking 2 on 11) buys ♡A for 2, counts 13 (now staking 4 on 13) twists ◇A, counts 14, twists ♣4 for 18 on a five-card trick.
Dealer is now facing three hands (out of four) on a count of 3 or 13. Draws ♠Q for 13, ♡7 for 20, announces 'Pay twenty-ones'.

*Result*

| | |
|---|---|
| Abel (20) pays 5 to Dealer . . . | −5 for A |
| Baker (21) receives 4 from Dealer . . . | +4 for B |
| Charlie Right (bust) pays 2 to Dealer . . . | |
| Charlie Left (five cards) receives 2 × 4 from Dealer | +6 for C |
| Total | −5 for D |

*Variants.* Gambling games vary more widely and change faster than any other type of game, which is why book descriptions of Vingt-un tend to sound archaic (it should be regarded as a forerunner of Pontoon rather than the same game).

In some circles, a pontoon is strictly defined as an Ace and a 'royal', Ace and Ten being only an ordinary 21. The objection to this is that it increases the banker's advantage by reducing a punter's chance to take over by 25 per cent.

Some permit the banker to look at his first card before dealing out any seconds, and, if he likes what he sees, to announce 'Double'. In this case all players must double the stake they have placed on their first card before the seconds are dealt. Again, it may be objected that this works to the banker's advantage.

There are various ways of changing the bankership. The least satisfactory, though clearly the fairest, is for each player to deal in turn. Or the banker may offer to sell the bankership, or entertain an offer to buy it, at any time, so long as the price is acceptable. This is usually followed when the banker has been playing so badly that he cannot afford to lose too heavily on the following round.

A Joker may be conveniently put to use as a marker card. Place it at the bottom of the pack before the first deal. When it appears at the top, shuffle the cards, or allow the bankership to pass to the left or be sold by auction.

# 34

## BRAG

**Wild East ancestor of Wild West Poker**

Brag has been one of Britain's most popular gambling games for centuries, a position confirmed in a survey conducted in the 1980s which showed it to rank fourth on a list of the most widely played card games. It can be traced back to the 16th-century game of Post, a relative of the Tudor court game of Primero. Later called Post and Pair, it first appeared under the name Brag in the 1720s, when it was still regarded as an aristocratic pastime. Since then it has suffered a social decline under the assault of its richer and more sophisticated American cousin Poker, from which it has borrowed a feature or two lacking from the original game.

Brag is an eminently non-standard game occurring in a variety of forms, of which the following are but a selection. All, however, are based on the same three-card combinations, namely:

- *Prial* (= *Pair Royal*). Three cards of the same rank. A prial of Aces beats a prial of Kings, and so on down to the lowest prial (Twos). A prial of Aces, however, is not the best hand but is beaten by a prial of Threes, although in most other respects Three ranks in its normal position between Two and Four.
- *Flush Run* (*or Running Flush*). Three cards in suit and sequence, such as 2–3–4 or Q–K–A. As between flush runs, the one with the highest-ranking top card wins. The Q–K–A hand, however, is not highest but is beaten by A–2–3, which can be beaten only by a prial.

- *Run.* Three cards in numerical sequence but not all of the same suit. The highest is A–2–3, followed by A–K–Q, and the lowest is 4–3–2.
- *Flush.* Any three cards of the same suit. As between competing flushes, the one with the highest top card wins, or second highest if tied, or third if tied again. Ace is highest, Two lowest, Three second lowest.
- *Pair.* Two cards of the same rank, the third one odd. A pair of Aces beats Kings, and so on down to Threes and then Twos (lowest). If tied, the rank of the odd card decides.
- *High card.* As between competing hands containing none of these combinations, the best is the one with the highest ranking top card, or second if tied, and so on. Ace is high, Three and Two are low.

*Wildcards.* One or more cards may be designated wild, standing for any card nominated by its holder. The Jack of clubs and/or any other Jack or Ace is traditional. Alternatively a Joker may be added to the pack as a wild card. Traditionally, a hand containing wild cards beats an equal hand containing none or fewer, but this seems now to have been reversed under the influence of Poker.

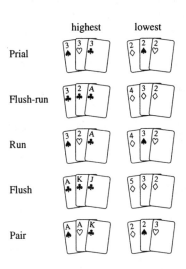

**Figure 25: Brag** Named Brag hands (as opposed to three unmatched cards) from highest to lowest – a prial of Threes to a pair of Twos.

# Three-card Brag

Decide first dealer by any agreed means. A game consists of any number of deals so long as all players deal the same number of times. Cards are shuffled at the start of play and immediately after any deal won with a prial, but not otherwise. Dealer puts up an agreed stake in advance (*ante*) and deals cards face down one at a time clockwise around the table until everyone has three. Place the remainder face *up* to the left to show the position of the deal.

Players now look at their cards (unless playing blind, as explained below). The first player to dealer's left must either bet any amount not less than the ante, or *stack*, i.e. throw his cards in, which he does by squaring them up and placing them face *up* on the top of the undealt portion of the pack.

Thereafter each player must do one of the following:

*Stack*  his cards if he does not wish to continue play;
*Stay*  by increasing his stake to equalise that of the previous active player on his right; or
*Raise*  by equalising (as above) and adding a further amount which subsequent players must meet if they wish to stay.

This continues until only two players are left in. Either of them may then stack (in which case the other wins without showing his cards), or raise, or *see* his opponent by equalising the stakes. The better hand then wins the pot, pool or kitty. If the caller admits defeat, he need not show his hand.

It should be noted that there is no 'showdown' with more than two players as there is at Poker. If all stakes are equalised when there are three or more players still in, the next to speak must either stack or raise.

*Betting blind.* Some schools permit players to bet *blind*, that is, without looking at their hand but leaving their cards face down on the table. A blind player may stack, stay or raise in the usual way, and may cease to play blind at any time by taking up his cards. So long as he does play blind, however, he need only bet half the appropriate stakes, while non-blind or 'open' players must be double the amount by which he raises. In this game there is a rule that 'you cannot see a blind man'. Consequently, if one of the last two left in is playing blind the other must either keep equalising the amount he bets, or raise it, until either of them stacks or the blind man takes up his cards.

If both continue to play blind the situation is even more amusing, though in some schools it is permitted for a blind man to 'see' a blind man. If everybody stacks, leaving a blind man to win the kitty with his unseen hand, he is permitted (if he wishes) to keep the same hand for his next deal, provided that he does not look at it until the betting is under way. In this case it is customary to deal him three cards in the usual way, but face up, in order to 'preserve the order of the cards'. These are then stacked before play begins.

# Five-card Brag

Five cards are dealt to each player, who rejects any two and plays the rest in the usual way. In this version there is nothing special about Threes, but the highest hand may be agreed to be a prial of Fives.

# Seven- and Nine-card Brag

In Seven-card, as the name implies, seven cards are dealt to each player. He forms six of these into two Brag hands, placing the higher of them to his left and the lower to his right, and rejecting the odd card. When ready, the player at dealer's left turns up his left (higher) hand. Each in turn after him either passes, if he cannot beat it, or turns his left hand face up if he can. When this round is complete, the player showing the highest hand then turns up his right hand, and the others then likewise if they can beat it. A player whose two hands are each highest in their turn wins the pool, to which everyone will have anted an agreed amount at the start of play. A player who wins on one hand and ties for best on the other also takes the pool, and in the unlikely event of two ties the pool is carried forward to the next deal.

Refinements: (*a*) there is nothing special about Threes, but a prial of Sevens is the top hand, beating a prial of Aces; (*b*) if anyone is dealt four of a kind among his seven cards he exposes them immediately, and the highest ranking four of a kind wins the pool. Four Aces may be beaten, in some circles, by four Fours or four Sevens (as agreed).

Nine-card Brag works on the same principle. Each player receives nine cards and arranges them into three Brag hands, which are revealed in order from highest to lowest as described above. A player must win all three hands to take the pool, or at least tie best on any he does not win outright, otherwise the pool is carried forward. The highest hand is four of a kind, which wins outright if dealt originally. Four Nines (or Fours, as agreed) beat any other four, and a prial of Nines (or Three) beats any other prial.

# Crash

A logical extension of Nine-card Brag, which became popular around Norwich some years ago. Four players receive thirteen cards each and form them into four Brag hands, which they place face down in a row, rejecting the odd card. Each hand is then revealed in turn, in order from left to right or right to left but not at random, and the winner marks one point on a special scoring board. In some circles the last hand only scores if it is a pair or better. The game is won – after as many deals as it takes – by the first player to mark seven points, but if one player wins all four hands in a deal it is a *crash* and he wins outright. Anyone who has made no score at the end of a game may be required to pay extra to the winner, or to ante double stakes to the next pool. (A Crash board for marking the points consists of a square of wood about five inches each side, with two lines of thirteen holes drilled from corner to corner like a St Andrew's cross, the middle hole being common to both. Each player starts with his peg or matchstick at one corner and advances it one hole per point towards the centre, which, of course, it takes seven steps to reach).

# American Brag

This is played like Poker but with three cards and Brag hands. All Jacks and Nines are wild cards (braggers). The highest hand is three braggers, since wild hands beat natural hands of the same degree.

# Bastard Brag

Also known as **Stop the Bus**.

Everyone antes an agreed amount. Three cards are dealt to each player and three face up to the middle of the table as a spare hand. Each player in turn may exchange any or all of his cards for the spare hand, and the process of exchanging with the cards in the middle continues until one player, satisfied with his hand, ends the game by knocking. The others may then stick or make one more exchange before the showdown, at which the best hand wins. In an improved version of the game, a player may exchange either one or all three cards, but not two, and/or each player following a knock *must* exchange one last time. This version renders the name of the game even more appropriate.

# Classical Brag

This is the old version of the game still described in the textbooks. There are no runs or flushes. The highest hand is a prial of Aces, followed by successively lower-ranking prials down to the Twos (nothing special about Threes). The next best hand is a pair, again ranking from Aces down to Twos, and with the odd card deciding in the event of a tie. Hands containing neither combination are decided on the highest cards as usual. There are three wild cards or braggers: ♣J, ♢A and ♢9. A hand with braggers beats an equal hand with none or fewer. Betting proceeds as at Poker rather than modern Brag, i.e. whenever all bets are equalised there is a showdown, regardless of how many are left in.

# Three-stake Brag

This is Classical Brag (see above) played in the following way: each player puts up three separate stakes before the deal, and receives two cards face down and one face up. The player with the highest-ranking upcard wins the first stake, or, if there is a tie for best, it goes to the first tied player to the dealer's left. Next, the hands are taken up and bet on in the normal way. The additional amounts go to augment the second stake, which is won by the player with the best hand or by the last remaining player if the others all drop. Finally, each player reveals his three cards and the third stake goes to the player whose cards total the nearest to 31 (counting Ace 11, courts 10, others face value). A player whose cards total under 31 may draw one or more cards in order to approach this total more nearly, but if he exceeds 31 he is bust and cannot win the stake. But it is not a bust if the original three cards exceed 31 – e.g. a hand worth 33 would win over a hand worth 28 and tie with a hand worth 29. In the event of a tie the stake is shared. This game is of some historic interest, being substantially the same as *Post and Pair* described in Cotton's *Compleat Gamester*, 1674.

# 35

## ─────── POKER ───────

### *The great leveller*

Contrary to the popular opinion of those who do not play it, Poker is a game of skill. It also happens to be a gambling game, but only in the technical sense of the word – that is, in the sense that it cannot be played for score-points, like Bridge, but only for hard score, i.e. cash, or at least for tokens representing cash ('chips'). It also differs from Bridge and other intellectual card games in the fundamental sense that the latter are played with cards whereas Poker is played with money. No physical card-play is involved at all in Poker. Playing-cards merely serve the purpose of providing raw material on which to exercise the skills of money management and practical psychology. In the absence of cards, which have the merit of being convenient and traditional, the play of Poker can be – and often is – applied equally well to dice, dominoes, Mah Jong tiles, Scrabble tiles, even pound notes and dollar bills. An understanding of the basic mathematical principles of probability is helpful to this game, but the skills involved are essentially psychological. It is the fact that you play the opponents and not the cards that makes Poker the great leveller.

A product of American genius, Poker is the most advanced and globally successful member of an ancient family of games including Brag and Primero. It originated around New Orleans during the 1820s, probably from a group of related games then chiefly represented by the French game of Poque. Further evolution during the course of the 19th century turned it into the highly sophisticated game that it is today – a game not to be taken or undertaken lightly.

Like most gambling games, and unlike Bridge, Poker is played in a variety of forms. All are based on the same five-card combinations or 'Poker hands', as described below, and are best played with proper Poker chips available from any good games shop. Chips come in various colours that may be used to represent any agreed scale of values. At least three colours are required, the lowest being white, the middle red, and the highest blue (whence the phrase 'blue chip' for an investment of high value). Typical scales of value are:

| white | 1 | 1 | 1 | 1 |
|--------|-----|-----|-----|-----|
| red | 2 | 2 | 5 | 5 |
| blue | 5 | 10 | 20 | 25 |
| yellow | 25 | 25 | 50 | 100 |
| black | 100 | 100 | 200 | 250 |

Beginners should start with Draw Poker on a scale of 1–2–5.

The five-card Poker hands rank from highest to lowest as follows. Note that individual cards rank 2 3 4 5 6 7 8 7 9 T J Q K A, with Ace optionally low in a numerical sequence, and that no suit is better than another. (The abbreviations in brackets are non-standard.)

*Straight flush (SF)*. Five cards in suit and sequence, Ace counting high or low. The lowest is A–2–3–4–5 of a suit. The highest, T–J–Q–K–A of a suit, is called a royal flush.

*Four of a kind, or Fours (4S)*. Four of the same rank, from 2–2–2–2–*x* to A–A–A–A–*x*. The fifth card (*x*) is immaterial.

*Full house (FH)*. Three of a kind and a pair, from 2–2–2–3–3 to A–A–A–K–K. Of two full houses, the one with the higher triplet prevails – e.g. 5–5–5–2–2 beats 4–4–4–K–K.

*Flush (FL)*. Five cards of the same suit but not all in sequence. The lowest would be 2–3–4–5–7 of a suit, the highest A–K–Q–J–9.

*Straight*. Five cards in sequence, but not all the same suit, from A–2–3–4–5 to A–K–Q–J–T.

*Triplet, three of a kind, threes (3S)*. Three of the same rank plus two of two different ranks, from 2–2–2–*x*–*y* to A–A–A–*x*–*y*.

*Two pairs (2P)*. Self-explanatory, from 2–2–3–3–*x* to A–A–K–K–*x*. Competing two pairs are decided on the higher pair, or the lower if equal, or the odd card if still equal. Thus J–J–7–7–3 beats J–J–6–6–4 or J–J–7–7–2.

*One pair (1P).* From 2–2–*x*–*y*–*z* to A–A–*x*–*y*–*z*. A higher pair beats a lower; if equal, the highest odd card decides.

*High card.* A hand containing no pair, flush or straight is called a high-card hand because when two or more of them compete the one with the highest card wins, or second highest if equal, and so on. Thus A–7–5–4–2 (Ace high) beats K–Q–J–T–8 (King high), which beats K–Q–J–T–7.

Poker cannot be successfully played without instant recognition of each type of hand for its true worth. The following table indicates their relative value by showing how rare or common they are. The first column of figures shows how many different hands there are of each type. The second expresses the same thing as a percentage of the total number of possible hands. The third shows the odds-to-one against being dealt such a hand straight from the pack (higher figures rounded to nearest 50):

**Table 8** *Poker odds*

| Hand | Number | Per cent | Odds-to-1 against |
|---|---|---|---|
| Straightflush | 40 | 0.0015 | 65,000 |
| Four of a kind | 624 | 0.024 | 4,150 |
| Fullhouse | 3,744 | 0.144 | 700 |
| Flush | 5,108 | 0.196 | 500 |
| Straight | 10,200 | 0.392 | 250 |
| Three of a kind | 54,912 | 2.13 | 46 |
| Twopair | 123,552 | 4.75 | 20 |
| Onepair | 1,098,240 | 42.25 | 1½ |
| Highcard | 1,302,540 | 50.12 | 1 |
| Total | 2,598,960 | (100%) | |

From this it will be seen that about half the hands dealt are nothing in particular, and most of the remainder are one pair. At an evening of ordinary Draw Poker, most of the pots will be won on two pair or threes, while anything higher than a Full House would be something of an event. In case this sounds unexciting, it may be worth noting that different types of Poker game increase the frequency of winning on higher hands – for example, by dealing seven or more cards and allowing the player to choose the best five from them.

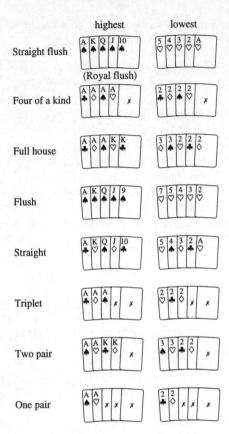

highest      lowest

Straight flush

(Royal flush)

Four of a kind

Full house

Flush

Straight

Triplet

Two pair

One pair

**Figure 26: Poker (1)** Named Poker hands (as opposed to five unmatched cards) from highest to lowest. Note that Ace counts high except in conjunction with 2−3−4−5, forming a straight. The top hand, an Ace high straight flush, is known as a royal flush. Cards marked 'x' are 'idlers' and count for nothing except to break a tie between otherwise equal two pairs.

# Draw Poker

With slight regional variations, this is the original form of the game and the most widely played throughout the world. It differs in some respects from the form described in many English books, which I refer to as

English Club Poker. It is also, but not quite accurately, sometimes known as Jackpots.

*Preliminaries.* From five to seven is a good number of players. With fewer, the game is dull; with more, there are not enough cards to go round in comfort. Each player should start with the equivalent of 200 chips in whites, reds and blues. Set a time limit on play and stop play at the end of the deal in which the limit expires. Agree on the value of the chips, the amount of the ante (ideally, one white chip), the maximum permitted raise in the first betting round (e.g. five whites or equivalent) and the maximum permitted in the second round (e.g. ten whites or equivalent). Alternatively, agree to play 'pot limits' – i.e. the maximum permitted raise is the size of the pot at the time it is made.

*Shuffling the cards.* Theoretically each new deal should be made from a thoroughly shuffled pack, and it is permissible to alternate between two packs so that one can be shuffled while the other is being dealt. In practice one pack is used continuously until a new one is called for – which anyone may do if he feels (rightly or wrongly) that the cards are 'running against him'. Also, in practice, there are people who prefer to play without shuffling the cards between deals, in order to produce 'more exciting hands'. There are such people who do this in all card games as a matter of course. It is a childish habit and has nothing to commend it.

Anybody who wishes has a right to shuffle, but the dealer has the right to shuffle last. Before dealing, he should have the cards cut by the player on his right. The purpose of this is to prevent the bottom card of the pack from being seen by anyone, as may sometimes happen at the end of a shuffle. For similar but less tenable reasons, some players insist that the top card of the pack be 'burned' immediately before dealing – that is, transferred from the top to the bottom of the pack. (I suspect that 'burned' originated as a mis-reading of 'buried'.)

*Ante.* Before the deal, each player contributes to the pot by paying an ante of one white chip, placing it in the centre of the table.

*Deal.* Deal cards one at a time, face down, in rotation, starting at dealer's left, until each player has received five cards.

*Opening.* Each player in turn, starting at dealer's left, may drop, check, or bet. A player *drops* if he has bad cards and does not wish to stay in the deal, by laying his cards face down on the table and announcing that he is out of the present pot. He *checks*, by announcing 'I check' or knocking on the table, if he wishes to stay in and play the hand but is either unwilling or unqualified to make the first or opening bet. The opening bet may only be made by a player whose hand contains a pair of Jacks or better (unless previous agreement has been made to 'open on anything'). He does so by announcing 'Open for two', or however many chips it may be, and pushes that number forwards towards the middle of the table – though not actually in it with the antes, as it is necessary during the course of the game to be able to see exactly how much each player has so far bet, and so determine whether or not the bets have been equalised.

If no player has opened the betting before the turn comes round again to the first to speak, the cards are thrown in and the next deal ensues. The antes stay in the middle of the table as part of the next pot, to which a fresh ante is made by each player.

*Continuation of first betting period.* Once somebody has opened, each player thereafter must do one of the following: drop out of play, 'stay' by increasing his stake so that it equals that of the previous player still in the game, or equal the last bet and 'raise'.

Example: Player A says 'Open for two'. Player B says 'Drop' and throws in his cards. Player C says 'Stay for two', staking two chips to equal the stake of the opener. Player D says 'Stay for two and raise two', pushing four chips towards the pot. Player E says 'Stay for four', since D has increased the amount necessary to stay in the pot and E does not wish to raise further. Back round to player A again, and he must pay two if he wishes to stay, since he is two short of the amount so far staked by E and D.

This continues until one of two things happens:

- Somebody raises and everybody else drops. The last raiser wins the pot without showing his hand and the deal is at an end.
- More usually, all bets are equalised between the two or more players who have stayed in the pot. Note: if one person raises and the others either drop or stay but do not re-raise, the betting period is at an end: a player may not re-raise himself.

When all bets are equalised it is time for the draw.

*The draw.* The dealer now addresses everybody in turn who is still in the game, starting at his left, and asks whether they want to 'stand pat' (keep the cards they were dealt) or exchange any. If not standing pat, each player discards from one to three cards, face down, and receives the same number dealt face down one at a time from the top of the pack. When the dealer gets round to himself he must announce clearly how many he is discarding and drawing.

Because it is nonsensical to exchange more than three cards in the draw, some players insist on a rule prohibiting the exchange of more, as implied in the paragraph above. Players should agree beforehand whether or not this rule applies. Serious players rarely, if ever, draw more than two.

If the player who opened the betting did so on a high pair – Jacks or better – it is quite possible that he may want to discard one of them in the draw. This is known as 'splitting openers'. He need not announce that he is doing so, but must keep track of his discards in case he wins the pot, for he may then be required to show that he was qualified to make the opening bet.

*Second betting period.* This time the first person to speak is not necessarily the player at dealer's left but the one who opened the first betting period. He may drop, bet, or check. Checking means that he wishes to stay in the pot but does not wish to open the betting this time round. If he checks, each player in turn after him has the same options. If everybody checks, then the original opener may not check again but must either drop or open the second period of betting.

Once the betting period has been opened, each player in turn after the opener may drop, meet the amount of the last bet, or meet it and raise again. This continues in exactly the same way as the first betting period. If all but one player drop out, the one left in wins the pot. Otherwise, betting continues until all bets have been equalised, at which point there is a showdown. All those still in the pot reveal their hands – they must do so, and must reveal them entirely – and the pot goes to the player with the best hand, or is divided equally if two have identical best hands. If the pot is won by the original opener and he cannot prove that he was qualified to open, it goes to the second best hand. If there is no second best (all but the opener having dropped), the pot is carried forward to the next deal.

*Irregularities.* In the event of a misdeal, such as exposing a card, dealing in the wrong order or with an imperfect or unshuffled pack, the cards are gathered in and the same dealer deals again after shuffling and cutting. If he misdeals twice in succession he forfeits the deal, which passes to the left.

If a player bets out of order, he must do whatever he said he was going to do (drop, bet or raise) when his proper turn comes round – he may not say one thing at the wrong time and do something different at the right.

If too many players exchange too many cards there may not be enough left in the pack to meet everyone's draw requirements. In this case the dealer deals cards from the pack as far as they will go short of the last card. This he keeps, and adds it to all the dropped hands and discards of the other players, except the discards of the original opener in case he split openers and has to prove it later. The new pack must be shuffled and cut, after which the draw can be continued from it.

If a player runs out of chips during the course of a hand he may (by previous agreement) be permitted to 'tap out'. This means that he may stay in the pot free of charge, provided that he does not raise but only notionally meets existing bets, and may even take part in the draw. All bets made after a player has tapped out are kept slightly apart from those made previously. If the tapper-out emerges the winner, he takes only the main pot: all the bets made after he tapped out constitute a second prize which goes to the second best hand. If not, he is out of the game, unless permitted to buy himself back in.

## Notes on play

Whole books can be written about strategy at Draw Poker, and have been, and pretty boring they are too. There is no substitute for experience, and in these pages no space to do more than outline the broadest of hints.

*Character of game.* How you play depends largely on how everyone else is playing. A 'loose' game is one in which players fool around, take reckless chances and reach bankruptcy at great speed. A 'tight' game is one in which the participants are either mathematicians or money grubbers or both: the game is played in expressionless silence, the draws are all of one card if any, and the action is only enlivened by long periods of rumination before each player makes a move. Needless to say, a sensible game steers a middle course between two extremes. A game is a social activity and players should be sociable without being silly, otherwise it will not serve its primary purpose of generating enjoyment at the exercise of skill. To any well balanced person the monetary aspect of the game is a secondary consideration, if it exists at all.

As a game progresses, it usually tends to get looser. It also gets looser if the table is a mixture of loose and tight players. In order to counterbalance this, I would recommend that you tend to err on the side of tightness, without going so far as to become a po-faced skinflint.

*Position.* Be conscious of your position during every deal. In the first betting period, the player at dealer's left may have a hand qualified to open, but if it is only a pair of Jacks (say), the bare minimum, he has as yet no way of knowing what the opposition is likely to hold. He may open and find himself raised all around the table, or he may check and find the deal passed up by everybody. The dealer, on the other hand, is in the best position to make a positive decision, because he will have heard all his opponents' initial reactions to their hands before he comes to speak. It is therefore sensible for a player in an early position to open with not less than a pair of Queens, Kings or even Aces, depending on how many there are at the table.

Throughout the game, it is useful to erase from your consciousness, from your vision if possible, those players who have dropped, and see only yourself in relation to those left in the pot. Your actions may then be guided by whether the players on your immediate right and left are tight or loose players, whether they are winning or losing, and so on.

*First betting period.* The first betting period is rather more mathematical than the second. First, you must assess the strength of your hand by whether it is probably the best, or the worst, or about middling. Since about half the hands dealt are nothing and most of the others are a pair, you can immediately assess a low or non-pair hand as worthless. On average, about half the people round the table should get a pair, which is why the minimum worthwhile opening hand is a pair of Jacks. Remember that the more players there are taking part, the greater likelihood there is of at least one opponent being dealt a strong hand, say two pair or three of a kind. Mathematics also enter into it because in the first period you are only partly betting on what your hand *is* – a greater consideration is what it may *become* after the draw. For this purpose the table below is worth being acquainted with. The first column shows the type of hand you may be dealt and the amount of it you would keep when discarding. (A 'kicker' is an Ace accompanying the main combination, which you may keep hold of in hope of pairing it. With three of a kind, the kicker may be any rank.) The next shows how many cards you might exchange from it, followed by the type of hand you hope to get as a result. For each type of desired result, the final column shows the odds against actually getting it.

A word about odds and probabilities. It is not worth attempting to commit them to memory if you haven't got that sort of mind, but sufficient to know which combinations are worth going for and which are very long shots. If you do remember any of the figures, one way

**Table 9** *Chances of improving the hand at 5-card Draw*

| Hand dealt | Cards drawn | Possible improvement | Odds-to-l against* |
|---|---|---|---|
| Ace high | 4 | 1P Aces | 3 |
| | | 2P Aces up | 14 |
| One pair | 3 | any | 2½ |
| | | 2P | 5 |
| | | 3S | 7† |
| | | FH | 97 |
| | | 4S | 360 |
| One pair + Ace kicker | 2 | any | 3 |
| | | 2P Aces up | 7½ |
| | | 2P other | 17 |
| | | 3S | 12 |
| | | FH | 120 |
| | | 4S | 1,080 |
| Two pair | 1 | FH only | 11 |
| Threes | 2 | any | 8½ |
| | | FH | 15½ |
| | | 4S | 22½ |
| Threes + Kicker | 1 | any | 11 |
| | | FH | 14½ |
| | | 4S | 46 |
| Fourstraight, double-ended | 1 | ST | 5 |
| Fourstraight, one place open | 1 | ST | 11 |
| Fourflush | 1 | FL | 4 |
| Four-card SF, double ended | 1 | ST or FL | 2 |
| | | SF | 22½ |
| Four-card SF, one place open | 1 | ST or FL | 3 |
| | | SF | 46 |

\* Odds over 100 are rounded.
† Often quoted as 8:1 against, but in fact 1 in 8 or 7:1 against (ignoring
  fractions).

of using them is this: if the odds offered you by the pot are greater
than those offered by the draw, make the draw; if not, don't. For
example, suppose there are 25 chips in the pot (including the ones you
have so far staked) and it costs you five to stay in. Then the pot is
offering odds of 25 to 5 or 5:1. It is therefore worth staying in on a
high pair, since the odds of improving after discarding three are 3:1
against, which is shorter than the odds offered by the pot. But it is
less worth while pursuing a two pair hand, as the odds against improvement are 11:1. Of course, the odds are not everything – they are only
a guide. Poker is primarily an intuitive game; but, just as there is no
reason why intuition should not enter your calculations, so there is no
reason why calculations should not form part of your intuition.

*Playing the dealt hand.* If you are dealt a high five-card combination
(straight, flush, full house or straight flush), you have no discarding
problems and will stand pat. Mathematics hardly enter into it: your
objective is the psychological one of betting hard enough to build up a
good pot but not so hard as to frighten everybody out of it.

Four of a kind is similar, except that you have the option of standing
pat or discarding the odd card just for fun – but make sure you don't
discard the wrong one or the joke will misfire badly. Some people deem
it immoral to discard one from four of a kind, but how often are you
likely to be in the happy position of so tussling with your conscience?

Any of these combinations are likely to be winners in the first round.
But what counts is not the first but the second round. Bear in mind
that players with worse hands may nevertheless convert them into
better as the result of the draw. You don't want to bet so hard as to
drive out such speculators, but you must remember that a pat hand,
though probably the best going in, is not necessarily the best coming
out.

Three of a kind is a good hand. It is usually the best going in and
quite often the best even after the draw. It also gives you the greatest
variety of options. You may discard two, giving yourself the best
chances of making any improvement, or one, which gives fair chances
and has the advantage of revealing no information about the shape of
your hand, since one card is the commonest and least tell-tale draw in

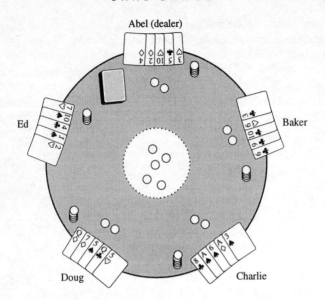

Abel (dealer)

Ed

Baker

Doug

Charlie

**Figure 27: Poker (2)** Opening deal in a five-player game to which Abel dealt. All have placed an agreed ante of 1 chip to the pot (represented here by the outlined circular area). Baker's pair of Sixes do not qualify as openers, but he may be willing to draw one to a flush, and checks. Charlie's Aces do so qualify, and he opens for two chips, which he pushes from his stack to a spot just outside the pot. Doug, with a very promising two pair, meets Baker's opening for two, but does not raise for fear of frightening subsequent players out. Ed, very properly, allows himself to be frightened out. Abel stays for 2, intending to draw one to his four-card straight, and Baker does likewise, holding four to a flush. The situation is now as illustrated, and the eight chips so far bet are now pushed into the pot with the original five. Note that these players are sufficiently experienced to hold their cards in the order dealt without arranging them by rank and suit, which would convey much useful information to the practised eye. (The cards are not exposed, of course.)

Charlie discards 3–6 and draws 2–9, making no improvement on his pair of Aces. Doug draws one – getting a Six for his Seven – not because he seriously expects to get a full house, but because his Queen-high two pair is probably the best hand, and standing pat might frighten others out. Abel draws a Two for his Ten, giving him a pair of Twos, and Baker the diamond Three for his heart Six, giving him a pair of Threes.

Charlie checks, Doug bets 2, and Abel throws in his pair of Twos. Baker tries a bluff, meeting Doug's 2 and raising 2 as if his one-card draw had made a straight or flush. Charlie now loses confidence in his Aces and folds. Doug sees Baker for 2 and, of course, his two pair wins. He gets 13 from the pot, 4 from Baker, and his own 4 back, yielding a net profit of 14 chips for 7 invested.

Not an exciting deal, but a typical and instructive one. Few hands at orthodox Draw Poker are won by anything higher than two pairs; the best hand going in is often the best hand going out; drawing one to a straight or flush rarely pays off; and if you (Baker) are really going to bluff, wait until you can afford to make it so big that no one dare call it.

sensible Poker. Or, if not too many remain in the pot, you may even take a chance and stand pat on it.

Two pair, by contrast, is the most awkward dealt hand to cope with, in many ways worse than a pair. The only sensible discard from two pair is one card, and the odds against improving (a full house being the only possible improvement) are 11:1. The only advantage is that the one-card discard at least gives nothing away. The problem, of course, is that two pair is usually the best hand going in, but rarely the best coming out. This applies especially if the pairs are low, since an opponent who went in with a high pair may well convert to a winning two pair. Hence the best thing to do with two pair is to bet hard in the first round if you bet at all, in order to drive out as much opposition as possible, and be prepared to relinquish it in the second period if it then seems unlikely to be the best round the table.

If you have a pair, discarding three is a dead give-away. However, you have the consolation of the best chances of making any improvement – 2½ to 1 according to the table, with a number of different hands as your ultimate prize. To give less away about your hand, you may keep the pair and a 'kicker' and merely exchange two. The higher the kicker, the better. With a pair and an Ace, few players would discard the Ace. If in the sort of company that invariably draws no cards or one, you could be ridiculously cheeky and discard one, keeping two kickers. The odds of making any improvement at all are about 5:1, specifically 7:1 against getting two pair and 22½:1 against threes. But don't make a habit of it.

The only combinationless hands worth taking seriously are four-flushes and open ended fourstraights, each of which is worthless in the first period and remains worthless in the second unless improved by the draw of one card, in which case they become very probable winners. If you have four cards of a suit the chances of drawing a fifth are about four to one against. If it fails you will either have to disown it in the second period or try to bluff it out, but at least it has the advantage of requiring the draw of only one card.

A hand containing four cards to a straight is only worth playing if they form an open ended sequence fillable by either of two cards, such as 7–8–9–T, which can be filled by a Six or a Jack. The odds are only 5:1 in this case, but are less worth playing in the case of an inside straight (e.g. 6–7–rubbish–8–9) or a closed straight (i.e. A–2–3–4–rubbish or A–K–Q–J–rubbish). Here only one rank will do, and the odds are 11:1 against.

Related hands are the pair-bobtail and four to a straight flush. If you have a four-card straight flush the odds against improvement are considerably shorter – 2:1 in the case of an open ended fourstraight and 3:1 if only one rank will fill the straight. In the former case, say 6–7–8–9 of spades, either of two cards will make a straight flush, any of six others will make a straight, and any of seven others a flush.

A pair-bobtail is a four-card straight or flush and a fifth card of the same rank as one of the others – for example, J–J–T–9–8 is a pair and an open ended straight, while ♠J–♡J–7–4–2 is a pair combined with a fourflush. The question in these cases is whether to keep the pair and discard the other three, or to go for the higher combination by breaking the pair up. In the first case you finish up with a pair, which is not a strong hand, but better than nothing and quite capable of winning a pot. In the second, you may finish up with a probably unbeatable hand, but only if you make it – if not, the loss of the pair leaves you worse off than when you started. The odds favour keeping the pair in most cases, and forgoing the chance of the higher hand, especially if the pair is as high as Aces or Kings.

*General.* The second betting period is less mathematical and more psychological. You will have seen how many cards are being drawn by your opponents, they will have seen how many are being drawn by you, and everyone will be trying to relate this to their knowledge of how everybody else thinks and behaves over the Poker table.

The two most useful generalisations that can be made for this period and for all other forms of Poker generally are as follows. First, if at any stage in the proceedings you really believe your hand is not the best round the table, drop it. You may be able to bluff your opponents into thinking your hand is better or worse than it really is, but you can't bluff the hand itself. The other side of the coin is that, having once decided that you are going to follow a hand through, do so with inner confidence. Never just string along in the hope that everyone else will drop out first and leave you to sweep the pot without showing your hand.

Second, the most dangerous property of a poor Poker player (in both senses of the word!) is predictability. Poker gives you plenty of opportunities for varying the way in which you draw cards and play the hands. If it becomes known that you always do the same thing – such as standing pat on two pair or betting too hard on a low straight, or holding your cards tight and close to the chest when you are sure you have a winner – then more observant players will note and remember it. I would say that the true meaning of the much misunderstood word 'bluff' lies in avoiding any sort of predictability in the way you play.

# Stud Poker

There is no draw in Stud Poker. Instead, some of your cards are dealt and kept face up, so that everyone can see part of everyone else's hand. For this reason Stud is more suitable than Draw for larger groups of players, eight being a good table. There are endless variations on the basic theme, but we will start with the simplest.

## Five-card or Short Stud

Everyone antes the minimum amount before the deal, or else (and preferably) the dealer *edges* by putting up as many chips as there are players.

After the shuffle and cut, deal a round of one card face down to each player followed by one card face up. Each player looks at his down-card and places it face down on the table before him as his hole card, partly covering it with his up-card.

The first betting interval follows, opened by the player showing the highest ranking up-card, or, in the case of a tie, by the tied player nearest to the dealer's left (dealer himself, if tied, counting as furthest from his own left). At this and each subsequent betting interval it is the dealer's responsibility to announce who is to bet first. The first to speak must either bet or *fold* (drop): at this stage it is not permitted to check or pass. Each subsequent player then folds, pays an equal amount to stay in, or raises by increasing that amount. After any raise there must be another complete round of announcements to enable each active player to fold, equalise or re-raise. This continues until all bets are equalised, or all but one player fold, in which case the one remaining wins the pot without exposing his hole card.

If two or more remain in the pot, deal each active player another up-card. Cards should be dealt with one hand from the top of the squared-up pack, which remains face down on the table. In some circles it is customary for the dealer to announce, as he deals each card, the best hand that could be held on the evidence of the player's up-cards at that moment, e.g. 'One 'pair', 'Ace high', 'Possible flush', etc.

The first to speak in this and subsequent betting intervals is the player showing the greatest number or highest value of paired cards if any, or the highest ranking individual card if not, followed by the second highest in the event of a tie and so on. First-to-speak may now check instead of folding or betting if he wishes, and if he checks each subsequent player has the same three options until someone bets, after which the others must fold, call or raise. If everyone checks the betting interval ends and the next card is dealt. A third and fourth upcard are dealt in this way, each followed by a betting interval.

A showdown is reached when the last person to raise has been called. All those in the pot must reveal their hole cards and the best hand wins the pot. If everyone checks there is an automatic showdown. If one player raises and everyone else folds he wins the pot without revealing his hole card.

Because there is no draw the winning hand is on average lower than in Draw Poker – often as low as a pair, sometimes merely a high card. Most of the action centres on paired combinations rather than straights and flushes. In practice this means you should not normally aim for, or bluff on, a possible straight or flush until you have your third up-card, unless your up-cards reveal a substantial threat – for instance, the possibility of a straight flush or at least a winning high pair.

## American Seven-card or Long Stud

Long Stud is played like Short Stud except that there are five betting intervals, which follow these deals:

1 Two cards down followed by one up
2 A second up-card
3 A third up-card
4 A fourth up-card
5 A third down-card.

By the last round, then, each player has four cards visible and three hole cards. When it comes to a showdown he selects any five cards from his seven to act as his final hand.

Strategy is the least of your worries. The first thing you have to do is recognise potential hands when you see them. Not for nothing is Long Stud known as *Down the River*, as you may gather when you note that a player showing four rubbish cards may actually be sitting on four of a kind. A useful exercise is to deal out seven hands without looking at the down-cards and then make a note of what is the best hand that each player could possibly be nursing.

## English Long Stud

Either everyone antes one chip, or (preferably) dealer edges as many chips as there are players. Assuming an ante and minimum bet of one chip, it may be agreed to limit raises to one chip in all betting intervals except the last, or to increase them gradually – say by one additional chip per interval until the last is reached, for which a maximum may be specified.

The difference between English and American Long Stud is that, in English, the sixth and seventh are not dealt in addition to the first five but as replacements for two discards from the first five. In effect, it is a cross between Stud and Draw, with a maximum buy of two cards.

A betting interval follows each of the following events:

1   Deal a first down-card to each player, then a second. When they have looked at their hole cards and placed them face down on the table, deal a third card face up to each player. Highest up-card speaks first. He may not check in this round.
2   Deal a second up-card. Highest visible pair speaks first, or best individual card if none. From now on first-to-speak may check, and if all players check the betting interval ends.
3   Deal a third up-card. At this and each subsequent deal first-to-speak is the player showing the highest number of paired cards, or highest ranking if tied.
4   Each player in rotation from the dealer's left now discards any one of his cards and receives a replacement from the top of the pack. The replacement is dealt face up if an up-card was thrown, down if a down-card was rejected. A player may stand pat if he wishes, but must then also stand pat on the next round.
5   A second discard is made and replaced, the replacement again being dealt up or down to match the discard. A player may stand pat if he wishes, and must do so if he stood pat before. This inaugurates the last interval.

As to strategy, the addition of what amounts to a two-card draw increases the mathematical skill factor of the game (not necessarily the psychological skill factor) and has an effect on the average final hands. The incidence of 2P and 3S is reduced because only two can be drawn to 1P instead of the three at Draw Poker, but that of ST and FL increased because two can be drawn to a bobtail instead of only one at Draw.

---

# Spit Poker

The varieties of Poker characterised under this heading are those in which one or more cards are dealt face up and may be used by any or all players as if they were part of their own hands. The original and simplest form was a variety of Draw known as Spit in the Ocean. One of countless modern developments of the theme is known as Hold 'em. And these two are all we have space for.

## Spit in the Ocean

This is basically five-card Draw except that the fifth card is a spit. Deal four cards to each player and one face up to the table. There is no minimum opening requirement, in fact the player at dealer's left may be required by previous agreement to open the betting regardless. When bets are equal in the first round, each player may discard and draw up to four replacements. In the event of a showdown the pot is won by the best five-card hand, counting the central spit as the fifth card. The average winning hand is lower than at ordinary Draw Poker, since everybody has the same fifth card and nobody can change it.

## Hold 'em

Deal two cards face down to each player, followed by a round of betting. Deal three cards face up to the centre of the table, and bet again. Then deal two more spits face up, one at a time, with a betting period after each one. When all bets are equalised, the pot is won by the player who can make the best five-card hand, counting for this purpose any five out of seven – i.e. his own two and the five spits. The average winning hand is in the straight-to-flush region, usually a full house if the spits include a pair.

## Wild cards

All forms of Poker may be played with one or more cards 'wild'. The original and dullest version involves adding a Joker to the pack and allowing it to count as any desired card. Any card or cards may be specified as wild, ranging from 'one-eyed Jacks' (i.e. those Jacks depicted in profile, with only one eye visible, which is interesting because of the wide variety of different designs now encountered in standard packs), to 'all the spades'.

Perhaps the most popular, and certainly the most sensible, is 'Deuces wild', in which all four Twos may count as anything specified by the holder(s). Fun and complication is introduced by making the wild card variable. For example, in Stud Poker it may be agreed that each player's first hole card is wild for his hand only, so that he may count this and any others he receives of the same rank as wild. In forms of Spit Poker it may be stated that the first spit is wild, together with all others of the same rank. And so on.

The more wild cards there are in a game, the higher the average winning hand. It should also be pointed out that the highest hand is five of a kind, the best possible being four Aces and a wild card, counting as five Aces. Between equal hands containing wild cards, the one with fewest wild cards wins – unless agreed otherwise.

## Dealer's Choice

If it's variety you're after in the game of Poker, the best way of introducing it is to play Dealer's Choice. This means that each player in turn, as he becomes the dealer, chooses the variety of Poker to be played, which may be a standard one or one invented by himself.

# —— GLOSSARY OF ——
# CARDPLAYING TERMS

**Ante** A fixed amount staked by the dealer, or by every player before cards are dealt.

**Auction** Procedure by which players bid for the right to specify certain conditions of the game (such as the trump suit) in return for an undertaking to achieve a higher valued objective than anyone else.

**Available** (Patience) Describes a card which, by the particular rules of the game, may be taken and used for building, packing, etc.

**Bid** Offer to achieve a higher valued objective than anyone else in return for the right to specify certain conditions of play, such as the trump suit.

**Combination** A set of matching cards for which a score or payment may be due by the rules of the particular game.

**Contract** An irrevocable undertaking to achieve a certain objective after bidding higher than anyone else and specifying conditions of play.

**Court (card)** A King, Queen or Jack (originally *coat* card). In America it is called *face card*.

**Declare** Various meanings according to context, but generally either (a) to announce the conditions of the game or the objective to be achieved, or (b) to show and score for a scoring combination of cards.

**Discard** To reject an unwanted card from the hand. Often used in the sense of **renounce** (see below).

**Eldest** The player sitting immediately next the dealer (on his left if the game is played clockwise round the table, his right otherwise), who normally has the privilege of bidding or playing first. In two-player games the non-dealer is elder.

**Exchange** To discard unwanted cards and replace them with fresh ones. In some games the discard is made before replacements are seen: in others, replacements are taken first and may form part of the discard.

**Flush** Cards of the same suit.

**Follow (suit)** Whoever plays first (e.g. to a trick) is said to lead, the others to follow. To play a card of the same suit as the leader is to follow suit.

**Forehand** Same as **eldest**.

**Game** Several related meanings. (a) Complete period of play at the end of which all scores are settled – may be anything from one deal to a whole session. (b) The target score which, when reached by at least one player, terminates the period of play and settlement, e.g. a game may be described as '500 up' – i.e., played up to a score of 500. (c) The stated objective and conditions of play for one particular deal – e.g. 'game in diamonds' means diamonds are trumps. (d) In Bridge, the number of points still needed to win a game by a side that may already have a part-score. (e) In contradiction of (a) above, several 'games' may constitute a larger self-contained period of play.

See **Rubber** below.

**Guard(ed)** In trick play a card in the hand is guarded by at least as many lower cards (guards) as there are cards above it lacking from the hand, e.g., if one's highest spade is the Queen it must be guarded by two lower cards to throw to leads of ♠A and ♠K in order to promote the Queen to top position.

**Hand** (a) The cards held in a player's hand. (b) A player (as in 'eldest hand'). (c) Period of play between the point at which all cards have been dealt and the point at which all have been played, none remaining in the hand.

**Head** In tricks, to play a higher ranking card of the suit led than any that have so far been played to the trick. In some games it is obligatory to head the trick if possible.

**Honours** Certain cards for which the rules of the game may prescribe a score of payment to their holder.

**Kitty** See **widow**.

**Lead** To play the first card of deal or to a trick.

**Long** Describes the holding of more than the average number of cards of a given suit, 'average' being the total number of that suit divided by the number of players.

**Meld** A winning or scoring set of cards that match one another by rank and or suit (see page 00). To show or declare such a set.

**Misère** An undertaking to lose every trick.

**Numerals** Cards other than court cards. (There is no general English term, but the American is *spot cards*.)

**Opponent** Sometimes has also the specialised meaning of one who is playing against a solo player or declarer. Thus the opponents of the soloist are not necessarily opponents of one another.

**Ouvert** A game played *ouvert* is one in which the principal player's hand of cards is exposed to the view of his opponents.

**Overcall** To make a higher bid than the preceding bidder.

**Overtrick** A trick in excess of the number required to win.

**Pass** To refrain from bidding.

**Pip (-value)** Literally, a pip is a suit symbol printed on a card. The pip value of a card is its value when captured, for example in a trick. The term avoids confusion with 'points' in the scoring sense.

**Plain suit** One that is not trumps.

**Rank** The denomination of a card – e.g. Ace, King, Two Three and so on.

**Renege** Sometimes used in the senses of ruff or revoke or renounce, but perhaps best used in the sense of failing to follow suit in games or circumstances in which there is no legal requirement to do so.

**Renounce** Loosely, to fail to follow suit; strictly, to play a card other than a trump when unable to follow suit.

**Revoke** To fail to follow suit, even though able and required to do so, for which a penalty may be exacted.

**Round** Circumstance in which everybody around the table has had one, or an equal number, of opportunities to bid, play, receive cards etc. Also, for example, 'third round of trumps' means 'third occasion on which a trump has been led to a trick.'

**Rubber** Equivalent to a match or tournament, the winner of a rubber being the first to win a certain number of games.

**Ruff** A trump. To play a trump to a non-trump lead.

**Sequence** A set of cards in numerical or ranking sequence, such as A–2–3 or T–J–Q–K–A. In some games a sequence only counts if the constituent cards are also of the same suit.

**Singleton** The holding of only one card in a given suit.

**Solo (ist)** A solo game is one in which one player (not usually called the soloist, though it seems the best word) undertakes to achieve his stated objective, without a partner, by playing against the combined efforts of everyone else to beat him.

**Stock** The undealt portion of the pack if not all cards are dealt.

**Trick** See Introduction page 1.

**Trump** See Introduction page 1.

**Vold** The holding of no cards in a given suit.

**Widow** A hand of cards dealt face down to the table (also called the *blind*, *skat*, *talon* or *kitty*), usually for the benefit of the highest bidder, who may exchange cards with them.

**Wild card** One that may represent any card its holder wishes.

# — INDEX OF GAMES —